Mrs. Powers wrote descriptive captions for each of the fifteen scenes represented on the quilt. These captions are as follows (from left to right, top to bottom of the quilt):

1. Job praying for his enemies. Jobs crosses. Jobs coffin.
2. The dark day of May, 19, 1780. The seven stars were seen 12. N. in the day. The cattle all went to bed, chickens to roost and the trumpet was blown. The sun went off to a small spot and then to darkness.
3. The serpent lifted up by Mosses and women bringing their children to look upon it to be healed.
4. Adam and Eve in the garden. Eve tempted by the serpent. Adam's rib by with which Eve was made. The *sun* and *moon*. God's all seeing *eye* and God's merciful hand.
5. John baptising Christ and the spirit of God descending and rested upon his shoulder like a dove.
6. Jonah casted over board of the ship and swallowed by a whale. Turtles.
7. God created two of every kind, Male and female
8. The falling of the stars on Nov. 13, 1833. The people were frighten and thought that the end of time had come. God's hand staid the stars. The varmints rushed out of their beds.
9. Two of every kind of animals continued. camels, elephants, "gheraffs" lions, etc.
10. The angels of wrath and the seven vials. The blood of fornications. Seven headed beast and 10 horns which arose out of the water.
11. Cold Thursday, 10. of Feb. 1895. A woman frozen while at prayer. A woman frozen at a gateway. A man with a sack of meal frozen. Isicles formed from the breath of a mule. All blue birds killed. A man frozen at his jug of liquor.
12. The red light night of 1846. A man tolling the bell to notify the people of the wonder. Women, children and fowls frightened but Gods merciful hand caused no harm to them.
13. Rich people who were taught nothing of God. Bob Johnson and Kate Bell of Virginia. They told their parents to stop the clock at one and to morrow it would strike one and so it did. This was the signal that they entered everlasting punishment. The independent hog which ran 500 miles from Ga. to Va. her name was Betts.
14. The creation of animals continues.
15. The crucifixtion of Christ between the two thieves. The sun went into darkness. Mary and Martha weeping at his feet. The blood and water run from his right side.

The Bible
as / in
Literature

JAMES S. ACKERMAN

Associate Professor of Religious Studies, Indiana University, Bloomington, Indiana; Director, Indiana University Institute on Teaching the Bible in Secondary English; recipient of the Indiana University Senior Class Teaching Excellence Award, 1974; senior author of *Teaching the Bible as Literature* and *Teaching the Old Testament in English Classes;* general coeditor for The Bible in Literature Courses, a five-volume series for teachers of the Bible in secondary English classes.

THAYER S. WARSHAW

Teacher of English and elective courses in Bible and in philosophy, Newton North High School, Newton, Massachusetts; Associate Director, Indiana University Institute on Teaching the Bible in Secondary English; recipient of Outstanding Teacher Award, Newton High School, 1970; general coeditor for The Bible in Literature Courses, a five-volume series for teachers of the Bible in secondary English classes; author of numerous articles on teaching about religion and on teaching the Bible in public schools.

JOHN SWEET
(Editorial Consultant)

Formerly, instructor in English, Horace Greeley High School, Chappaqua, New York; Assistant Professor of English, Bowdoin College, Brunswick, Maine. Recipient of Fulbright Fellowship and East-West Fellowship; actor and community theater director; author of numerous articles on teaching drama and writing.

SCOTT, FORESMAN AND COMPANY
Glenview, Illinois • Dallas, Texas • Oakland, New Jersey
Palo Alto, California • Tucker, Georgia • Brighton, England

ACKNOWLEDGMENTS
The Scripture quotations in this publication
are from the Revised Standard Version Bible,
copyright 1946, 1952, and © 1971
by the Division of Christian Education of the National
Council of the Churches of Christ in the U.S.A.
and used by permission.
Judith and Susanna from the Revised Standard Version
of the Apocrypha, copyright © 1957, by the Division
of Christian Education, National Council of the
Churches of Christ in the U.S.A. and
used by permission.

Contents

4 ISRAEL'S YOUTHFUL DAYS

5 ANOINTED KINGS

6 SPOKESMEN OF GOD

7 VARIETIES OF BIBLICAL POETRY

8 WHY DO THE RIGHTEOUS SUFFER?

9 IN THE MIDST OF THE ENEMY

10 JESUS: BIRTH AND EARLY MINISTRY

11 JESUS: TEACHINGS, DEATH, AND RESURRECTION

12 IN THE END OF DAYS

INTRODUCTION

As the title suggests, this book has a two-fold purpose: to study the literary craftsmanship of passages from the Bible (the Bible *as* literature) and to explore the relationship of a variety of other stories, poems, and plays to the Bible (the Bible *in* literature). Some of these latter selections are directly influenced by the Bible, openly retelling or quietly alluding to specific biblical passages. Other nonbiblical selections, while not connected explicitly to a biblical passage, have a similar theme or situation.

Most selections are followed by three types of student aids:

1. *For close reading.* Factual questions to help the student focus upon and grasp important or subtle details. The answers may be found by simply rereading the relevant portion of the text.

2. *For thought and discussion.* Discussion questions—not the "guess-what's-in-our-minds" variety but questions as open-ended as we can make them. Here the student's written or oral answers are meant to be judged not as either "right" or "wrong," but as "more appropriate" and "less appropriate."

3. *Activities.* Suggestions for imaginative responses, both verbal and nonverbal—individual or group "projects" in such fields as art, acting, music, handcrafts, and other audio-visual media.

In addition, marginal notes are intended to clarify customs and explain difficult words.

These questions, suggestions, and notes are only initial stimuli to the imaginations and resources of teacher and student; interests and abilities will, we hope, lead still further out from, or more deeply into, the text.

A word about the Bible *as* literature. Literary craftsmanship is only one aspect of the Bible, a work that has had an immeasurable influence on the western world and is sacred to three of the world's major religions. Concentration on the literary aspects of the Bible does not imply any intent to ignore or diminish its cultural, historical, moral, and religious content. Rather, focus on the Bible as literature provides a common ground for people of all traditions and attitudes to examine and appreciate the Bible in the same classroom. Furthermore, craftsmanship is only one aspect of literature. The study of any literature may lead to a consideration of its relevance to the reader's own experience and values. In this respect biblical and Bible-related literature, more than most, can present problems for a pluralistic society. (For example, what is actually in "the Bible" varies for different religious traditions.) But such problems are not barriers; they are, instead, welcome reminders that teachers and students must be aware of the sensibilities of other people.

We hope you will read and enjoy and think and learn.

James S. Ackerman
Thayer S. Warshaw

1

stories
from
the
beginning

CREATION: HEAVEN AND EARTH

Genesis

In the beginning God created the heavens and the earth. The earth was without form and void, and darkness was upon the face of the deep; and the Spirit of God was moving over the face of the waters.

void: i.e. a disordered waste.

And God said, "Let there be light"; and there was light. And God saw that the light was good; and God separated the light from the darkness. God called the light Day, and the darkness he called Night. And there was evening and there was morning, one day.

And God said, "Let there be a firmament in the midst of the waters, and let it separate the waters from the waters." And God made the firmament and separated the waters which were under the firmament from the waters which were above the firmament. And it was so. And God called the firmament Heaven. And there was evening and there was morning, a second day.

firmament: arched roof of heaven; sky.

And God said, "Let the waters under the heavens be gathered together into one place, and let the dry land appear." And it was so. God called the dry land Earth, and the waters that were gathered together he called Seas. And God saw that it was good. And God said, "Let the earth put forth vegetation, plants yielding seed, and fruit trees bearing fruit in which is

---

Genesis 1:1–2:4a (RSV).
LEFT: *The Hand of Creation,* brush drawing by Ben Shahn. Courtesy Bernarda Bryson Shahn.

their seed, each according to its kind, upon the earth." And it was so. The earth brought forth vegetation, plants yielding seed according to their own kinds, and trees bearing fruit in which is their seed, each according to its kind. And God saw that it was good. And there was evening and there was morning, a third day.

And God said, "Let there be lights in the firmament of the heavens to separate the day from the night; and let them be for signs and for seasons and for days and years, and let them be lights in the firmament of the heavens to give light upon the earth." And it was so. And God made the two great lights, the greater light to rule the day, and the lesser light to rule the night; he made the stars also. And God set them in the firmament of the heavens to give light upon the earth, to rule over the day and over the night, and to separate the light from the darkness. And God saw that it was good. And there was evening and there was morning, a fourth day.

And God said, "Let the waters bring forth swarms of living creatures, and let birds fly above the earth across the firmament of the heavens." So God created the great sea monsters and every living creature that moves, with which the waters swarm, according to their kinds, and every winged bird according to its kind. And God saw that it was good. And God blessed them, saying, "Be fruitful and multiply and fill the waters in the seas, and let birds multiply on the earth." And there was evening and there was morning, a fifth day.

And God said, "Let the earth bring forth living creatures according to their kinds: cattle and creeping things and beasts of the earth according to their kinds." And it was so. And God made the beasts of the earth according to their kinds and the cattle according to their kinds, and everything that creeps upon the ground according to its kind. And God saw that it was good.

us . . . our: may refer to lesser beings in God's heavenly court.

have dominion: rule.

Then God said, "Let us make man in our image, after our likeness; and let them have dominion over the fish of the sea, and over the birds of the air, and over the cattle, and over all the earth, and over every creeping thing that creeps upon the earth." So God created man in his own image, in the image of God he created him; male and female he created them. And God blessed them, and God said to them, "Be fruitful and multiply, and fill the earth and subdue it; and have dominion over the fish of the sea and over the birds of the air and over every living thing that moves upon the earth." And God said, "Behold, I have given you every plant yielding seed which is upon the face of all the earth, and every tree with seed in its fruit; you shall have them for food. And to every beast of the earth, and to every bird of the air, and to everything that creeps on the earth, everything that has the breath of life, I have given every green plant for food." And it was so. And God saw everything that he had made, and behold, it was very good. And there was evening and there was morning, a sixth day.

Thus the heavens and the earth were finished, and all the host of them. And on the seventh day God finished his work which he had done, and he rested on the seventh day from all his work which he had done. So God blessed the seventh day and hallowed it, because on it God rested from all his work which he had done in creation.

hallowed: made holy.

These are the generations of the heavens and the earth when they were created.

For close reading

1 Make a list of what is created on each of the first six days. What are the main differences between the seventh day and the first six?
2 What kinds of food does God feel that his creatures will need?
3 Certain phrases are repeated for almost every day and every creative act. What are they?
4 Make a list of the verbs that describe what God does.

For thought and discussion

5 Look at your list of each day's creations. Can you see any logic to the order? Explain. Why do you think human beings are created last?

6 According to the Bible story, the seventh day may be considered a rest from work or a completion of work. In what ways are weekends today like God's day of rest?

7 As each part of the process of creation is presented, God makes a statement. After the statement comes an almost exact restatement of God's language. What do you think is the purpose of this restatement?

8 Look at the "and it was good" sequence. Why do you think the last instance differs from the others?

9 The first day concerns light and darkness; so does the fourth day. In what ways might the second and fifth days also be similar to each other? The third and sixth days?

10 Consider the verbs describing God's actions. What sense of the personality or character of God do you get from these words and other details? What seems to be his relation to the world and its creatures? Use specific phrases to show how his personal qualities are revealed.

11 Certain phrases in this passage have called up vivid images or emotions for many readers. (For example, creeping things don't usually suggest cheery thoughts to the modern mind, yet here the phrase seems appealing. Why?) Can you find other phrases which appeal to you? Can you say why?

12 Human beings are created "in the image of God." What do you think this means?

Activities

1 Create something—art, diagram, music, etc.—that will help you explain one or more stages of the biblical creation story to a small child. If possible, make your presentation to a group of children and report to the class how the children reacted.

2 For a group. Each student takes a piece of clay to shape into anything he or she wishes. You are all "creating." Now try to decide which is the most "creative" creation. How did you decide? What criteria did you agree upon?

CREATION: IN THE GARDEN

Genesis

In the day that the Lord God made the earth and the heavens, when no plant of the field was yet in the earth and no herb of the field had yet sprung up (for the Lord God had not caused it to rain upon the earth, and there was no man to till the ground; but a mist went up from the earth and watered the whole face of the ground) then the Lord God formed man of dust from the ground, and breathed into his nostrils the breath of life; and man became a living being. And the Lord God planted a garden in Eden, in the east; and there he put the man whom he had formed. And out of the ground the Lord God made to grow every tree that is pleasant to the sight and good for food, the tree of life also in the midst of the garden, and the tree of the knowledge of good and evil.

A river flowed out of Eden to water the garden, and there it divided and became four rivers. The name of the first is Pishon; it is the one which flows around the whole land of Havilah, where there is gold; and the gold of that land is good; bdellium and onyx stone are there. The name of the second river is Gihon; it is the one which flows around the whole land of Cush. And the name of the third river is Tigris, which flows east of Assyria. And the fourth river is the Euphrates.

The Lord God took the man and put him in the garden of Eden to till it and keep it. And the Lord God commanded the man, saying, "You may freely eat of every tree of the garden; but of the tree of the

ground, man: In the original Hebrew, the word for ground is *adamah* and the word for mankind is *adam.*

tree of life: its fruit was believed to bring eternal life.

bdellium (del′ ē əm): fragrant tree resin.
onyx (on′ iks): precious stone.

Genesis 2:4b–25 (RSV).

knowledge of good and evil you shall not eat, for in the day that you eat of it you shall die."

Then the Lord God said, "It is not good that the man should be alone; I will make him a helper fit for him." So out of the ground the Lord God formed every beast of the field and every bird of the air, and brought them to the man to see what he would call them; and whatever the man called every living creature, that was its name. The man gave names to all cattle, and to the birds of the air, and to every beast of the field; but for the man there was not found a helper fit for him. So the Lord God caused a deep sleep to fall upon the man, and while he slept took one of his ribs and closed up its place with flesh; and the rib which the Lord God had taken from the man he made into a woman and brought her to the man. Then the man said,

man, woman: The Hebrew words are *ish* and *ishshah*.

"This at last is bone of my bones
and flesh of my flesh;
she shall be called Woman,
because she was taken out of Man."

cleaves: clings.

Therefore a man leaves his father and his mother and cleaves to his wife, and they become one flesh. And the man and his wife were both naked, and were not ashamed.

For close reading

1 According to the opening sentence, what two things were lacking for the plants and herbs to grow? Of these two things, which did God create first?

2 According to this part of the Bible story what is the order of creation of our world? Why, and from what, did God create the beasts? The woman?

3 The Lord gives man two instructions. What must he not do? What is the first job he is given to do?

4 According to the story, why do people get married?

5 What new verbs, not used in part one, describe God's actions in part two? Make a list of the new ones.

For thought and discussion

6 The tree that has to do with wisdom is forbidden to Adam and Eve. What danger might God have seen in their being "wise"? Since men and women have been created in the divine image, why must any limitation be put upon them?

7 In the story woman is made to seem quite secondary to man (being created second, called a helper, taken from his rib, her name based on his). Some women today feel that these details are offensive, a "put-down." Do you agree?

8 The description of the relationship between a man and a woman seems to imply a greater responsibility on the part of the man: he is the one who leaves his father and mother; he does the cleaving. In recent times, it has been assumed by many that a woman makes the greater sacrifice and has more responsibility for the success of a marriage. How do you account for this shift? How do things stand now, in your opinion?

9 Look at your list of new verbs describing God's actions. What new sense of the personality or character of God do you get from these words and other details of the story? What new relation does God seem to have to the world and its creatures? Give instances from the text to support your opinion.

10 There are several variations between this part of the biblical creation story and the preceding passage on page 3. How many have you noticed? How might one explain these variations?

Activity

Suppose that you can overhear Adam and Eve thinking as well as speaking. Write what you hear in one of the following instances: *(a)* Some of what goes on in Adam's mind between the time when he is created and the time he finds his "helper." *(b)* What goes on in Eve's mind from her creation until she becomes Adam's wife.

THE
CREATION

James Weldon Johnson

And God stepped out on space,
And He looked around and said,
"I'm lonely——
I'll make me a world."

5   And far as the eye of God could see
Darkness covered everything,
Blacker than a hundred midnights
Down in a cypress swamp.

Then God smiled,
10   And the light broke,
And the darkness rolled up on one side,
And the light stood shining on the other,
And God said, *"That's good!"*

Then God reached out and took the light in His
    hands,
15   And God rolled the light around in His hands,
Until He made the sun;
And He set that sun a-blazing in the heavens.
And the light that was left from making the sun
God gathered up in a shining ball
20   And flung against the darkness,
Spangling the night with the moon and stars.
Then down between
The darkness and the light
He hurled the world;
25   And God said, *"That's good!"*

Then God himself stepped down——
And the sun was on His right hand,

And the moon was on His left;
The stars were clustered about His head,
30 and the earth was under His feet.
And God walked, and where He trod
His footsteps hollowed the valleys out
And bulged the mountains up.

Then He stopped and looked and saw
35 That the earth was hot and barren.
So God stepped over to the edge of the world
And He spat out the seven seas;
He batted His eyes, and the lightnings flashed;
He clapped His hands, and the thunders rolled;
40 And the waters above the earth came down,
The cooling waters came down.

Then the green grass sprouted,
And the little red flowers blossomed,
The pine-tree pointed his finger to the sky,
45 And the oak spread out his arms;
The lakes cuddled down in the hollows of the
       ground,
And the rivers ran down to the sea;
And God smiled again,
And the rainbow appeared,
50 And curled itself around His shoulder.

Then God raised His arm and He waved His hand
Over the sea and over the land,
And He said, *"Bring forth! Bring forth!"*
And quicker than God could drop His hand,
55 Fishes and fowls
And beast and birds
Swam the rivers and the seas,
Roamed the forests and the woods,
And split the air with their wings,
60 And God said, *"That's good!"*

Then God walked around
And God looked around
On all that He had made.
He looked at His sun,
65 And He looked at His moon,
And He looked at His little stars;
He looked on His world
With all its living things,
And God said, *"I'm lonely still."*

70 Then God sat down
On the side of a hill where He could think;
By a deep, wide river He sat down;
With His head in His hands,
God thought and thought,
75 Till He thought, *"I'll make me a man!"*

Up from the bed of the river
God scooped the clay;
And by the bank of the river
He kneeled Him down;
80 And there the great God Almighty,
Who lit the sun and fixed it in the sky,
Who flung the stars to the most far corner of the
night,
Who rounded the earth in the middle of His
hand—
This Great God,
85 Like a mammy bending over her baby,
Kneeled down in the dust
Toiling over a lump of clay
Till He shaped it in His own image;

Then into it He blew the breath of life,
90 And man became a living soul.
Amen. Amen.

For thought and discussion

1 In what ways is the God of Genesis different from
the God portrayed in this poem? Compare the verbs
used to describe God's actions in the poem with the
verbs used in Genesis.
2 Do the Genesis stories suggest *why* God created
the world? What reason or reasons are suggested in
this poem?

HEAVEN AND EARTH IN JEST

Annie Dillard

A couple of summers ago I was walking along the edge of the island to see what I could see in the water, and mainly to scare frogs. Frogs have an inelegant way of taking off from invisible positions on the bank just ahead of your feet, in dire panic, emitting a froggy "Yike!" and splashing into the water. Incredibly, this amused me, and, incredibly, it amuses me still. As I walked along the grassy edge of the island, I got better and better at seeing frogs both in and out of the water. I learned to recognize, slowing down, the difference in texture of the light reflected from mudbank, water, grass, or frog. Frogs were flying all around me. At the end of the island I noticed a small green frog. He was exactly half in and half out of the water, looking like a schematic diagram of an amphibian, and he didn't jump.

He didn't jump; I crept closer. At last I knelt on the island's winterkilled grass, lost, dumbstruck, staring at the frog in the creek just four feet away. He was a very small frog with wide, dull eyes. And just as I looked at him, he slowly crumpled and began to sag. The spirit vanished from his eyes as if snuffed. His skin emptied and drooped; his very skull seemed to collapse and settle like a kicked tent. He was shrinking before my eyes like a deflating football. I watched the taut, glistening skin on his shoulders ruck, and rumple, and fall. Soon, part of his skin, formless as a pricked balloon, lay in floating folds like bright scum on top of the water: it was a monstrous and terrifying thing. I gaped bewildered, appalled. An oval shadow hung in the water behind the drained frog; then the shadow glided away. The frog skin bag started to sink.

I had read about the giant water bug, but never seen one. "Giant water bug" is really the name of the creature, which is an enormous, heavy-bodied brown beetle. It eats insects, tadpoles, fish, and frogs. Its grasping forelegs are mighty and hooked inward. It seizes a victim with these legs, hugs it tight, and paralyzes it with enzymes injected during a vicious bite. That one bite is the only bite it ever takes. Through the puncture shoot the poisons that dissolve the victim's muscles and bones and organs—all but the skin—and through it the giant water bug sucks out the victim's body, reduced to a juice. This event is quite common in warm fresh water. The frog I saw was being sucked by a giant water bug. I had been kneeling on the island grass; when the unrecognizable flap of frog skin settled on the creek bottom, swaying, I stood up and brushed the knees of my pants. I couldn't catch my breath.

Of course, many carnivorous animals devour their prey alive. The usual method seems to be to subdue the victim by downing or grasping it so it can't flee, then eating it whole or in a series of bloody bites. Frogs eat everything whole, stuffing prey into their mouths with their thumbs. People have seen frogs with their wide jaws so full of live dragonflies they couldn't close them. Ants don't even have to catch their prey: in the spring they swarm over newly hatched, featherless birds in the nest and eat them tiny bite by bite.

That it's rough out there and chancy is no surprise. Every live thing is a survivor on a kind of extended emergency bivouac. But at the same time we are also created. In the Koran, Allah asks, "The heaven and the earth and all in between, thinkest thou I made them *in jest?*" It's a good question. What do we think of the created universe, spanning an unthinkable void with an unthinkable profusion of forms? Or what do we think of nothingness, those sickening reaches of time in either direction? If the giant water bug was not made in jest, was it then made in earnest? Pascal uses a nice term to describe

enzymes: complex digestive substances.

bivouac (biv′wak): outdoor camp, usually without tents.

Koran: the sacred book of the Moslems. *Allah* is the Moslem name of God.

profusion: abundancy.

the notion of the creator's, once having called forth the universe, turning his back to it: *Deus Absconditus.* Is this what we think happened? Was the sense of it there, and God absconded with it, ate it, like a wolf who disappears round the edge of the house with the Thanksgiving turkey? "God is subtle," Einstein said, "but not malicious." Again, Einstein said that "nature conceals her mystery by means of her essential grandeur, not by her cunning." It could be that God has not absconded but spread, as our vision and understanding of the universe have spread, to a fabric of spirit and sense so grand and subtle, so powerful in a new way, that we can only feel blindly of its hem. In making the thick darkness a swaddling band for the sea, God "set bars and doors" and said, "Hitherto shalt thou come, but no further." But have we come even that far? Have we rowed out to the thick darkness, or are we all playing pinochle in the bottom of the boat?

Cruelty is a mystery, and the waste of pain. But if we describe a world to compass these things, a world that is a long, brute game, then we bump against another mystery: the inrush of power and light, the canary that sings on the skull. Unless all ages and races of men have been deluded by the same mass hypnotist (who?), there seems to be such a thing as beauty, a grace wholly gratuitous. About five years ago I saw a mockingbird make a straight vertical descent from the roof gutter of a four-story building. It was an act as careless and spontaneous as the curl of a stem or the kindling of a star.

The mockingbird took a single step into the air and dropped. His wings were still folded against his sides as though he were singing from a limb and not falling, accelerating thirty-two feet per second per second, through empty air. Just a breath before he would have been dashed to the ground, he unfurled his wings with exact, deliberate care, revealing the broad bars of white, spread his elegant, white-banded tail, and so floated onto the grass. I had just rounded a corner when his insouciant step caught my eye; there was no one else in sight. The fact of his free fall was like the old philosophical conundrum about the tree that falls in the forest. The answer must be, I think, that beauty and grace are performed whether or not we will or sense them. The least we can do is try to be there.

Deus Absconditus: (Latin) the hidden God. **absconded:** left quickly.

insouciant (in süˈsē ənt): carefree. **conundrum** (kə nunˈdrəm): puzzle.

Another time I saw another wonder: sharks off the Atlantic coast of Florida. There is a way a wave rises above the ocean horizon, a triangular wedge against the sky. If you stand where the ocean breaks on a shallow beach, you see the raised water in a wave is translucent, shot with lights. One late afternoon at low tide a hundred big sharks passed the beach near the mouth of a tidal river in a feeding frenzy. As each green wave rose from the churning water, it illuminated within itself the six- or eight-foot-long bodies of twisting sharks. The sharks disappeared as each wave rolled toward me; then a new wave would swell above the horizon, containing in it, like scorpions in amber, sharks that roiled and heaved. The sight held awesome wonders: power and beauty, grace tangled in a rapture with violence.

We don't know what's going on here. If these tremendous events are random combinations of matter run amok, the yield of millions of monkeys at millions of typewriters, then what is it in us, hammered out of those same typewriters, that they ignite? We don't know. Our life is a faint tracing on the surface of mystery, like the idle, curved tunnels of leaf miners on the face of a leaf. We must somehow take a wider view, look at the whole landscape, really see it, and describe what's going on here. Then we can at least wail the right question into the swaddling band of darkness, or, if it comes to that, choir the proper praise.

At the time of Lewis and Clark, setting the prairies on fire was a well-known signal that meant, "Come down to the water." It was an extravagant gesture, but we can't do less. If the landscape reveals one certainty, it is that the extravagant gesture is the very stuff of creation. After the one extravagant gesture of creation in the first place, the universe has continued to deal exclusively in extravagances, flinging intricacies and colossi down aeons of emptiness, heaping profusions on profligacies with everfresh vigor. The whole show has been on fire from the word go. I come down to the water to cool my eyes. But everywhere I look I see fire; that which isn't flint is tinder, and the whole world sparks and flames.

run amok: behaving wildly.

millions of monkeys: the speculation that a million monkeys at typewriters for a million years could type all the great literary works ever written—by sheer chance.

leaf miners: insect larvae that feed on leaves.

aeons (ē′əns): thousands of years.

For close reading

1 The author focuses on frogs, a water bug, a mockingbird, and sharks. How does she respond to each?

2 Dillard is especially skilled in making fresh comparisons. For instance, "his very skull seemed to collapse and settle *like a kicked tent.*" Find several others.

For thought and discussion

3 From your own knowledge and experience of nature, describe one or two things that suggest *(a)* the harshness and *(b)* the beauty of the universe.

4 What part of this selection most affected you? Why?

5 What are the author's feelings about the universe?

FORBIDDEN FRUIT

Genesis

subtle: crafty, sly.

Now the serpent was more subtle than any other wild creature that the Lord God had made. He said to the woman, "Did God say, 'You shall not eat of any tree of the garden'?" And the woman said to the serpent, "We may eat of the fruit of the trees of the garden; but God said, 'You shall not eat of the fruit of the tree which is in the midst of the garden, neither shall you touch it, lest you die.' " But the serpent said to the woman, "You will not die. For God knows that when you eat of it your eyes will be opened, and you will be like God, knowing good and evil." So when the woman saw that the tree was good for food, and that it was a delight to the eyes, and that the tree was to be desired to make one wise, she took of its fruit and ate; and she also gave some to her husband, and he ate. Then the eyes of both were opened, and they knew that they were naked; and they sewed fig leaves together and made themselves aprons.

And they heard the sound of the Lord God walking in the garden in the cool of the day, and the man and his wife hid themselves from the presence of the Lord God among the trees of the garden. But the Lord God called to the man, and said to him, "Where are you?" And he said, "I heard the sound of thee in the garden, and I was afraid, because I was naked; and I hid myself." He said, "Who told you that you were naked? Have you eaten of the tree of

Genesis 3:1–24 (RSV).

which I commanded you not to eat?" The man said, "The woman whom thou gavest to be with me, she gave me fruit of the tree, and I ate." Then the Lord God said to the woman, "What is this that you have done?" The woman said, "The serpent beguiled me, and I ate." The Lord God said to the serpent,

beguiled: tricked.

"Because you have done this,
cursed are you above all cattle,
and above all wild animals;
upon your belly you shall go,
and dust you shall eat
all the days of your life.
I will put enmity between you and the woman,
and between your seed and her seed;
he shall bruise your head,
and you shall bruise his heel."

seed: children, descendants.

To the woman he said,

"I will greatly multiply your pain in child-
    bearing;
in pain you shall bring forth children;
yet your desire shall be for your husband,
and he shall rule over you."

And to Adam he said,

"Because you have listened to the voice of
    your wife,
and have eaten of the tree
of which I commanded you,
'You shall not eat of it,'
cursed is the ground because of you;
in toil you shall eat of it all the days of your
    life;
thorns and thistles it shall bring forth to you;
and you shall eat the plants of the field.
In the sweat of your face
you shall eat bread
till you return to the ground,
for out of it you were taken;
you are dust,
and to dust you shall return."

The man called his wife's name Eve, because she was the mother of all living. And the Lord God made

Eve: very close to the Hebrew word for "living."

for Adam and for his wife garments of skins, and clothed them.

Then the Lord God said, "Behold, the man has become like one of us, knowing good and evil; and now, lest he put forth his hand and take also of the tree of life, and eat, and live for ever"—therefore the Lord God sent him forth from the garden of Eden, to till the ground from which he was taken. He drove out the man; and at the east of the garden of Eden he placed the cherubim, and a flaming sword which turned every way, to guard the way to the tree of life.

cherubim (cher′ ə bim): winged angels.

For close reading

1 For what three reasons does Eve eat the fruit?
2 What do Adam and Eve "learn" from eating the fruit?
3 What punishments are given to the serpent? To Eve? To Adam?
4 Many parts of the Bible explain why certain aspects of life are hard or painful. What aspects of life can you find explained in this passage?

For thought and discussion

5 Eve's answer to the serpent includes an addition to God's original command. Do you think Eve made up the new part? If she did, what clue to Eve's personality might this addition have given to the serpent?
6 Both the serpent and God begin with questions to which they already know the answers. Why do you suppose they ask questions instead of making statements? Do they do so for the same reason? What do the questions show about the serpent? About God? About Adam and Eve?

7 Who do you think receives the harshest punishment? Why?

8 Earlier we are told that "the man and his wife were both naked, and were not ashamed." How does this attitude compare with: *(a)* Adam and Eve's behavior after they have eaten the forbidden fruit and *(b)* contemporary attitudes about sexuality?

9 Some have argued that it was unfair of God to place a tempting but forbidden tree in the Garden. Others feel that without the presence of the tree and the possibility of disobeying God, Adam and Eve would not have been fully human. What are your views?

10 Note the phrase "cursed is the ground." How would you explain its meaning? Originally, God had told man to "fill the earth and subdue it." How are these and other phrases in the creation story related to ecology problems in our own time?

11 Ever since Adam and Eve left the Garden it seems that human beings have wished that they could return to a paradise, to a state of innocence. What would people gain or lose if this were possible?

Activities

1 Construct a model of the Garden as a small stage set, or draw or paint the Garden, or make a clay model of one of the figures in the story. Construct a mobile which deals with elements of the story.

2 Write a version of the story in which Eve is offered the fruit and talks things over with Adam before making up her mind.

3 If you could create your own paradise, what would it be like? Make up a travel brochure that emphasizes the attractive features of "your" paradise.

4 Stitch in needlepoint or crewel embroidery an element from this story.

5 Design a theater poster for a play titled *The Forbidden Fruit.*

6 Retell this story from the point of view of the serpent.

ORIGINAL SEQUENCE

Philip Booth

Time was the apple Adam ate.
Eve bit, gave seconds to his mouth,
and then they had no minute left
to lose. Eyes opened in mid-kiss,
5 they saw, for once, raw nakedness,
and hid that sudden consequence
behind an hour's stripped leaves.

This is one sequence in the plot,
the garden where God came, that time,
10 to call. Hands behind him, walking
to and fro, he counted how
the fruit fell, bruised on frozen sod.
This was his orchard, his to pace;
the day was cool, and he was God.

15 Old Adam heard him humming, talking
to himself: *Winesap, King,*
ripen in sun,
McIntosh and
Northern Spy
20   *fall one by one,*
ripen to die.

Adam heard him call his name,
but Adam, no old philosopher,
was not sure what he was after.

25 *We're naked, Lord, and can't come out.*
Eve nudged him with the bitter fruit.
God paused. *How do you know? Where is*
that woman that I sprung from you?

Eve held the twisted stem, the pulp;
30 she heard the low snake hiss, and let fly
blindly with a woman arm, careless
where her new-won anger struck.
The fodder for that two-fold flock
fell, an old brown core, at God's
35 stopped feet. He reached, and wound the clock.

For thought and discussion

1 You will recall that after Adam and Eve eat of the tree of the knowledge of good and evil, God expels them from the Garden lest they also eat of the tree of life and live eternally. How does this help to explain the first line of the poem?
2 What impression do you get of God when he talks to himself? When he talks to Adam?
3 What does Eve's flinging of the apple core suggest about her? Why does the poet describe her anger as "new-won"?
4 Reread the last line. What does God reach for? How does "and wound the clock" tie in with the first line of the poem? What kind of clock is the poet talking about?

EDEN
IS THAT
OLD-FASHIONED
HOUSE

Emily Dickinson

RIGHT: *The Hand of God,* Romanesque fresco from St. Climent de Taull. Museo de Arte de Cataluña, Barcelona.

abode: place where one lives

sauntered: walked slowly and happily; strolled.

Eden is that old-fashioned House
We dwell in every day
Without suspecting our abode
Until we drive away.

5 How fair on looking back, the Day
We sauntered from the Door—
Unconscious our returning,
But discover it no more.

For thought and discussion

1 How does Dickinson define Eden? What, besides an actual building, might one's abode be?
2 How do you interpret line 7?
3 What does the author say about people's attitudes toward what they have? When do these attitudes change?

ABOVE: *God Creating Adam,* color print, watercolor by William Blake, 1795. The Tate Gallery, London.

RIGHT: *The Tree of Life,* cut-out gouache maquette for a window in the Vence Chapel by Henri Matisse, 1949. Paris, private collection. Photo Studio Adrion, Paris/ZIOLO. © SPADEM, Paris, 1975.

BELOW: *Adam and Eve in Paradise,* detail from an oil painting by Peter Paul Rubens. Mauritshuis, The Hague, The Netherlands.

EXTRACTS FROM ADAM'S DIARY

Samuel Clemens

Monday. This new creature with the long hair is a good deal in the way. It is always hanging around and following me about. I don't like this; I am not used to company. I wish it would stay with the other animals. . . . Cloudy today, wind in the east; think we shall have rain. . . . *We?* Where did I get that word?—I remember now—the new creature uses it.

Tuesday. Been examining the great waterfall. It is the finest thing on the estate, I think. The new creature calls it Niagara Falls—why, I am sure I do not know. Says it *looks* like Niagara Falls. That is not a reason, it is mere waywardness and imbecility. I get no chance to name anything myself. The new creature names everything that comes along, before I can get in a protest. And always that same pretext is offered—it *looks* like the thing. There is the dodo, for instance. Says the moment one looks at it one sees at a glance that it "looks like a dodo." It will have to keep that name, no doubt. It wearies me to fret about it, and it does no good, anyway. Dodo! It looks no more like a dodo than I do.

Wednesday. Built me a shelter against the rain, but could not have it to myself in peace. The new creature intruded. When I tried to put it out it shed water out of the holes it looks with, and wiped it away with the back of its paws, and made a noise such as some of the other animals make when they are in distress. I wish it would not talk; it is always talking. That sounds like a cheap fling at the poor creature, a slur; but I do not mean it so. I have never heard the human voice before, and any new and

imbecility: stupidity.

pretext: excuse.

strange sound intruding itself here upon the solemn hush of these dreaming solitudes offends my ear and seems a false note. And this new sound is so close to me; it is right at my shoulder, right at my ear, first on one side and then on the other, and I am used only to sounds that are more or less distant from me.

Friday. The naming goes recklessly on, in spite of anything I can do. I had a very good name for the estate, and it was musical and pretty—GARDEN OF EDEN. Privately, I continue to call it that, but not any longer publicly. The new creature says it is all woods and rocks and scenery, and therefore has no resemblance to a garden. Says it *looks* like a park, and does not look like anything *but* a park. Consequently, without consulting me, it has been new-named—NIAGARA FALLS PARK. This is sufficiently high-handed, it seems to me. And already there is a sign up:

KEEP OFF
THE GRASS

My life is not as happy as it was.

Saturday. The new creature eats too much fruit. We are going to run short, most likely. "We" again—that is *its* word; mine, too, now, from hearing it so much. Good deal of fog this morning. I do not go out in the fog myself. The new creature does. It goes out in all weathers, and stumps right in with its muddy feet. And talks. It used to be so pleasant and quiet here.

Sunday. Pulled through. This day is getting to be more and more trying. It was selected and set apart last November as a day of rest. I had already six of them per week before. This morning found the new creature trying to clod apples out of that forbidden tree.

Monday. The new creature says its name is Eve. That is all right, I have no objections. Says it is to call it by, when I want it to come. I said it was superfluous, then. The word evidently raised me in its respect; and indeed it is a large, good word and will bear repetition. It says it is not an It, it is a She. This is probably doubtful; yet it is all one to me; what she is were nothing to me if she would but go by herself and not talk.

superfluous: unnecessary.

Tuesday. She has littered the whole estate with execrable names and offensive signs:

THIS WAY TO THE WHIRLPOOL
THIS WAY TO GOAT ISLAND
CAVE OF THE WINDS THIS WAY

She says this park would make a tidy summer resort if there was any custom for it. Summer resort—another invention of hers—just words, without any meaning. What is a summer resort? But it is best not to ask her, she has such a rage for explaining.

Friday. She has taken to beseeching me to stop going over the Falls. What harm does it do? Says it makes her shudder. I wonder why; I have always done it—always liked the plunge, and coolness. I supposed it was what the Falls were for. They have no other use that I can see, and they must have been made for something. She says they were only made for scenery—like the rhinoceros and the mastodon.

I went over the Falls in a barrel—not satisfactory to her. Went over in a tub—still not satisfactory. Swam the Whirlpool and the Rapids in a fig-leaf suit. It got much damaged. Hence, tedious complaints about my extravagance. I am too much hampered here. What I need is change of scene.

Saturday. I escaped last Tuesday night, and traveled two days, and built me another shelter in a secluded place, and obliterated my tracks as well as I could, but she hunted me out by means of a beast which she has named and calls a wolf, and came making that pitiful noise again, and shedding that water out of the places she looks with. I was obliged to return with her, but will presently emigrate again when occasion offers. She engages herself in many foolish things; among others, to study out why the animals called lions and tigers live on grass and flowers, when, as she says, the sort of teeth they wear would indicate that they were intended to eat each other. This is foolish, because to do that would be to kill each other, and that would introduce what, as I understand it, is called "death"; and death, as I have been told, has not yet entered the Park. Which is a pity, on some accounts.

Sunday. Pulled through.

Monday. I believe I see what the week is for; it is

to give time to rest up from the weariness of Sunday. It seems a good idea. . . . She has been climbing that tree again. Clodded her out of it. She said nobody was looking. Seems to consider that a sufficient justification for chancing any dangerous thing. Told her that. The word justification moved her admiration—and envy, too, I thought. It is a good word.

justification: reason.

Tuesday. She told me she was made out of a rib taken from my body. This is at least doubtful, if not more than that. I have not missed any rib. . . . She is in much trouble about the buzzard; says grass does not agree with it; is afraid she can't raise it; thinks it was intended to live on decayed flesh. The buzzard must get along the best it can with what it is provided. We cannot overturn the whole scheme to accommodate the buzzard.

Saturday. She fell in the pond yesterday when she was looking at herself in it, which she is always doing. She nearly strangled, and said it was most uncomfortable. This made her sorry for the creatures which live in there, which she calls fish, for she continues to fasten names on to things that don't need them and don't come when they are called by them, which is a matter of no consequence to her, she is such a numskull, anyway; so she got a lot of them out and brought them in last night and put them in my bed to keep warm, but I have noticed them now and then all day and I don't see that they are any happier there than they were before, only quieter. When night comes I shall throw them outdoors. I will not sleep with them again, for I find them clammy and unpleasant to lie among when a person hasn't anything on.

Sunday. Pulled through.

Tuesday. She has taken up with a snake now. The other animals are glad, for she was always experimenting with them and bothering them; and I am glad because the snake talks, and this enables me to get a rest.

Friday. She says the snake advises her to try the fruit of that tree, and says the result will be a great and fine and noble education. I told her there would be another result, too—it would introduce death into the world. That was a mistake—it had been better to keep the remark to myself; it only gave her an idea—she could save the sick buzzard, and furnish fresh meat to the despondent lions and tigers. I advised her to keep away from the tree. She said she wouldn't. I foresee trouble. Will emigrate.

Wednesday. I have had a variegated time. I escaped last night, and rode a horse all night as fast as he could go, hoping to get clear out of the Park and hide in some other country before the trouble should begin; but it was not to be. About an hour after sun-up, as I was riding through a flowery plain where thousands of animals were grazing, slumbering, or playing with each other, according to their wont, all of a sudden they broke into a tempest of frightful noises, and in one moment the plain was a frantic commotion and every beast was destroying its neighbor. I knew what it meant—Eve had eaten that fruit, and death was come into the world. . . . The tigers ate my horse, paying no attention when I ordered them to desist, and they would have eaten me if I had stayed—which I didn't, but went away in much haste. . . . I found this place, outside the Park, and was fairly comfortable for a few days, but she has found me out. Found me out, and has named the place Tonawanda—says it *looks* like that. In fact I was not sorry she came, for there are but meager pickings here, and she brought some of those apples. I was obliged to eat them, I was so hungry. It was against my principles, but I find that principles have no real force except when one is well fed. . . . She came curtained in boughs and bunches of leaves, and when I asked her what she meant by such nonsense, and snatched them away and threw them down, she tittered and blushed. I had never seen a person titter and blush before, and to me it seemed unbecoming and idiotic. She said I would soon know how it was myself. This was correct. Hungry as I was, I laid down the apple half-eaten—certainly the best one I ever saw, considering the lateness of the season—and arrayed myself in the discarded boughs and branches, and then spoke to her with some severity and ordered her to go and get some more and not make such a spectacle of herself. She did it, and after this we crept down to where the wild-beast battle had been, and collected some skins, and I made her patch together a couple of suits proper for public occasions. They are uncomfortable, it is true, but stylish, and that is the main point about clothes. . . . I find

variegated: varied; diverse.

wont: habit.

she is a good deal of a companion. I see I should be lonesome and depressed without her, now that I have lost my property. Another thing, she says it is ordered that we work for our living hereafter. She will be useful. I will superintend.

Ten days later. She accuses *me* of being the cause of our disaster! She says, with apparent sincerity and truth, that the Serpent assured her that the forbidden fruit was not apples, it was chestnuts. I said I was innocent, then, for I had not eaten any chestnuts. She said the Serpent informed her that "chestnut" was a figurative term meaning an aged and moldy joke. I turned pale at that, for I have made many jokes to pass the weary time, and some of them could have been of that sort, though I had honestly supposed that they were new when I made them. She asked me if I had made one just at the time of the catastrophe. I was obliged to admit that I had made one to myself, though not aloud. It was this. I was thinking about the Falls, and I said to myself, "How wonderful it is to see that vast body of water tumble down there!" Then in an instant a bright thought flashed into my head, and I let it fly, saying, "It would be a deal more wonderful to see it tumble *up* there!"—and I was just about to kill myself with laughing at it when all nature broke loose in war and death and I had to flee for my life. "There," she said, with triumph, "that is just it; the Serpent mentioned that very jest, and called it the First Chestnut, and said it was coeval with the creation." Alas, I am indeed to blame. Would that I were not witty; oh, that I had never had that radiant thought!

Next year. We have named it Cain. She caught it while I was up country trapping on the north shore of the Erie; caught it in the timber a couple of miles from our dug-out—or it might have been four, she isn't certain which. It resembles us in some ways, and may be a relation. That is what she thinks, but this is an error, in my judgment. The difference in size warrants the conclusion that it is a different and new kind of animal—a fish, perhaps, though when I put it in the water to see, it sank, and she plunged in and snatched it out before there was opportunity for the experiment to determine the matter. I still think it is a fish, but she is indifferent about what it is, and will not let me have it to try. I do not understand

coeval with: the same age as.

this. The coming of the creature seems to have changed her whole nature and made her unreasonable about experiments. She thinks more of it than she does of any of the other animals, but is not able to explain why. Her mind is disordered—everything shows it. Sometimes she carries the fish in her arms half the night when it complains and wants to get to the water. At such times the water comes out of the places in her face that she looks out of, and she pats the fish on the back and makes soft sounds with her mouth to soothe it, and betrays sorrow and solicitude in a hundred ways. I have never seen her do like this with any other fish, and it troubles me greatly. She used to carry the young tigers around so, and play with them, before we lost our property, but it was only play; she never took on about them like this when their dinner disagreed with them.

Sunday. She doesn't work, Sundays, but lies around all tired out, and likes to have the fish wallow over her; and she makes fool noises to amuse it, and pretends to chew its paws, and that makes it laugh. I have not seen a fish before that could laugh. This makes me doubt. . . . I have come to like Sunday myself. Superintending all the week tires a body so. There ought to be more Sundays. In the old days they were tough, but now they come handy. . . .

solicitude: concern

For thought and discussion

1 A number of things seem "out of place" in this account—the first one being that Adam is setting down his thoughts in English, presumably with pen and paper. What are some other incongruities? Why do you think the author included them?

2 What kind of person is Adam? Describe him in two sentences.

3 God is never mentioned in this account. Can you find any places where his presence is implied?

4 What stereotypes of masculinity and femininity are presented in the "Diary"? In what ways might the "Diary" be different if it were written by Eve? (Clemens later wrote "Eve's Diary"; you may wish to find and read it.)

MURDER

Genesis

Cain: the Hebrew
word for "gotten."

tiller: one who plows;
a farmer.
fruit: produce.
firstlings: first
offspring.

countenance: face.

couching: crouching.

Now Adam knew Eve his wife, and she conceived and bore Cain, saying, "I have gotten a man with the help of the Lord." And again, she bore his brother Abel. Now Abel was a keeper of sheep, and Cain a tiller of the ground. In the course of time Cain brought to the Lord an offering of the fruit of the ground, and Abel brought of the firstlings of his flock and of their fat portions. And the Lord had regard for Abel and his offering, but for Cain and his offering he had no regard. So Cain was very angry, and his countenance fell. The Lord said to Cain, "Why are you angry, and why has your countenance fallen? If you do well, will you not be accepted? And if you do not do well, sin is couching at the door; its desire is for you, but you must master it."

Cain said to Abel his brother, "Let us go out to the field." And when they were in the field, Cain rose up against his brother Abel, and killed him. Then the Lord said to Cain, "Where is Abel your brother?" He said, "I do not know; am I my brother's keeper?" And the Lord said, "What have you done? The voice of your brother's blood is crying to me from the ground. And now you are cursed from the ground, which has opened its mouth to receive your brother's blood from your hand. When you till the ground, it shall no longer yield to you its strength; you shall be a fugitive and a wanderer on the earth." Cain said to the Lord, "My punishment is greater than I can bear. Behold, thou hast driven me this day away from the ground; and from thy face I shall be hidden; and I shall be a fugitive and a wanderer on the earth, and whoever finds me will slay me." Then the Lord said to him, "Not so! If any one slays Cain, vengeance shall be taken on him sevenfold." And

Genesis 4:1–16 (RSV).

the Lord put a mark on Cain, lest any who came upon him should kill him. Then Cain went away from the presence of the Lord, and dwelt in the land of Nod, east of Eden.

mark: according to tradition, borne on his forehead.

Nod: the Hebrew word for "wandering."

For close reading

1 Brothers sometimes compete with each other; they have certain responsibilities for each other; and there are limits to what they may do to each other. Where are these three themes dealt with in the story?
2 What do you think is meant by the word *keeper?*
3 What is Cain told about the future?
4 What protection does the Lord offer Cain after his crime?

For thought and discussion

5 This story suggests a competition between two ways of living: herding (Abel) and farming (Cain). Can you think of other examples where people are set against each other because of their different livelihoods? Explain.
6 The Bible gives no reasons for God's rejection of Cain's offering. What reasons can you suggest?
7 Do you think the killing of Abel was planned

before the brothers went to the field? Explain. Which do you think is worse, a planned act of revenge or an angry, thoughtless attack? Why?

8 Cain has done a fearful thing, yet the Lord gives him a guarantee of protection. Why? If you committed a crime, would you prefer to have a mark which would protect you from others, or to have no mark at all? Explain.

9 What do you suppose is meant by a "sevenfold" punishment? Is Cain's punishment sevenfold for his killing of Abel? If so, how? If not, why is his punishment made less than that of those who might kill him in the future?

Activities

1 The most famous line in the story is the question, "Am I my brother's keeper?" Look for a moment at your classmates. Do you feel obligations to "keep" them? If so, in what ways? In what other ways would you deny your obligations? Write out your answer or prepare notes for a talk in class.

2 Tell the story from the point of view of Adam or Eve.

3 Write out an imagined dialogue in the field between Abel and Cain.

4 Guitar player. Study the story until you can remember the incidents well enough to tell the story from memory. With gentle guitar strumming as background, tell the story to the class in the mood of the blues, or as a simple country tragedy.

CAIN

Howard Nemerov

(A field at the edge of a forest. Two altars, or fireplaces anyhow, one blackened and smoking, the other clean stone. To the second altar, enter **CAIN** *carrying vegetables.)*

CAIN. The corn is coming along,
Tomatoes ripening up nicely, in a week
There should be melons. The apples
Are still green, but, then, after what happened
5   It might be as well if apples were not mentioned.
There is a good deal I don't understand
About that story, often as I've heard it told.
Mother doesn't like to discuss it, of course.
And I suspect that Adam my father
10   Is not entirely clear himself as to what happened
Though he wears a very wise expression.
(Enter **ABEL.***)*
ABEL. Well! My sacrifices accepted for the day, I
    see.
And nothing more to be done for the moment.
Not bad. But you, brother,
15   I don't see any flames at your offering.
It's blood and meat the Lord likes,
Charred on the outside, red and juicy inside;
There's something unmanly about vegetables,
I always say. That's probably your trouble.
20   **CAIN.** Go on, amuse yourself at my expense,

I guess you have the right, for certainly
God favors your offerings of meat,
And leaves my vegetables alone. He leaves
The flowers too, that I bring
25   Because they are lovely, a something extra
To ornament the altar, and do Him honor
These lilies that are blooming now.
ABEL *(laughing)*. You can't imagine the mighty God of All
Eating a lily! What God wants
30   Is strength. Strong men want strong meat.
CAIN. If He made All, He made the lilies too.
And He can't be like a man.
ABEL. I'm not arguing, I'm telling you,
It's simply a matter of fact.
35   The Lord has put His blessing on blood and
meat.
Therefore He prefers me before you,
And I prosper greatly, and sit on the hillside
Watching my flocks, while you
Sweat in your vegetable patch.
40   **CAIN.** You have to kill those poor little lambs.
ABEL. Well, it's a man's work anyhow.
CAIN. It's horrible. I've heard them bleat
Before you cut the throat, and I've seen
The fear dumb in their eyes. What must it be
like,
45   I wonder, to die?
ABEL. We can't tell, till one of us does.
I expect you'll be the first.
CAIN. Me? Why me?
ABEL. It's perfectly simple. Death is a punishment.
50   In dying we are punished for our sin.
CAIN. *Our* sin? I haven't sinned. What have I done?
ABEL. We have all sinned, and all will die.
But God's not respecting your offerings
Is a sign that you will be the first.
55   **CAIN.** You sound rather pleased about it.
ABEL. Do you suppose I want to be the first?
No, I am essentially a conservative person.
And I can see, looking at my lambs,
That dying's a grim business. I'm in no hurry.
60   It's only fit that you go first—you were born
first.
Vegetarian!
CAIN. I don't understand. What have I done
That was wrong, or you that was right?

Father and Mother began the fault,
65   I know the story as well as you do.
ABEL. You don't accept life as it is, that's
        your trouble.
     Things are the way they are, that's all.
     They've been that way from the beginning.
CAIN. Which isn't so very long ago.
70   **ABEL.** And they will always be as they are.
     Accept it, Cain. Face up to reality.
CAIN. That's easy for a winner to say.
(Enter **ADAM** *and* **EVE.***)*
CAIN and **ABEL.** Father! Mother!
(They bow their heads.)
ADAM. That's right, respect. It's a proper respect
75   As from the children to the parents
     That keeps the world going round. It's a fine
        day,
     And life is what you make it, isn't that so?
     And both boys working hard, yes, that's right.
     "In the sweat of thy face shalt thou eat
        thy bread"
80   Is what He said to me, but it's not so bad
     When the children sweat for the father's bread.
(He picks a tomato from **CAIN'S** *altar and eats it.)*
CAIN. Father, that is my offering to the Lord.
ADAM. Don't worry, I won't eat it all. Anyhow,
     The Lord seems to prefer the flesh and fat
85   That Abel provides. I must say
     That I agree. I'm eating this
     Only to stave off hunger till mealtime.
     Abel, I smell roast lamb. Good!
ABEL. Yes, the Lord God has received the essence,
90   And we may eat whatever is left over.
CAIN. It seems to me that everything is left except
        the smoke.
ABEL. Don't talk of what you don't understand.
ADAM. It is obvious, Cain, that you don't know
     The first principle of sacrifice. It is
95   The divine effluvium of the beast that rises
     To God in heaven, and does Him honor.
     A spiritual essence Himself, He feeds on spirit.
     The grosser parts are the leftovers of His meal,
     Which we may eat, if we do so with humble
        hearts.
100 **EVE.** Why doesn't He eat the divine effluvium
     Of Cain's vegetables?
ABEL.   Whoever heard

effluvium: vapor or odor.

essence: concentration.

Of burning vegetables? Our God
Is an eater of meat, meat, meat.
ADAM. Mother, don't mix in the relations of man
with God.
105 Remember what happened last time.
(There is a silence.)
EVE. It wasn't my fault. It was only a mistake.
ADAM. A mistake to end all mistakes.
EVE. You listened to me, wise as you are.
ADAM. It proves the wisdom of my not doing so
again.
110 He for God alone, and she for God in him;
Remember that, and there won't be any trouble.
CAIN. Sir, what really did happen last time,
I mean in the Garden?
ABEL. What's past is past. Cain still believes
115 There's something that he doesn't understand,
Or that you haven't told us, which would make
Some difference to his situation.
EVE *(to Cain).* My poor boy, my poor, dear boy,
I too
Go over it and over it in my mind, I too,
120 Though what I did is said to be so dreadful,
Feel that the Lord's way with me
Was very arbitrary, to say the least.
ADAM. Woman, enough. You'll make us more
trouble.
ABEL. And as for Cain, he should have the tact
125 Not to pursue a subject which so evidently
Causes his mother pain.
(to **CAIN***)*
Also, our food is ready.
You may do as you please about that slop of
yours,
But *this family* is going to eat.
*(***CAIN*** sits to one side, the rest to the other.* **CAIN**
starts eating a tomato.)
ADAM. Not, however, before properly rendering
thanks
130 To the Most High. Cain, have the decency
To control your appetite until Abel
Has sanctified our meal with prayer. Abel.
ABEL. Permit us, O Lord, this tender beast
Slain in Thy Holy Name, Amen.
(All eat.)
135 **ADAM.** Mm, good.

arbitrary: based on
chance or one's own
wishes; unreasonable.

CAIN. Won't you let me have some? It smells
    good,
And I would give you all this fruit.
ADAM. Dear boy, don't let us go all over this
    again.
It's not that we don't care for you personally,
140   But we simply cannot afford to offend the Lord.
If He does not respect your offering, Cain,
It would be presumptuous in us to do so,
If He means to separate you by this sign,
We must not disobey.
145 **ABEL.** To each according to his labor, you know.
CAIN. But I haven't done anything wrong—
    As far as I'm aware, that is.
ADAM. As far as you're aware, or we. Who knows
The hidden meaning of God's mysteries?
150   By the sign you are set off, and that's enough.
ABEL. I'd set him further off. Suppose that God
In His displeasure should strike Cain
With fire from Heaven? I know that God
Can do whatever He will, but still
155   If we sit this close there might just be
    an accident.
CAIN *(moving a bit further away).*
    I don't want to be a danger to you, you all
Seem to understand things so much better
    than I do.
But what have I done wrong? Answer me that.
ADAM. Ah, as to that, you would have to ask Him.
(He points upward.)
160 **CAIN.** Did He really speak to you, Himself—then?
ADAM. He did indeed, yes. Your father has
    spoken with God.
CAIN. What does He look like?
ADAM. Oh, you don't really see Him, you know,
He doesn't have a form. There was a Voice.
165 **EVE** *(covering her ears).* Don't. Don't remind me.
    That Voice!
ADAM. Mother, have more respect. We are
    talking
Of divine things. Besides, who was responsible
For His talking to us in that voice,
And saying what He said? Remember that,
170   Consider your sin, be quiet.
ABEL. Cain thinks, because he is a gardener,
That he would have been at home in a Garden.

It's illogical, Cain, to suppose
The Garden of the Lord would be anything like
   yours.
175 **CAIN.** Illogical, yes. Yet if I reason it out,
It does appear that God did once favor gardens,
Since, after all, He put our parents there.
And if I ask myself why He has turned against
Garden and gardener, I will have to answer
180 That what our parents did while they were there
Was the thing that changed His mind.

blasphemy: contempt
for God.

ADAM. I will not have blasphemy, Cain,
And particularly not while we are at meat.
As for disrespect for your father,
185 I will not have that at any time. After all,
Your mother went through much suffering
To bring you into the world, while I
Labored to give you food and all good things.
For you to reward us with ingratitude
190 Proves, to my mind, a hidden fault in you,
And sufficiently explains why the All-Wise
Does not respect your offerings as Abel's;
Some wickedness, my boy, which is bringing
   you to sin.
EVE. But truly, father, it was our fault.
195 It was my fault first, then it was yours.
ADAM. We may have made an error of judgment.
Does Cain suppose he could have done better?
We tried our best to give you boys
A decent life and bring you up to be honest,
200 Industrious, pleasing in the sight of the Lord.
As a matter of fact, I am convinced
It was a piece of luck to have got out of
   that garden.
It was no place to bring up children in.
You would have had everything provided for
   you,
205 No need to learn the manly virtues,
The dignity of toil, the courage of independence.
No, Cain, hard work never hurt anybody.
What happened to us was the will of God,
Which shows He did not mean us to sit around
210 On our behinds in a garden all our lives,
But to get out in the world and become
The masters of it.
ABEL.   Inventors of the knife,
The wheel, the bow.
ADAM. Sometimes I could bless that serpent!

215 **EVE.** Stop! What dreadful things you are saying.
　　　Shame, labor, and the pains of birth
　　　The woman knows. Those are the fruits
　　　That grew on the forbidden tree, and I,
　　　The first to sin, was the first to know them.
220 　　　I shall be the first to know death also.
　　ADAM. Mother, don't excite yourself. What's
　　　　done is done.
　　　As for death, no need to talk of that, I hope,
　　　For many years.
　　ABEL. The little lambs are peaceful after death,
225 　　　Mother. There's only a moment of fright,
　　　And then it's over.
　　CAIN. But there's that moment, that small
　　　　moment.
　　　A man might do anything, if he thought enough
　　　How there's no way out but through that
　　　　moment.
230 　　　He might become wild, and run away,
　　　Knowing there was nowhere to run, he
　　　　might . . .
　　ABEL. Might what?
　　CAIN. Kill.
　　ABEL. He might leave off babbling in that manner,
235 　　　And remember he is a man, if not a very good
　　　　one.
　　CAIN. But if a man, even if not a very good one,
　　　Is turned away by his God, what does he do?
　　　Where does he go? What could he do
　　　Worse than what is already done to him?
240 　　　For there is God on the one hand,
　　　And all the world on the other, and this man
　　　Between them. Why should he care,
　　　Seeing he cannot save himself?
　　ADAM. These are dangerous thoughts, Cain.
245 　　　That man might better think
　　　Wherein he has offended.
　　*(The sky darkens. Thunder is heard, and lightning
　　　seen.)*
　　ABEL. Aha! he's done it now, with his talk.
　　　Did you think He would not have heard?
　　　Did you consider the rest of us?
250 **CAIN.** I only meant to ask.
　　ABEL. You are being answered.
　　(He points to the sky.)
　　ADAM. I am afraid, Cain, that Abel is right.
　　　I have faced up to God one time in my life,

It was enough. The coming storm
255 You brought down on yourself, and you must face
The consequences. I am sorry for you.
Eve, come. Come, Abel. We shall seek shelter elsewhere.
(They leave, and **CAIN** *stands alone. Lightning flashes, sounds of thunder, then a stillness.)*
CAIN. Ah, they are right. I am going to die,
And I deserve to die. As Abel said,
260 There is no argument, the uneasy fear
I feel in my stomach tells me I am wrong,
Am guilty of everything, everything,
Though I cannot say what it is. Lord!
Lord God! Master! I am a wicked man,
265 The thoughts of my heart are wicked
And I don't know why. Punish me, Lord,
Punish me, but do not let me die.
*(***CAIN** *kneels.)*
THE VOICE OF GOD *(in the silence).*
Cain.
Cain.
Cain.
CAIN. Here I am.
270 **GOD.** What do you want?
CAIN. I want to know.
GOD. Ask.
CAIN. Why do You respect my brother's offerings and not mine?
GOD. That is not the question you want to ask.
275 **CAIN.** Why do You prefer Abel to me?
GOD. That again is not it. You must ask to the end.
(A long silence)
CAIN. Why are things as they are?
GOD. I will debate it with you. Do you know
That things are as they are?
280 **CAIN.** But—but they *are,* they just *are.* Besides,
My father says they are.
GOD. Cain, I am your father.
CAIN. Sir, as you say.
GOD. Do you want things to be other than as they are?
285 **CAIN.** I want my offering to be acceptable, Sir.
I want my offering to be preferred over Abel's.
I want to be respected, even as he is now.
GOD. Why do you trouble yourself about it, then?

The thing is easy. If you do well,
290   Will you not be accepted? And if you do not
       do well,
Look, sin lies at the door.
CAIN. Sir, I do not understand.
GOD. Cain, Cain, I am trying to tell you.
All things can be done, you must only
295   Do what you will. Things are as they are
Until you decide to change them,
But do not be surprised if afterward
Things are as they are again. What is to stop
      you
From ruling over Abel?
(Again after a silence)
300 **CAIN.** I do not know.
(Thunder)
    I do not know. I said I do not know.
    He is not there and I am alone.
(The sky clears, the light grows stronger.)
    And this is Abel's knife, which he left here
    In his hurry to escape the storm he hoped
       would slay me.
305   And that storm was God.
    And this is the knife which cuts the throats
    Of acceptable sacrifices.
*(Enter **ABEL**.)*
ABEL. You're still alive. Surely the ways of the
      Lord
Are past understanding. Have you seen my knife?
310 **CAIN** *(still kneeling).* I have it here.
ABEL. Throw it to me then. I'm still uneasy
    About coming close to you.
CAIN. I have spoken with God, Abel. If you want
      your knife,
Come over here and have it. God said things,
315   Abel, such as I never heard from you. He told
      me
About the will. Do what you will, He said.
And more than that. He said: You must
Do what you will. Abel, do you understand
That saying?
320 **ABEL** *(approaching).* The knife, I want the knife.
CAIN. Here, then.
*(He rises, stabbing **ABEL**, who falls.)*
    My sacrifices shall be acceptable.
ABEL. My God, what have you done?
(He dies.)

CAIN *(standing over him).* I have done what I
willed. I have changed
325 The way things are, and the first man's death
is done.
It was not much, I have seen some of his lambs
Die harder.

GOD *(speaking casually, conversationally, without
thunder).*
Do you find it good, what you've done? Or bad?

CAIN *(as though talking to himself).*
Good? Bad? It was my will that I did.
330 I do not know anything of good or bad.

GOD. Do you find that you have changed
Things as they are?

CAIN *(staring at* **ABEL***).* There is this difference,
certainly.
And I have changed inside myself. I see now
335 That a man may be the master here.

GOD. Like that man on the ground?

CAIN. A man. Myself.

GOD. How peaceful he is, lying there.

CAIN. That's true, I feel uneasy, myself.
340 Abel, what have you to say to me now?
Well, speak up.

GOD. He will not speak.

CAIN. He is very quiet now, considering
How much he used to talk. How lonely
345 Everything has become! Mother! Father!
(He shouts.)

GOD. They will do to you as you have done to
him.

CAIN. Then I must run away.

GOD. Where will you run?

CAIN. Anywhere, to be alone.
350 There are no other people.

GOD. You're wrong about that. Everywhere
Men are beginning, and everywhere they
believe
Themselves to be alone, and everywhere
They are making the discovery of the conditions
355 Under which they are as they are. One of these
Discoveries has just been made, by you.
You will be alone, but alone among many,
Alone in every crowd.

CAIN. Seeing me set apart, they will kill me.
360 **GOD.** They would. But I have set my sign
Upon your forehead, that recognizing you,

Men will be afeared. Shunning you, scorning
      you,
Blaming you, they may not kill you.
CAIN *(kneeling)*. Lord God! You spoke, and I did
      not know.
365 GOD. I send you away, Cain. You are one
Of my holy ones, discoverer of limits,
Your name is the name of one of the ways,
And you must bear it. You must bear
The everlasting fear no one can stop,
370 The everlasting life you do not want,
The smell of blood forever on your hand.
You are the discoverer of power, and you
Shall be honored among men that curse you.
And honored even in the moment of the curse.
375 From your discovery shall proceed
Great cities of men, and well defended,
And these men, your descendants, shall make
Weapons of war, and instruments of music,
Being drawn thereto by the nature of power;
380 But they will not be happy, and they will
      not know
Peace or any release from fear.
CAIN. May I not die?
GOD. Because of My sign, only you
May destroy yourself. And because of your fear,
385 You won't. For you have found
An idea of Me somewhat dangerous to consider,
And mankind will, I believe, honor your name
As one who has faced things as they are,
And changed them, and found them still the
      same.
390 CAIN. If I were sorry, would you raise Abel up?
GOD. No.
CAIN. Then I am not sorry. Because You have
      saved me
From everything but the necessity of being me,
I say it is Your fault. None of this need have
      happened.
395 And even my mother's temptation by the
      serpent in the Garden
Would not have happened but for You; I see
      now,
Having chosen myself, what her choice must
      have been.
GOD. Cain, I will tell you a secret.
CAIN. I am listening.

400 **GOD.** I was the serpent in the Garden.
CAIN. I can believe that, but nobody else will.
   I see it so well, that You are the master of the
      will
   That works two ways at once, whose action
   Is its own punishment, the cause
405 That is its own result. It will be pain to me
   To reject You, but I do it, in Your own world,
   Where everything that is will speak of You.
   And I will be deaf.
GOD. You do not reject Me. You cannot.
410 **CAIN.** I do not expect it to be easy.
(After a silence)
   I said: I do not expect it to be easy.
   But He is gone, I feel His absence.
   As, after the storm's black accent,
   The light grows wide and distant again,
415 So He is gone. Of all He said to me,
   Only one thing remains. I send you away,
   He said: Cain, I send you away.
   But where is *Away?* Is it where Abel is,
   My brother, as lonely and still as that?
*(Enter **ADAM** and **EVE**; **CAIN** turns away his face.)*
420 **ADAM** *(at a distance).* Was it the thunder, Abel,
      the lightning?
*(Coming closer, he sees that **ABEL** is on the
   ground.)*
   It can't be. There has been a mistake.
EVE. Abel, my son, my lamb.
(She runs to the corpse and throws herself down.)
ADAM. Monster! Unnatural child! Did you do
      this?
   Lord God, let it not go unpunished,
425 Let it be swiftly visited.

visited: i.e. inflicted.

CAIN *(still turned away).* Suppose it was God that
      struck Abel down?
   Cannot the Lord do as He will do?
ADAM. Liar! I will never believe it, never.
CAIN. Well, then, it was a lie. I did it.
430 But had it been the other way, and I
   The brother lying there, would you not have
      said,
   As I have heard you say so many times,
   What the Lord does is well done?
ADAM. Vicious boy! Have you not done enough?
435 Would you go on to stand against your father?

EVE. Leave off, leave off. One son and the other
son,
All that I had, all that I cared to have,
One son and the other son, and from the
beginning
This was the end I carried, the end we lay
together
440   Taking our pleasure for, is now accomplished.
CAIN. I stand, it seems, alone. Neither against
Nor for father or mother or anything.
ADAM. If the Lord God will not punish. I must.
EVE. Leave off, leave off. All that we had
445   Is halved, and you would destroy the other half?
Abel my son and Cain my son. Old man,
It is your seed that from the beginning
Was set at odds. You ate the fruit
Of the tree of knowledge as well as I,
450   And sickened of it as well as I, and excited
with lust
As I swelled with the fruit of lust,
And have you yet no knowledge?
ADAM. Woman, be quiet. This is not woman's
work.
EVE. Oh, fool, what else if not woman's work?
455   The fruit of the curse has ripened till it fell,
Can you refuse to swallow it? But you will
swallow it,
I tell you, stone and all, one son and the other
son.
ADAM. Cain, I am an old man, but it comes to me
That I must do to you as you did to your brother.
460   **EVE.** Fooled in the Garden, and fooled out of it!
CAIN (turning his face to **ADAM,** who falls back).
Sir, you will do nothing. I am young and strong,
And I have the knife—but no, that's not it,
I do not want to stand against you, but I must.
ADAM. There is a sign, a wound, there on your
brow
465   Between the eyes. Cain, I am afraid of you.
There is a terror written on your face.
CAIN. And I am afraid of you. That is my fear
You see written upon me, that your fear
answers to.
I am forbidden to be sorry for what I did.
470   Forbidden to pity you, forbidden to kiss
My mother's tears, and everywhere

In everything forbidden. I feel myself filled
With this enormous power that I do not want.
This force that tells me I am to go,
475　To go on, always to go on, to go away
And see you both, and this place, never again.
EVE. My son, my only one, you won't go away?
I'll face the fear I see upon your face.
And you'll comfort me for what you did to me.
480　**ADAM.** And stay me in my age? Cain, I accept it,
Though I shall never understand it, this
That you have done, this final thing
In a world where nothing seemed to end,
Is somehow the Lord God's doing. I fear you,
485　My son, but I will learn to still my fear,
If you will stay.
CAIN. No. I would change things if I could.
I tried to change things once, and the change
Is as you see; we cannot change things back,
490　Which may be the only change worth having,
So the future must be full of fear, which I
Would spare you. If this is riddling talk,
Let it go by; or, to speak plainly,
I am afraid my fear would make me kill you
495　If I stayed here.
EVE.　　　　　　This is the end
That we began with. Why should we not
Curse God and die?
ADAM. Woman, be careful.
EVE. I have been careful, full of care.
500　My son, my darling, why not kill us both?
It would be only what we did to you;
And that was only what was done to us.
CAIN. Mother, Mother, I must not hear you.
You and I, we understand things alike,
505　And that is curse enough, maybe. But he
May have his own curse, which we
Don't understand, that is, to go on.
Into the darkness, into the light,
Having the courage not to know
510　That what I do to him is what he does to me,
And both of us compelled, or maybe
It is a blessing, the blindness of too much light
That comes from staring at the sun.
　　　　　　　　　　　　　Father,
I'd bless you if I could, but I suspect
515　That God believes in you.
And now farewell,

If that is possible; try not to remember me.
(CAIN goes. The scene begins to darken.)
ADAM. Old woman, we are alone again, and the
    night
Beginning to come down. Do you remember
520   The first night outside the Garden?
EVE. We slept in the cold sparkle of the
    angel's sword,
Having cried ourselves asleep.
ADAM. If we went back, do you think, and stood
At the gate, and said plainly, kill us
525   Or take us back, do you think . . . ?
EVE. No.
ADAM. You're right, we couldn't any more go
    back
Than you could be my rib again, in my first
    sleep.
The water in the rivers running out of Eden,
530   Where must that water be now, do you think?
EVE. It must be elsewhere, somewhere in the
    world;
And yet I know those rivers glitter with water
    still.
Abel my son and my son Cain, all that we had
    is gone.
Old as we are, we come to the beginning again.
535 ADAM. Doing as we would, and doing as we
    must. . . .
The darkness is so lonely, lonelier now
Than on the first night, even, out of Eden.
Having what we've had, and knowing what
  we know. . . .
EVE. What have we had, and what do we know?
540   The years are flickering as a dream, in which
Our sons are grown and gone away. Husband,
Take courage, come to my arms, husband and
    lord.
It is the beginning of everything.
ADAM. Must we take the terrible night into our-
    selves
545   And make the morning of it? Again?
Old woman, girl, bride of the first sleep,
In pleasure and in bitterness all ways
I love you till it come death or daylight.

For close reading

1 How does Cain feel about killing at the beginning of the play?

2 According to Adam, who or what was responsible for his and Eve's ejection from the Garden? What are Eve's thoughts about this?

3 Why does Cain kill Abel?

For thought and discussion

4 What do we learn about Cain, Abel, Adam, and Eve from the opening speeches of each? With which character or characters did you sympathize most? Why?

5 In lines 278–279, God asks a question. Try putting emphasis on "you" and then on "know" as you read the question. Considering Cain's answer, which is the better way to read the question?

6 Reread lines 387–389. What things do you think are "still the same"?

7 God tells Cain that he is the "discoverer of limits" (line 366). What "limit" has Cain discovered?

8 Is it significant in your opinion that God speaks only to Cain? Why or why not?

9 Does Cain change by the end of the play? Does Adam? Does Eve? If so, how?

10 Complete the following sentence: "Howard Nemerov's play "Cain" is about . . . ." Write down as many answers as you can think of. Check the two or three which seem the most important to you.

THE GREAT FLOOD

Genesis

These are the generations of Noah. Noah was a righteous man, blameless in his generation; Noah walked with God. And Noah had three sons, Shem, Ham, and Japheth.

Now the earth was corrupt in God's sight, and the earth was filled with violence. And God saw the earth, and behold, it was corrupt; for all flesh had corrupted their way upon the earth. And God said to Noah, "I have determined to make an end of all flesh; for the earth is filled with violence through them; behold, I will destroy them with the earth. Make yourself an ark of gopher wood; make rooms in the ark, and cover it inside and out with pitch. This is how you are to make it: the length of the ark three hundred cubits, its breadth fifty cubits, and its height thirty cubits. Make a roof for the ark, and finish it to a cubit above; and set the door of the ark in its side; make it with lower, second, and third decks. For behold, I will bring a flood of waters upon the earth, to destroy all flesh in which is the breath of life from under heaven; everything that is on the earth shall die. But I will establish my covenant with you; and you shall come into the ark, you, your sons, your wife, and your sons' wives with you. And of every living thing of all flesh, you shall bring two of every sort into the ark, to keep them alive with you; they shall be male and female. Of the birds according to their kinds, and of the animals

gopher wood: possibly a kind of cypress; durable light wood.

pitch: tar.

cubit: about eighteen inches.

covenant: agreement.

according to their kinds: of all kinds.

Genesis 6:9–22; 7:11–24; 8:6–12, 20–22; 9:1–19 (RSV).

according to their kinds, of every creeping thing of the ground according to its kind, two of every sort shall come in to you, to keep them alive. Also take with you every sort of food that is eaten, and store it up; and it shall serve as food for you and for them." Noah did this; he did all that God commanded him. . . .

In the six hundredth year of Noah's life, in the second month, on the seventeenth day of the month, on that day all the fountains of the great deep burst forth, and the windows of the heavens were opened. And rain fell upon the earth forty days and forty nights. On the very same day Noah and his sons, Shem and Ham and Japheth, and Noah's wife and the three wives of his sons with them entered the ark, they and every beast according to its kind, and all the cattle according to their kinds, and every creeping thing that creeps on the earth according to its kind, and every bird according to its kind, every bird of every sort. They went into the ark with Noah, **two and two:** two by two of all flesh in which there was the breath of life. And they that entered, male and female of all flesh, went in as God had commanded him; and the Lord shut him in.

two and two: two by two.

The flood continued forty days upon the earth; and the waters increased, and bore up the ark, and it rose high above the earth. The waters prevailed and increased greatly upon the earth; and the ark floated on the face of the waters. And the waters prevailed so mightily upon the earth that all the high mountains under the whole heaven were covered; the waters prevailed above the mountains, covering them fifteen cubits deep. And all flesh died that moved upon the earth, birds, cattle, beasts, all swarming creatures that swarm upon the earth, and every man; everything on the dry land in whose nostrils was the breath of life died. He blotted out every living thing that was upon the face of the ground, man and animals and creeping things and birds of the air; they were blotted out from the earth. Only Noah was left, and those that were with him in the ark. And the waters prevailed upon the earth a hundred and fifty days. . . .

prevailed: swelled, crested.

At the end of forty days Noah opened the window of the ark which he had made, and sent forth a raven; and it went to and fro until the waters were dried up from the earth. Then he sent forth a dove from him, to see if the waters had subsided from the face of the ground; but the dove found no place to set her foot, and she returned to him to the ark, for the waters were still on the face of the whole earth. So he put forth his hand and took her and brought her into the ark with him. He waited another seven days, and again he sent forth the dove out of the ark; and the dove came back to him in the evening, and lo, in her mouth a freshly plucked olive leaf; so Noah knew that the waters had subsided from the earth. Then he waited another seven days, and sent forth the dove; and she did not return to him any more. . . .

Then Noah built an altar to the Lord, and took of every clean animal and of every clean bird, and offered burnt offerings on the altar. And when the Lord smelled the pleasing odor, the Lord said in his heart, "I will never again curse the ground because of man, for the imagination of man's heart is evil from his youth; neither will I ever again destroy every living creature as I have done. While the earth remains, seedtime and harvest, cold and heat, summer and winter, day and night, shall not cease."

And God blessed Noah and his sons, and said to them, "Be fruitful and multiply, and fill the earth. The fear of you and the dread of you shall be upon every beast of the earth, and upon every bird of the air, upon everything that creeps on the ground and all the fish of the sea; into your hand they are delivered. Every moving thing that lives shall be food for you; and as I gave you the green plants, I give you everything. Only you shall not eat flesh with its life, that is, its blood. For your lifeblood I will surely require a reckoning; of every beast I will require it and of man; of every man's brother I will require the life of man. Whoever sheds the blood of man, by man shall his blood be shed; for God made man in his own image. And you, be fruitful and multiply, bring forth abundantly on the earth and multiply in it."

Then God said to Noah and to his sons with him, "Behold, I establish my covenant with you and your descendants after you, and with every living creature that is with you, the birds, the cattle, and every beast of the earth with you, as many as came out of the ark. I establish my covenant with you, that never again shall all flesh be cut off by the waters of a flood, and never again shall there be a flood to destroy the earth." And God said, "This is the sign of the covenant which I make between me and you and every living creature that is with you, for all future generations: I set my bow in the cloud, and it shall be a sign of the covenant between me and the earth. When I bring clouds over the earth and the bow is seen in the clouds, I will remember my covenant which is between me and you and every living creature of all flesh; and the waters shall never again become a flood to destroy all flesh. When the bow is in the clouds, I will look upon it and remember the everlasting covenant between God and every living creature of all flesh that is upon the earth." God said to Noah, "This is the sign of the covenant which I have established between me and all flesh that is upon the earth."

bow: rainbow.

The sons of Noah who went forth from the ark were Shem, Ham, and Japheth. Ham was the father of Canaan. These three were the sons of Noah; and from these the whole earth was peopled.

For close reading

1 What seem to be the reasons for God's selection of Noah to build the ark?
2 Two birds are sent forth from the ark to test the earth. Which of the two brought the good news that the Flood had subsided? What does that bird symbolize today? What does the olive branch symbolize?
3 God makes promises to Noah before the Flood and again after the Flood subsides. Compare and contrast the two statements.

For thought and discussion

4 The Great Flood may be one of the two or three stories most memorable to young children. What elements in it contribute to that appeal?

5 In his instructions to Noah, what does God say about the relationship between people and other living creatures? Is this a change from earlier times? Explain. What would you say is the relationship between people and other living creatures today?

6 The word *every* occurs over twenty times in this passage. Why do you suppose this word is used so frequently? What other words and phrases are repeated often in this story? Sometimes repetitions are dull, other times they are forceful. What is the effect here? Why?

7 Which do you think is stronger in the story of Noah, warning or reassurance? Explain.

Activities

1 Look up the word *kind* in a large dictionary and report on it to the class. You will find it a long entry. What do you think are the reasons for its having so many meanings?

2 Write a description of life aboard the ark. Or write the monologue which might run through Noah's mind at several points in the story. Conclude this activity by playing Bill Cosby's Noah monologues from the album *Bill Cosby Is A Very Funny Fellow, Right!*

3 Construct a model ark.

NOAH

David Ignatow

RIGHT: *The Story of Cain and Abel*, detail from
The Gates of Paradise (east door) of the Baptistry,
Florence. Bronze gilt relief by Lorenzo Ghiberti,
c. 1436. SCALA/Florence.

He must wade out to a high point
and build an ark of the trees,
take two of each kind of happiness.
And send out
5 a pigeon that shall not return,
after the bubbling shriek of the drowned;
it shall land upon a rock.
God of his crying shall have made the flood
   subside.
10 He shall emerge
upon the earth, brown for grief
of its dead, and know no better
than before, save there is a promise
to cling to when the floods rise.

For thought and discussion

1 What would you say is the mood of this poem?
What details help create this mood?
2 According to the poet, what knowledge does
Noah have when he emerges from the ark?

ABOVE: *Noah Releasing the Dove from the Ark,* mosaic from St. Mark's Cathedral, Venice, before 1220. Erich Lessing from Magnum.
RIGHT: *Dove with Olive Leaf* from Noah's Ark panel, Verdun Altar, the Abbey Klosterneuberg, Austria, by Nicholas of Verdun, 1180. Enamel and copper gilt. Erich Lessing from Magnum.
The Dove Sent Forth from the Ark, detail from an illustration by Gustave Doré, 1866.
Page 64: *The Tower of Babel,* detail from an oil on wood painting by Pieter Bruegel the Elder, 1563. The Kunsthistorisches Museum, Vienna.

[*These four poems are from
a series of simple prayers by Noah
and the animals in the ark.*]

Carmen Bernos de Gasztold
Translated by Rumer Godden

NOAH'S PRAYER

Lord,
what a menagerie!
Between Your downpour and these animal cries
one cannot hear oneself think!
5 The days are long,
Lord.
All this water makes my heart sink.
When will the ground cease to rock under my
     feet?
The days are long.
10 Master Raven has not come back.
Here is Your dove.
Will she find us a twig of hope?
The days are long,
Lord.
15 Guide Your Ark to safety,
some zenith of rest,   **zenith:** highest point.
where we can escape at last
from this brute slavery.
The days are long,
20 Lord.
Lead me until I reach the shore of Your covenant.

Amen

THE PRAYER OF THE BUTTERFLY

Lord!
Where was I?
Oh yes! This flower, this sun,
thank You! Your world is beautiful!
5   This scent of roses . . .
Where was I?
A drop of dew
rolls to sparkle in a lily's heart.
I have to go . . .
10 Where? I do not know!
The wind has painted fancies
on my wings.
Fancies . . .
Where was I?
15 Oh yes! Lord,
I had something to tell you:

Amen

THE PRAYER OF THE OX

Dear God, give me time.
Men are always so driven!
Make them understand that I can never hurry.
Give me time to eat.
5   Give me time to plod.
Give me time to sleep.
Give me time to think.

Amen

THE PRAYER OF THE COCK

Do not forget, Lord,
it is I who make the sun rise.
I am Your servant
but, with the dignity of my calling,
5   I need some glitter and ostentation.
Noblesse oblige. . . .
All the same,
I am Your servant,
only . . . do not forget, Lord,
10   I make the sun rise.

                                    Amen

ostentation: showiness.

noblesse oblige: the
obligation of the rich or
highly ranked to be
kind to those less
fortunate.

For thought and discussion

1 Why does time weigh so heavily on Noah?
2 The cock has something mixed up. What is it?
3 In what way is the *content* of the butterfly's prayer
appropriate to a butterfly? In what way is the structure of the poem appropriate? Apply these same
questions to "The Prayer of the Ox."
4 What irony can you find in line 2 of "The Prayer of
the Ox"?
5 The Bible story of the Flood does not mention
Noah's thoughts and feelings. Do the portrayals of
Noah in "Noah's Prayer" and Ignatow's "Noah"
seem reasonable to you? Why or why not?

BABEL:
THE CITY
AND THE
TOWER

Genesis

Shinar (shi/när): in what was later Babylonia; today southern Iraq.

bitumen (bə tü/mən): asphalt, used to cement bricks together.

Babel (bā/bəl): "gate of God" in Babylonian. It is also similar to the Hebrew word meaning "to confuse."

Now the whole earth had one language and few words. And as men migrated in the east, they found a plain in the land of Shinar and settled there. And they said to one another, "Come, let us make bricks, and burn them thoroughly." And they had brick for stone, and bitumen for mortar. Then they said, "Come, let us build ourselves a city, and a tower with its top in the heavens, and let us make a name for ourselves, lest we be scattered abroad upon the face of the whole earth." And the Lord came down to see the city and the tower, which the sons of men had built. And the Lord said, "Behold, they are one people, and they have all one language; and this is only the beginning of what they will do; and nothing that they propose to do will now be impossible for them. Come, let us go down, and there confuse their language, that they may not understand one another's speech." So the Lord scattered them abroad from there over the face of all the earth, and they left off building the city. Therefore its name was called Babel, because there the Lord confused the language of all the earth; and from there the Lord scattered them abroad over the face of all the earth.

Genesis 11:1–9 (RSV).

For close reading

1 This story is told in ten sentences. Under the following headings indicate the sentences: *(a)* which are speeches by the people; *(b)* which are speeches by the Lord; *(c)* which describe the situation before construction of the tower; *(d)* which describe the situation after the Lord's actions; and *(e)* the sentence that links the two speakers in the episode.

2 What phrase is repeated by the people and then by the Lord? What other repetitions do you find?

3 What reason did the people give for building the tower?

For thought and discussion

4 Why do you think the people wanted to "make a name for themselves"?

5 In what ways is this story similar to the episode of the forbidden fruit in the Garden of Eden? In what ways is it different?

6 Examine the chart you made for question one. What patterns do you find? What might these patterns of structure and language contribute to the story?

7 Which do you think is the uppermost concern of this story: the warning against extreme ambition, the explanation of why people speak different languages, or something else? Explain.

8 Until modern times, the tallest buildings of a society were usually places of worship. How might this fact be related to the Babel story?

Activities

1 James Thurber once said, "We use only one quarter of our brain cells, and a good thing too." What do you think he meant? What is your response to that opinion? Write about it.

2 Using whatever materials you wish, build a model of the tower of Babel.

2

forefathers
of
israel

ABRAHAM: A PROMISE, A TEST

Genesis

Now the Lord said to Abram, "Go from your country and your kindred and your father's house to the land that I will show you. And I will make of you a great nation, and I will bless you, and make your name great, so that you will be a blessing. I will bless those who bless you, and him who curses you I will curse; and by you all the families of the earth shall bless themselves."

So Abram went, as the Lord had told him; and Lot went with him. Abram was seventy-five years old when he departed from Haran. And Abram took Sarai his wife, and Lot his brother's son, and all their possessions which they had gathered, and the persons that they had gotten in Haran; and they set forth to go to the land of Canaan. . . .

After these things the word of the Lord came to Abram in a vision, "Fear not, Abram, I am your shield; your reward shall be very great." But Abram said, "O Lord God, what wilt thou give me, for I continue childless, and the heir of my house is Eliezer of Damascus?" And Abram said, "Behold, thou hast given me no offspring; and a slave born in my house will be my heir." And behold, the word of the Lord came to him, "This man shall not be your heir; your own son shall be your heir." And he brought him outside and said, "Look toward heaven, and number the stars, if you are able to number

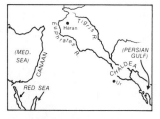

Canaan (kā′nən): the region between the Jordan River and the Mediterranean.

heir . . . Eliezer: probably by adoption to carry on Abram's name.

Genesis 12:1–5; 15:1–12, 17–21; 18:1–15; 21:1–7; 22:1–14 (RSV).
LEFT: *Sacrifice of Abraham* (Oshogbo), lino-cut by Jacob Afolabi, 1964. Courtesy of Ulli Beier.

them." Then he said to him, "So shall your descendants be." And he believed the Lord; and he reckoned it to him as righteousness.

And he said to him, "I am the Lord who brought you from Ur of the Chaldeans, to give you this land to possess." But he said, "O Lord God, how am I to know that I shall possess it?" He said to him, "Bring me a heifer three years old, a she-goat three years old, a ram three years old, a turtledove, and a young pigeon." And he brought him all these, cut them in two, and laid each half over against the other; but he did not cut the birds in two. And when birds of prey came down upon the carcasses, Abram drove them away.

As the sun was going down, a deep sleep fell on Abram; and lo, a dread and great darkness fell upon him. . . .

When the sun had gone down and it was dark, behold, a smoking fire pot and a flaming torch passed between these pieces. On that day the Lord made a covenant with Abram, saying, "To your descendants I give this land, from the river of Egypt to the great river, the river Euphrates, the land of the Kenites, the Kenizzites, the Kadmonites, the Hittites, the Perizzites, the Rephaim, the Amorites, the Canaanites, the Girgashites and the Jebusites." . . .

And the Lord appeared to him by the oaks of Mamre, as he sat at the door of his tent in the heat of the day. He lifted up his eyes and looked, and behold, three men stood in front of him. When he saw them, he ran from the tent door to meet them, and bowed himself to the earth, and said, "My lord, if I have found favor in your sight, do not pass by your servant. Let a little water be brought, and wash your feet, and rest yourselves under the tree, while I fetch a morsel of bread, that you may refresh yourselves, and after that you may pass on—since you have come to your servant." So they said, "Do as you have said." And Abraham hastened into the tent to Sarah, and said, "Make ready quickly three measures of fine meal, knead it, and make cakes." And Abraham ran to the herd, and took a calf, tender and good, and gave it to the servant, who hastened to prepare it. Then he took curds, and milk, and the calf which he had prepared, and set it before them; and he stood by them under the tree while they ate.

They said to him, "Where is Sarah your wife?" And he said, "She is in the tent." The Lord said, "I will surely return to you in the spring, and Sarah your wife shall have a son." And Sarah was listening at the tent door behind him. Now Abraham and Sarah were old, advanced in age; it had ceased to be with Sarah after the manner of women. So Sarah laughed to herself, saying, "After I have grown old, and my husband is old, shall I have pleasure?" The Lord said to Abraham, "Why did Sarah laugh, and say, 'Shall I indeed bear a child, now that I am old?' Is anything too hard for the Lord? At the appointed time I will return to you, in the spring, and Sarah shall have a son." But Sarah denied, saying, "I did not laugh"; for she was afraid. He said, "No, but you did laugh." . . .

ceased to be . . . : she was beyond child-bearing age.

The Lord visited Sarah as he had said, and the Lord did to Sarah as he had promised. And Sarah conceived, and bore Abraham a son in his old age at the time of which God had spoken to him. Abraham called the name of his son who was born to him, whom Sarah bore him, Isaac. . . . Abraham was a hundred years old when his son Isaac was born to him. And Sarah said, "God has made laughter for me; every one who hears will laugh over me." And she said, "Who would have said to Abraham that Sarah would suckle children? Yet I have borne him a son in his old age." . . .

Isaac: Hebrew word meaning "he laughs."

suckle: nurse.

After these things God tested Abraham, and said to him, "Abraham!" And he said, "Here am I." He said, "Take your son, your only son Isaac, whom you love, and go to the land of Moriah, and offer him there as a burnt offering upon one of the mountains of which I shall tell you." So Abraham rose early in the morning, saddled his ass, and took two of his young men with him, and his son Isaac; and he cut the wood for the burnt offering, and arose and went to the place of which God had told him. On the third day Abraham lifted up his eyes and saw the place afar off. Then Abraham said to his young men, "Stay here with the ass; I and the lad will go yonder and worship, and come again to you." And Abraham took the wood of the burnt offering, and laid it on Isaac his son; and he took in his hand the fire and the knife. So they went both of them together. And

Moriah (mō ri'ə): according to tradition, Jerusalem.

Isaac said to his father Abraham, "My father!" And he said, "Here am I, my son." He said, "Behold, the fire and the wood; but where is the lamb for a burnt offering?" Abraham said, "God will provide himself the lamb for a burnt offering, my son." So they went both of them together.

When they came to the place of which God had told him, Abraham built an altar there, and laid the wood in order, and bound Isaac his son, and laid him on the altar, upon the wood. Then Abraham put forth his hand, and took the knife to slay his son. But the angel of the Lord called to him from heaven, and said, "Abraham, Abraham!" And he said, "Here am I." He said, "Do not lay your hand on the lad or do anything to him; for now I know that you fear God, seeing you have not withheld your son, your only son, from me." And Abraham lifted up his eyes and looked, and behold, behind him was a ram, caught in a thicket by his horns; and Abraham went and took the ram, and offered it up as a burnt offering instead of his son. So Abraham called the name of that place The Lord will provide; as it is said to this day, "On the mount of the Lord it shall be provided."

fear: respect, obey, have confidence in.

For close reading

1 God mentions three things Abram must leave. What are they?

2 What does the Lord do to seal his agreement with Abram?

3 In what ways is the promise made to Abram different from the one made earlier to Noah?

4 The birth of Isaac has many supernatural or miraculous details. What are they? How does Sarah react when she is told she will have a son?

5 In the sacrifice episode Abraham is spoken to once by God, once by his son, and once by an angel. How does he answer each one?

For thought and discussion

6 The Lord is very clear about what Abram is to leave. What difference would it make if Abram were simply told to leave the country? In what tone of voice do you think the Lord's statement should be read? How might you have reacted in Abram's situation?

7 After the covenant, Abram sleeps in a "dread and great darkness." Sleep, dreams, darkness—all are connected with momentous events throughout the Bible and in much other literature. Why do you think people are so affected by these experiences?

8 What might have been Abraham's arguments against the sacrifice of his son? If Abraham had objected to the sacrifice, how do you think your attitude toward him would have been affected?

9 At crucial points in the sacrifice story, there occur passages of carefully described activity. What is the effect of these detailed descriptions? What is the climax or most intense moment of this story? What incidents and phrases build the tension toward this climax?

10 Why do you think the story contains no description of the emotions of Abraham and Isaac? How do you think the father and son felt about each other after the sacrifice?

Activities

1 Write a monologue in which you give the thoughts and feelings of the son before the sacrifice. Or write about the thoughts of the father, or of Sarah, or of a servant who had remained below the mountain.

2 Act out some part of the story for the class. Improvise the words without memorization.

SARAH

Delmore Schwartz

The angel said to me: "Why are you laughing?"
"Laughing! Not me! Who was laughing? I did not
   laugh. It was
A cough. I was coughing. Only hyenas laugh.
It was the cold I caught nine minutes after
5 Abraham married me: when I saw
How I was slender and beautiful, more and more
Slender and beautiful.
                I was also
Clearing my throat; something inside of me
Is continually telling me something
10 I do not wish to hear: A joke: A big joke:
But the joke is always just on me.
He said: you will have more children than the
   sky's stars
And the seashore's sands, if you just wait patiently.
Wait: patiently: ninety years? You see
15 The joke's on me!"

For thought and discussion

Does laughter always express amusement and happiness? In what other situations do people laugh?
What does laughter express in the Bible story of
Isaac's birth? What does laughter express in this
poem?

THE PARABLE OF THE OLD MEN AND THE YOUNG

Wilfred Owen

So Abram rose, and clave the wood, and went,
And took the fire with him, and a knife.
And as they sojourned both of them together,
Isaac the first-born spake and said, "My Father,
5 Behold the preparations, fire and iron,
But where the lamb for this burnt-offering?"
Then Abram bound the youth with belts and straps,
And builded parapets and trenches there,
And stretched forth the knife to slay his son.
10 When lo! an angel called him out of heaven,
Saying, "Lay not thy hand upon the lad,
Neither do anything to him. Behold,
A ram, caught in a thicket by its horns;
Offer the Ram of Pride instead of him."
15 But the old man would not so, but slew his son,—
And half the seed of Europe, one by one.

clave: split.

sojourned: stayed for a while.

parapets: walls, fortifications.

For thought and discussion

1 A parable is a story which illustrates a truth or lesson in a symbolic way. In this poem Abram and Isaac are "themselves," but each also stands for something else. Who or what do you think they represent? What do you think is the "lesson"?
2 What effects are achieved by the phrases "fire and iron," "belts and straps," and "parapets and trenches"?
3 In this poem, what does the angel tell Abram to sacrifice? Is such a sacrifice likely to prevent bloodshed? Explain.

THE FATHER

Björnstjerne Björnson
Translated by Rasmus B. Anderson

The man whose story is here to be told was the wealthiest and most influential person in his parish; his name was Thord Överaas. He appeared in the priest's study one day, tall and earnest.

"I have gotten a son," said he, "and I wish to present him for baptism."

"What shall his name be?"

"Finn,—after my father."

"And the sponsors?"

They were mentioned, and proved to be the best men and women of Thord's relations in the parish.

"Is there anything else?" inquired the priest, and looked up.

The peasant hesitated a little.

"I should like very much to have him baptized by himself," said he, finally.

"That is to say on a weekday?"

"Next Saturday, at twelve o'clock noon."

"Is there anything else?" inquired the priest.

"There is nothing else"; and the peasant twirled his cap, as though he were about to go.

Then the priest rose. "There is yet this, however," said he, and walking toward Thord, he took him by the hand and looked gravely into his eyes: "God grant that the child may become a blessing to you!"

One day sixteen years later, Thord stood once more in the priest's study.

From *The Bridal March and Other Stories* by Björnstjerne Björnson. Translated from the Norse by Rasmus B. Anderson. First published 1882.

"Really, you carry your age astonishingly well, Thord," said the priest; for he saw no change whatever in the man.

"That is because I have no troubles," replied Thord.

To this the priest said nothing, but after a while he asked: "What is your pleasure this evening?"

"I have come this evening about that son of mine who is to be confirmed to-morrow."

confirmed: formally admitted to full membership in a church.

"He is a bright boy."

"I did not wish to pay the priest until I heard what number the boy would have when he takes his place in church tomorrow."

"He will stand number one."

"So I have heard; and here are ten dollars for the priest."

"Is there anything else I can do for you?" inquired the priest, fixing his eyes on Thord.

"There is nothing else."

Thord went out.

Eight years more rolled by, and then one day a noise was heard outside of the priest's study, for many men were approaching, and at their head was Thord, who entered first.

The priest looked up and recognized him.

"You come well attended this evening, Thord," said he.

"I am here to request that the banns may be published for my son; he is about to marry Karen Storliden, daughter of Gudmund, who stands here beside me."

banns: notices of intent to marry.

"Why, that is the richest girl in the parish."

"So they say," replied the peasant, stroking back his hair with one hand.

The priest sat a while as if in deep thought, then entered the names in his book, without making any comments, and the men wrote their signatures underneath. Thord laid three dollars on the table.

"One is all I am to have," said the priest.

"I know that very well; but he is my only child; I want to do it handsomely."

The priest took the money.

"This is now the third time, Thord, that you have come here on your son's account."

"But now I am through with him," said Thord, and folding up his pocketbook he said farewell and walked away.

The men slowly followed him.

A fortnight later, the father and son were rowing across the lake, one calm, still day, to Storliden to make arrangements for the wedding.

"This thwart is not secure," said the son, and stood up to straighten the seat on which he was sitting.

At the same moment the board he was standing on slipped from under him; he threw out his arms, uttered a shriek, and fell overboard.

"Take hold of the oar!" shouted the father, springing to his feet and holding out the oar.

But when the son had made a couple of efforts he grew stiff.

"Wait a moment!" cried the father, and began to row toward his son.

Then the son rolled over on his back, gave his father one long look, and sank.

Thord could scarcely believe it; he held the boat still, and stared at the spot where his son had gone down, as though he must surely come to the surface again. There rose some bubbles, then some more, and finally one large one that burst; and the lake lay there as smooth and bright as a mirror again.

For three days and three nights people saw the father rowing round and round the spot, without taking either food or sleep; he was dragging the lake for the body of his son. And toward morning of the third day he found it, and carried it in his arms up over the hills to his gard.

gard: fenced property; farm.

It might have been about a year from that day, when the priest, late one autumn evening, heard some one in the passage outside of the door, carefully trying to find the latch. The priest opened the door, and in walked a 'l, thin man, with bowed form and white hair. The , riest looked long at him before he recognized him. It was Thord.

"Are you out walking so late?" said the priest, and stood still in front of him.

"Ah, yes! it is late," said Thord, and took a seat.

The priest sat down also, as though waiting. A long, long silence followed. At last Thord said,—

"I have something with me that I should like to give to the poor; I want it to be invested as a legacy in my son's name."

legacy: bequest; money or property left to a person by someone who has died.

He rose, laid some money on the table, and sat down again. The priest counted it.

"It is a great deal of money," said he.

"It is half the price of my gard. I sold it today."

The priest sat long in silence. At last he asked, but gently,—

"What do you propose to do now, Thord?"

"Something better."

They sat there for a while, Thord with downcast eyes, the priest with his eyes fixed on Thord. Presently the priest said, slowly and softly,—

"I think your son has at last brought you a true blessing."

"Yes, I think so myself," said Thord, looking up, while two big tears coursed slowly down his cheeks.

For close reading

1 What question does the priest repeat on Thord's first two visits?

2 What details show the father's great pride in his son?

3 How has Thord's appearance changed by the end of the story?

For thought and discussion

4 Did you anticipate that something would happen to Thord's son? Why or why not?

5 Compare Thord's experiences with Abraham's. What did each man's son mean to him? What "sacrifice" does Thord make at the end of the story?

6 Both "The Father" and "The Parable of the Old Men and the Young" emphasize a father's pride. Is pride an element of the biblical story of Abraham and Isaac? Explain.

JOSEPH:
THE DREAMER
CAST
DOWN

Genesis

[*God's blessing was passed on to Isaac and to Isaac's son, Jacob. As a sign of blessing, Jacob was given the name Israel; from his twelve sons descended the twelve tribes of Israel.*

The following Bible passages focus on Joseph, the favorite son of Jacob.]

sojournings: i.e., places where his father had stayed.

Jacob dwelt in the land of his father's sojournings, in the land of Canaan. This is the history of the family of Jacob.

Joseph, being seventeen years old, was shepherding the flock with his brothers; he was a lad with the sons of Bilhah and Zilpah, his father's wives; and Joseph brought an ill report of them to their father. Now Israel loved Joseph more than any other of his children, because he was the son of his old age; and

with sleeves: i.e., expensive. Other versions call this a "coat of many colors."

he made him a long robe with sleeves. But when his brothers saw that their father loved him more than all his brothers, they hated him, and could not speak peaceably to him.

Now Joseph had a dream, and when he told it to his brothers they only hated him the more. He said to them, "Hear this dream which I have dreamed:

sheaves: bundles of cut grain.

behold, we were binding sheaves in the field, and lo, my sheaf arose and stood upright; and behold, your sheaves gathered round it, and bowed down to my sheaf." His brothers said to him, "Are you indeed to reign over us? Or are you indeed to have

have dominion: rule.

dominion over us?" So they hated him yet more for

Genesis 37:1–14a, 17b–35; 39:1–23 (RSV).

his dreams and for his words. Then he dreamed another dream, and told it to his brothers, and said, "Behold, I have dreamed another dream; and behold, the sun, the moon, and eleven stars were bowing down to me." But when he told it to his father and to his brothers, his father rebuked him, and said to him, "What is this dream that you have dreamed? Shall I and your mother and your brothers indeed come to bow ourselves to the ground before you?" And his brothers were jealous of him, but his father kept the saying in mind.

saying: what Joseph had said.

Now his brothers went to pasture their father's flock near Shechem. And Israel said to Joseph, "Are not your brothers pasturing the flock at Shechem? Come, I will send you to them." And he said to him, "Here I am." So he said to him, "Go now, see if it is well with your brothers, and with the flock; and bring me word again." . . . So Joseph went after his brothers, and found them at Dothan. They saw him afar off, and before he came near to them they conspired against him to kill him. They said to one another, "Here comes this dreamer. Come now, let us kill him and throw him into one of the pits; then we shall say that a wild beast has devoured him, and we shall see what will become of his dreams." But when Reuben heard it, he delivered him out of their hands, saying, "Let us not take his life." And Reuben said to them, "Shed no blood; cast him into this pit here in the wilderness, but lay no hand upon him"—that he might rescue him out of their hand, to restore him to his father. So when Joseph came to his brothers, they stripped him of his robe, the long robe with sleeves that he wore; and they took him and cast him into a pit. The pit was empty, there was no water in it.

Reuben: the oldest brother.

Then they sat down to eat; and looking up they saw a caravan of Ishmaelites coming from Gilead, with their camels bearing gum, balm, and myrrh, on their way to carry it down to Egypt. Then Judah said to his brothers, "What profit is it if we slay our brother and conceal his blood? Come, let us sell him to the Ishmaelites, and let not our hand be upon him, for he is our brother, our own flesh." And his brothers heeded him. Then Midianite traders passed by; and they drew Joseph up and lifted him out of the pit, and sold him to the Ishmaelites for twenty shekels of silver; and they took Joseph to Egypt.

caravan: a group of travelers.

gum, balm, myrrh: various products derived from plants.

Judah: another of the older brothers.

shekels: coins worth approximately one dollar each.

rent: tore.

The goat was killed
instead of the boy.
Where has this
occurred before?

sackcloth: rough cloth
worn as a sign of
mourning.

loins: the middle
portions of the body.

Sheol (shē′ōl): the
underworld; place of
the dead.

Pharaoh: title of
ancient Egyptian kings.

When Reuben returned to the pit and saw that
Joseph was not in the pit, he rent his clothes and
returned to his brothers, and said, "The lad is gone;
and I, where shall I go?" Then they took Joseph's
robe, and killed a goat, and dipped the robe in the
blood; and they sent the long robe with sleeves and
brought it to their father, and said, "This we have
found; see now whether it is your son's robe or
not." And he recognized it, and said, "It is my son's
robe; a wild beast has devoured him; Joseph is
without doubt torn to pieces." Then Jacob rent his
garments, and put sackcloth upon his loins, and
mourned for his son many days. All his sons and all
his daughters rose up to comfort him; but he
refused to be comforted, and said, "No, I shall go
down to Sheol to my son, mourning." Thus his
father wept for him. . . .

Now Joseph was taken down to Egypt, and Poti-
phar, an officer of Pharaoh, the captain of the guard,
an Egyptian, bought him from the Ishmaelites who
had brought him down there. The Lord was with
Joseph, and he became a successful man; and he
was in the house of his master the Egyptian, and his
master saw that the Lord was with him, and that the
Lord caused all that he did to prosper in his hands.
So Joseph found favor in his sight and attended him,
and he made him overseer of his house and put him
in charge of all that he had. From the time that he
made him overseer in his house and over all that he
had the Lord blessed the Egyptian's house for Joseph's sake; the blessing of the Lord was upon all
that he had, in house and field. So he left all that he
had in Joseph's charge; and having him he had no
concern for anything but the food which he ate.

Now Joseph was handsome and good-looking.
And after a time his master's wife cast her eyes upon
Joseph, and said, "Lie with me." But he refused and
said to his master's wife, "Lo, having me my master
has no concern about anything in the house, and he
has put everything that he has in my hand; he is not
greater in this house than I am; nor has he kept back
anything from me except yourself, because you are
his wife; how then can I do this great wickedness,
and sin against God?" And although she spoke to
Joseph day after day, he would not listen to her, to
lie with her or to be with her. But one day, when he

went into the house to do his work and none of the men of the house was there in the house, she caught him by his garment, saying, "Lie with me." But he left his garment in her hand, and fled and got out of the house. And when she saw that he had left his garment in her hand, and had fled out of the house, she called to the men of her household and said to them, "See, he has brought among us a Hebrew to insult us; he came in to me to lie with me, and I cried out with a loud voice; and when he heard that I lifted up my voice and cried, he left his garment with me, and fled and got out of the house." Then she laid up his garment by her until his master came home, and she told him the same story, saying, "The Hebrew servant, whom you have brought among us, came in to me to insult me; but as soon as I lifted up my voice and cried, he left his garment with me, and fled out of the house."

When his master heard the words which his wife spoke to him, "This is the way your servant treated me," his anger was kindled. And Joseph's master took him and put him into the prison, the place where the king's prisoners were confined, and he was there in prison. But the Lord was with Joseph and showed him steadfast love, and gave him favor in the sight of the keeper of the prison. And the keeper of the prison committed to Joseph's care all the prisoners who were in the prison; and whatever was done there, he was the doer of it; the keeper of the prison paid no heed to anything that was in Joseph's care, because the Lord was with him; and whatever he did, the Lord made it prosper.

For close reading

1 Why do Joseph's brothers dislike him?
2 In this passage, which of the brothers cares most about Joseph? What sentence shows this most clearly?
3 On three occasions Joseph is put into a low position. List those times and describe the situations.

For thought and discussion

4 When the brothers are plotting to kill Joseph they say, "Here comes this dreamer." Why do you suppose they use that word to show their hatred? People generally seem to be a little uneasy with those who have or claim to have unusual mental powers. Why do you think this is so?

5 What is your initial impression of Joseph? Write down three words that describe Joseph at seventeen.

6 What part does Joseph's clothing play in his success and misfortune?

7 To what extent is Joseph to blame for his difficulties? To what extent is he personally responsible for his successes?

Activities

1 "Coat of many colors" or "long robe with sleeves," Joseph's garment symbolized that he was special to his father. Sketch or describe an article of clothing that you think would express Joseph's special status if he lived in today's world.

2 Depict in some medium (painting, collage, sculpture, needlepoint, etc.) one of Joseph's dreams.

JOSEPH: HIS BROTHERS' KEEPER

Genesis

After two whole years, Pharaoh dreamed that he was standing by the Nile, and behold, there came up out of the Nile seven cows sleek and fat, and they fed in the reed grass. And behold, seven other cows, gaunt and thin, came up out of the Nile after them, and stood by the other cows on the bank of the Nile. And the gaunt and thin cows ate up the seven sleek and fat cows. And Pharaoh awoke. And he fell asleep and dreamed a second time; and behold, seven ears of grain, plump and good, were growing on one stalk. And behold, after them sprouted seven ears, thin and blighted by the east wind. And the thin ears swallowed up the seven plump and full ears. And Pharaoh awoke, and behold, it was a dream. So in the morning his spirit was troubled; and he sent and called for all the magicians of Egypt and all its wise men; and Pharaoh told them his dream, but there was none who could interpret it to Pharaoh.

Then the chief butler said to Pharaoh, "I remember my faults today. When Pharaoh was angry with his servants, and put me and the chief baker in custody in the house of the captain of the guard, we dreamed on the same night, he and I, each having a dream with its own meaning. A young Hebrew was there with us, a servant of the captain of the guard; and when we told him, he interpreted our dreams to us, giving an interpretation to each man according

blighted: withered, dried up.

Genesis 41:1–16, 25–43, 53–57; 42:1–28, 35–38; 43:1–44:18a; 44:30b–45:28 (RSV).

to his dream. And as he interpreted to us, so it came to pass; I was restored to my office, and the baker was hanged."

Then Pharaoh sent and called Joseph, and they brought him hastily out of the dungeon; and when he had shaved himself and changed his clothes, he came in before Pharaoh. And Pharaoh said to Joseph, "I have had a dream, and there is no one who can interpret it; and I have heard it said of you that when you hear a dream you can interpret it." Joseph answered Pharaoh, "It is not in me; God will give Pharaoh a favorable answer." . . .

the dream . . . is one: the two dreams are the same.

Then Joseph said to Pharaoh, "The dream of Pharaoh is one; God has revealed to Pharaoh what he is about to do. The seven good cows are seven years, and the seven good ears are seven years; the dream is one. The seven lean and gaunt cows that came up after them are seven years, and the seven empty ears blighted by the east wind are also seven

famine: food shortage due to crop failure.

years of famine. It is as I told Pharaoh, God has shown to Pharaoh what he is about to do. There will come seven years of great plenty throughout all the land of Egypt, but after them there will arise seven years of famine, and all the plenty will be forgotten in the land of Egypt; the famine will consume the

consume: ruin

land, and the plenty will be unknown in the land by reason of that famine which will follow, for it will be very grievous. And the doubling of Pharaoh's dream means that the thing is fixed by God, and God will shortly bring it to pass. Now therefore let Pharaoh select a man discreet and wise, and set him over the

Where else did two dreams seem to say the same thing?

discreet: showing good judgment.

land of Egypt. Let Pharaoh proceed to appoint overseers over the land, and take the fifth part of the produce of the land of Egypt during the seven plenteous years. And let them gather all the food of these good years that are coming, and lay up grain under the authority of Pharaoh for food in the cities, and let them keep it. That food shall be a reserve for the land against the seven years of famine which are to befall the land of Egypt, so that the land may not perish through the famine."

This proposal seemed good to Pharaoh and to all his servants. And Pharaoh said to his servants, "Can we find such a man as this, in whom is the Spirit of God?" So Pharaoh said to Joseph, "Since God has shown you all this, there is none so discreet and wise as you are; you shall be over my house, and all my people shall order themselves as you command; only as regards the throne will I be greater than you." And Pharaoh said to Joseph, "Behold, I have set you over all the land of Egypt." Then Pharaoh took his signet ring from his hand and put it on Joseph's hand, and arrayed him in garments of fine linen, and put a gold chain about his neck; and he made him to ride in his second chariot; and they cried before him, "Bow the knee!" Thus he set him over all the land of Egypt. . . .

signet ring: ring bearing official seal, symbol of authority.

arrayed: dressed.

The seven years of plenty that prevailed in the land of Egypt came to an end; and the seven years of famine began to come, as Joseph had said. There was famine in all lands; but in all the land of Egypt there was bread. When all the land of Egypt was famished, the people cried to Pharaoh for bread; and Pharaoh said to all the Egyptians, "Go to Joseph; what he says to you, do." So when the famine had spread over all the land, Joseph opened all the storehouses, and sold to the Egyptians, for the famine was severe in the land of Egypt. Moreover, all the earth came to Egypt to Joseph to buy grain, because the famine was severe over all the earth.

When Jacob learned that there was grain in Egypt, he said to his sons, "Why do you look at one another?" And he said, "Behold, I have heard that there is grain in Egypt; go down and buy grain for us there, that we may live, and not die." So ten of Joseph's brothers went down to buy grain in Egypt. But Jacob did not send Benjamin, Joseph's brother, with his brothers, for he feared that harm might befall him. Thus the sons of Israel came to buy among the others who came, for the famine was in the land of Canaan.

Benjamin: of the twelve brothers, only Joseph and Benjamin, who was the youngest, were sons of Rachel, Jacob's favorite wife.

Now Joseph was governor over the land; he it was who sold to all the people of the land. And Joseph's brothers came, and bowed themselves before him with their faces to the ground. Joseph saw his brothers, and knew them, but he treated them like strangers and spoke roughly to them. "Where do you come from?" he said. They said, "From the land of Canaan, to buy food." Thus Joseph knew his brothers, but they did not know him. And Joseph remembered the dreams which he had dreamed of them; and he said to them, "You are spies, you have come to see the weakness of the land." They said to him, "No, my lord, but to buy food have your servants come. We are all sons of one man, we are honest men, your servants are not spies." He said to them, "No, it is the weakness of the land that you have come to see." And they said, "We, your servants, are twelve brothers, the sons of one man in the land of Canaan; and behold, the youngest is this day with our father, and one is no more." But Joseph said to them, "It is as I said to you, you are spies. By this you shall be tested: by the life of Pharaoh, you shall not go from this place unless your youngest brother comes here. Send one of you, and let him bring your brother, while you remain in prison, that your words may be tested, whether there is truth in you; or else, by the life of Pharaoh, surely you are spies." And he put them all together in prison for three days.

fear: respect, obey.

On the third day Joseph said to them, "Do this and you will live, for I fear God: if you are honest men, let one of your brothers remain confined in your prison, and let the rest go and carry grain for the famine of your households, and bring your youngest brother to me; so your words will be verified, and you shall not die." And they did so.

verified: proved.

Then they said to one another, "In truth we are guilty concerning our brother, in that we saw the distress of his soul, when he besought us and we would not listen; therefore is this distress come upon us." And Reuben answered them, "Did I not tell you not to sin against the lad? But you would not listen. So now there comes a reckoning for his blood." They did not know that Joseph understood them, for there was an interpreter between them. Then he turned away from them and wept; and he returned to them and spoke to them. And he took Simeon from them and bound him before their eyes. And Joseph gave orders to fill their bags with grain, and to replace every man's money in his sack, and to give them provisions for the journey. This was done for them.

besought: begged.

reckoning: payment.

Then they loaded their asses with their grain, and departed. And as one of them opened his sack to give his ass provender at the lodging place, he saw his money in the mouth of his sack; and he said to his brothers, "My money has been put back; here it is in the mouth of my sack!" At this their hearts failed them, and they turned trembling to one

provender (prov′ən dər): grain, food.

another, saying, "What is this that God has done to us?" . . .

As they emptied their sacks, behold, every man's bundle of money was in his sack; and when they and their father saw their bundles of money, they were dismayed. And Jacob their father said to them, "You have bereaved me of my children: Joseph is no more, and Simeon is no more, and now you would take Benjamin; all this has come upon me." Then Reuben said to his father, "Slay my two sons if I do not bring him back to you; put him in my hands, and I will bring him back to you." But he said, "My son shall not go down with you, for his brother is dead, and he only is left. If harm should befall him on the journey that you are to make, you would bring down my gray hairs with sorrow to Sheol."

Now the famine was severe in the land. And when they had eaten the grain which they had brought from Egypt, their father said to them, "Go again, buy us a little food." But Judah said to him, "The man solemnly warned us, saying, 'You shall not see my face, unless your brother is with you.' If you will send our brother with us, we will go down and buy you food; but if you will not send him, we will not go down, for the man said to us, 'You shall not see my face, unless your brother is with you.' " Israel said, "Why did you treat me so ill as to tell the man that you had another brother?" They replied, "The man questioned us carefully about ourselves and our kindred, saying, 'Is your father still alive? Have you another brother?' What we told him was in answer to these questions; could we in any way know that he would say, 'Bring your brother down'?" And Judah said to Israel his father, "Send the lad with me, and we will arise and go, that we may live and not die, both we and you and also our little ones. I will be surety for him; of my hand you shall require him. If I do not bring him back to you and set him before you, then let me bear the blame for ever; for if we had not delayed, we would now have returned twice."

Then their father Israel said to them, "If it must be so, then do this: take some of the choice fruits of the land in your bags, and carry down to the man a present, a little balm and a little honey, gum, myrrh, pistachio nuts, and almonds. Take double the money with you; carry back with you the money that

bereaved me of: taken away.

kindred: family.

be surety: take responsibility.

was returned in the mouth of your sacks; perhaps it was an oversight. Take also your brother, and arise, go again to the man; may God Almighty grant you mercy before the man, that he may send back your other brother and Benjamin. If I am bereaved of my children, I am bereaved." So the men took the present, and they took double the money with them, and Benjamin; and they arose and went down to Egypt, and stood before Joseph.

When Joseph saw Benjamin with them, he said to the steward of his house, "Bring the men into the house, and slaughter an animal and make ready, for the men are to dine with me at noon." The man did as Joseph **bade** him, and brought the men to Joseph's house. And the men were afraid because they were brought to Joseph's house, and they said, "It is because of the money, which was replaced in our sacks the first time, that we are brought in, so that he may seek occasion against us and fall upon us, to make slaves of us and seize our asses." So they went up to the steward of Joseph's house, and spoke with him at the door of the house, and said, "Oh, my lord, we came down the first time to buy food; and when we came to the lodging place we opened our sacks, and there was every man's money in the mouth of his sack, our money in full weight; so we have brought it again with us, and we have brought other money down in our hand to buy food. We do not know who put our money in our sacks." He replied, "Rest assured, do not be afraid; your God and the God of your father must have put treasure in your sacks for you; I received your money." Then he brought Simeon out to them. And when the man had brought the men into Joseph's house, and given them water, and they had washed their feet, and when he had given their asses provender, they made ready the present for Joseph's coming at noon, for they heard that they should eat bread there.

When Joseph came home, they brought into the house to him the present which they had with them, and bowed down to him to the ground. And he inquired about their welfare, and said, "Is your father well, the old man of whom you spoke? Is he still alive?" They said, "Your servant our father is well, he is still alive." And they bowed their heads and made obeisance. And he lifted up his eyes, and saw his brother Benjamin, his mother's son, and

bade: commanded.

made obesiance:
bowed low.

said, "Is this your youngest brother, of whom you spoke to me? God be gracious to you, my son!" Then Joseph made haste, for his heart yearned for his brother, and he sought a place to weep. And he entered his chamber and wept there. Then he washed his face and came out; and controlling himself he said, "Let food be served." They served him by himself, and them by themselves, and the Egyptians who ate with him by themselves, because the Egyptians might not eat bread with the Hebrews, for that is an abomination to the Egyptians. And they sat before him, the first-born according to his birthright and the youngest according to his youth; and the men looked at one another in amazement. Portions were taken to them from Joseph's table, but Benjamin's portion was five times as much as any of theirs. So they drank and were merry with him.

abomination: hated thing.

Then he commanded the steward of his house, "Fill the men's sacks with food, as much as they can carry, and put each man's money in the mouth of his sack, and put my cup, the silver cup, in the mouth of the sack of the youngest, with his money for the grain." And he did as Joseph told him. As soon as the morning was light, the men were sent away with their asses. When they had gone but a short distance from the city, Joseph said to his steward, "Up, follow after the men; and when you overtake them, say to them, 'Why have you returned evil for good? Why have you stolen my silver cup? Is it not from this that my lord drinks, and by this that he divines? You have done wrong in so doing.' "

divines: foretells the future.

When he overtook them, he spoke to them these words. They said to him, "Why does my lord speak such words as these? Far be it from your servants that they should do such a thing! Behold, the money which we found in the mouth of our sacks, we brought back to you from the land of Canaan; how then should we steal silver or gold from your lord's house? With whomever of your servants it be found, let him die, and we also will be my lord's slaves." He said, "Let it be as you say: he with whom it is found shall be my slave, and the rest of you shall be blameless." Then every man quickly lowered his sack to the ground, and every man opened his sack. And he searched, beginning with the eldest and ending with the youngest; and the cup was found in

Benjamin's sack. Then they rent their clothes, and every man loaded his ass, and they returned to the city.

When Judah and his brothers came to Joseph's house, he was still there; and they fell before him to the ground. Joseph said to them, "What deed is this that you have done? Do you not know that such a man as I can indeed divine?" And Judah said, "What shall we say to my lord? What shall we speak? Or how can we clear ourselves? God has found out the guilt of your servants; behold, we are my lord's slaves, both we and he also in whose hand the cup has been found." But he said, "Far be it from me that I should do so! Only the man in whose hand the cup was found shall be my slave; but as for you, go up in peace to your father."

Then Judah went up to him and said, "O my lord, let your servant, I pray you, speak a word in my lord's ears, and let not your anger burn against your servant; . . . when I come to your servant my father, and the lad is not with us, then, as his life is bound up in the lad's life, when he sees that the lad is not with us, he will die; and your servants will bring down the gray hairs of your servant our father with sorrow to Sheol. For your servant became surety for the lad to my father, saying, 'If I do not bring him back to you, then I shall bear the blame in the sight of my father all my life.' Now therefore, let your servant, I pray you, remain instead of the lad as a slave to my lord; and let the lad go back with his brothers. For how can I go back to my father if the lad is not with me? I fear to see the evil that would come upon my father."

Then Joseph could not control himself before all those who stood by him; and he cried, "Make every one go out from me." So no one stayed with him when Joseph made himself known to his brothers. And he wept aloud, so that the Egyptians heard it, and the household of Pharaoh heard it. And Joseph said to his brothers, "I am Joseph; is my father still alive?" But his brothers could not answer him, for they were dismayed at his presence.

So Joseph said to his brothers, "Come near to me, I pray you." And they came near. And he said, "I am your brother, Joseph, whom you sold into Egypt. And now do not be distressed, or angry with yourselves, because you sold me here; for God sent me before you to preserve life. For the famine has been in the land these two years; and there are yet five years in which there will be neither plowing nor harvest. And God sent me before you to preserve for you a remnant on earth, and to keep alive for you many survivors. So it was not you who sent me here, but God; and he has made me a father to Pharaoh, and lord of all his house and ruler over all the land of Egypt. Make haste and go up to my father and say to him, 'Thus says your son Joseph, God has made me lord of all Egypt; come down to me, do not tarry; you shall dwell in the land of Goshen, and you shall be near me, you and your children and your children's children, and your flocks, your herds, and all that you have; and there I will provide for you, for there are yet five years of famine to come; lest you and your household, and all that you have, come to poverty.' And now your eyes see, and the eyes of my brother Benjamin see, that it is my mouth that speaks to you. You must tell my father of all my splendor in Egypt, and of all that you have seen. Make haste and bring my father down here.'' Then he fell upon his brother Benjamin's neck and wept; and Benjamin wept upon his neck. And he kissed all his brothers and wept upon them; and after that his brothers talked with him.

When the report was heard in Pharaoh's house, "Joseph's brothers have come," it pleased Pharaoh and his servants well. And Pharaoh said to Joseph, "Say to your brothers, 'Do this: load your beasts and go back to the land of Canaan; and take your father and your households, and come to me, and I will give you the best of the land of Egypt, and you shall eat the fat of the land.' Command them also, 'Do this: take wagons from the land of Egypt for your little ones and for your wives, and bring your father, and come. Give no thought to your goods, for the best of all the land of Egypt is yours.' "

The sons of Israel did so; and Joseph gave them wagons, according to the command of Pharaoh, and gave them provisions for the journey. To each and all of them he gave festal garments; but to Benjamin he gave three hundred shekels of silver and five festal garments. To his father he sent as follows: ten asses loaded with the good things of Egypt, and ten she-asses loaded with grain, bread, and provision for his father on the journey. Then he sent his

remnant: remaining survivors.

father to: chief under.

tarry: delay.
Goshen (gō'shən): a very fertile area in Egypt.

fell upon . . . his neck: embraced, put his arms around him.

fat of the land: best foods.

festal garments: clothing worn to celebrations.

brothers away, and as they departed, he said to them, "Do not quarrel on the way." So they went up out of Egypt, and came to the land of Canaan to their father Jacob. And they told him, "Joseph is still alive, and he is ruler over all the land of Egypt." And his heart fainted, for he did not believe them. But when they told him all the words of Joseph, which he had said to them, and when he saw the wagons which Joseph had sent to carry him, the spirit of their father Jacob revived; and Israel said, "It is enough; Joseph my son is still alive; I will go and see him before I die."

For close reading

1 How does Pharaoh learn of Joseph's special talents?

2 When the brothers first come to get grain from Joseph, he is actually glad to see them. Where is this shown? What other passages show Joseph's strong feeling for his family?

3 What argument does Joseph use to remove the feelings of guilt his brothers feel toward him?

4 Six dreams occur in the complete story of Joseph. List the people who have the dreams and what the dreams foretell.

5 On several occasions in both parts of the story, Joseph becomes the favorite of an authority. Cite the occasions, the name of the authority, and the kinds of people subordinate to Joseph.

6 Which scene would you choose as the most important turning point in Joseph's fortunes? Which scene is the point of strongest emotional tension?

For thought and discussion

7 What effect does each of the three pairs of dreams have on Joseph's life? In times past, people attached great importance to dreams. How are dreams regarded today?

8 When the brothers find the money in their sacks on the first trip home they say, "What is this that God has done to us?" Why do you think they assume God is responsible for their problem?

9 Explain the significance of the following events: (a) Joseph imprisons his brothers; (b) Joseph has Simeon bound before his brothers' eyes; (c) Joseph threatens Benjamin with slavery. In what ways is the story of Joseph and his brothers a story of revenge? How does this story differ from most revenge stories?

10 How does the brothers' response to Benjamin's predicament compare with their earlier attitude toward the young Joseph? In what ways have the brothers changed?

11 Joseph says, "God sent me before you to preserve for you a remnant, and to keep alive for you many survivors." What does this quote indicate about Joseph? What is your impression of Joseph at the conclusion of this passage? Has he changed over the course of the story? Explain.

12 Certain images and situations occur several times throughout the story of Joseph; for example, "clothing" and being "cast down." What others can you find? What effect do these recurring images have as you read?

Activities

1 Draw a plot line of the action in the story of Joseph as it goes up and down. Label each turning point with the name of the situation which occurs there. Place on the drawing a small sketch of any object which seems significant during each turning point (bloody coat, a cup, etc.).

2 Write an obituary notice which might have been written about Joseph at his death.

3

---

from
slavery
to
freedom

MOSES: THE CALLING OF A LEADER

Exodus

Now there arose a new king over Egypt, who did not know Joseph. And he said to his people, "Behold, the people of Israel are too many and too mighty for us. Come, let us deal shrewdly with them, lest they multiply, and, if war befall us, they join our enemies and fight against us and escape from the land." Therefore they set taskmasters over them to afflict them with heavy burdens; and they built for Pharaoh store-cities, Pithom and Raamses. But the more they were oppressed, the more they multiplied and the more they spread abroad. And the Egyptians were in dread of the people of Israel. So they made the people of Israel serve with rigor, and made their lives bitter with hard service, in mortar and brick, and in all kinds of work in the field; in all their work they made them serve with rigor.

taskmasters: bosses for forced labor.
store-cities: supply depots (pī′thəm; rä am′sēz).

with rigor: harshly.

Then the king of Egypt said to the Hebrew midwives, one of whom was named Shiphrah and the other Puah, "When you serve as midwife to the Hebrew women, and see them upon the birthstool, if it is a son, you shall kill him; but if it is a daughter, she shall live." But the midwives feared God, and did not do as the king of Egypt commanded them, but let the male children live. So the king of Egypt called the midwives, and said to them, "Why have you done this, and let the male children live?" The midwives said to Pharaoh, "Because the Hebrew women are not like the Egyptian women; for they

midwives: women who assist in childbirth.

upon the birthstool: giving birth.

Exodus 1:8–3:14; 4:10–15, 18–20 (RSV).
LEFT: *Moses*, granite sculpture by William Zorach, 1956. Collection of Columbia University, New York, Gift of Armand G. Erpf. Geoffrey Clements, photography.

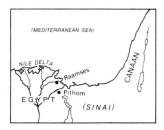

are vigorous and are delivered before the midwife comes to them." So God dealt well with the midwives; and the people multiplied and grew very strong. And because the midwives feared God he gave them families. Then Pharaoh commanded all his people, "Every son that is born to the Hebrews you shall cast into the Nile, but you shall let every daughter live."

house of Levi (lē′vi): the tribe of Levi.

Now a man from the house of Levi went and took to wife a daughter of Levi. The woman conceived and bore a son; and when she saw that he was a goodly child, she hid him three months. And when she could hide him no longer she took for him a basket made of bulrushes, and daubed it with bitumen and pitch; and she put the child in it and placed it among the reeds at the river's brink. And his sister stood at a distance, to know what would be done to him. Now the daughter of Pharaoh came down to bathe at the river, and her maidens walked beside the river; she saw the basket among the reeds and sent her maid to fetch it. When she opened it she saw the child; and lo, the babe was crying. She took pity on him and said, "This is one of the Hebrews' children." Then his sister said to Pharaoh's daughter, "Shall I go and call you a nurse from the Hebrew women to nurse the child for you?" And Pharaoh's daughter said to her, "Go." So the girl went and called the child's mother. And Pharaoh's daughter said to her, "Take this child away, and nurse him for me, and I will give you your wages." So the woman took the child and nursed him. And the child grew, and she brought him to Pharaoh's daughter, and he became her son; and she named him Moses, for she said, "Because I drew him out of the water."

basket: the Hebrew word is the same one used for Noah's ark.

bitumen: asphalt.

pitch: tar.

Moses: the Hebrew word, *Mosheh*, means "he draws out," but Pharaoh's daughter seems to think it means "he is drawn out."

his people: the Hebrews.

One day, when Moses had grown up, he went out to his people and looked on their burdens; and he saw an Egyptian beating a Hebrew, one of his people. He looked this way and that, and seeing no one he killed the Egyptian and hid him in the sand. When he went out the next day, behold, two Hebrews were struggling together; and he said to the man that did the wrong, "Why do you strike your fellow?" He answered, "Who made you a prince and a judge over us? Do you mean to kill me as you killed the Egyptian?" Then Moses was afraid, and thought, "Surely the thing is known." When Pharaoh heard of it, he sought to kill Moses.

But Moses fled from Pharaoh, and stayed in the land of Midian; and he sat down by a well. Now the priest of Midian had seven daughters; and they came and drew water, and filled the troughs to water their father's flock. The shepherds came and drove them away; but Moses stood up and helped them, and watered their flock. When they came to their father Reuel, he said, "How is it that you have come so soon today?" They said, "An Egyptian delivered us out of the hand of the shepherds, and even drew water for us and watered the flock." He said to his daughters, "And where is he? Why have you left the man? Call him, that he may eat bread." And Moses was content to dwell with the man, and he gave Moses his daughter Zipporah. She bore a son, and he called his name Gershom; for he said, "I have been a sojourner in a foreign land."

In the course of those many days the king of Egypt died. And the people of Israel groaned under their bondage, and cried out for help, and their cry under bondage came up to God. And God heard their groaning, and God remembered his covenant with Abraham, with Isaac, and with Jacob. And God saw the people of Israel, and God knew their condition.

Now Moses was keeping the flock of his father-in-law, Jethro, the priest of Midian; and he led his flock to the west side of the wilderness, and came to Horeb, the mountain of God. And the angel of the Lord appeared to him in a flame of fire out of the midst of a bush; and he looked, and lo, the bush was burning, yet it was not consumed. And Moses said, "I will turn aside and see this great sight, why the bush is not burnt." When the Lord saw that he turned aside to see, God called to him out of the bush, "Moses, Moses!" And he said, "Here am I." Then he said, "Do not come near; put off your shoes from your feet, for the place of which you are standing is holy ground." And he said, "I am the God of your father, the God of Abraham, the God of Isaac, and the God of Jacob." And Moses hid his face, for he was afraid to look at God.

Then the Lord said, "I have seen the affliction of my people who are in Egypt, and have heard their cry because of their taskmasters; I know their sufferings, and I have come down to deliver them out of the hand of the Egyptians, and to bring them up out of that land to a good and broad land, a land flowing

Midian: the Midianites and Hebrews had common ancestors.

Reuel (rü'əl): also called Jethro.

Gershom (gėr' shəm): from the Hebrew words *ger* (stranger, alien) and *shom* (there).

Horeb (hôr' eb): also called Sinai (si' ni).

sons: descendants.

sign: proof.

I AM: the Hebrew word is close to the word which is translated "The Lord" in this translation (RSV).

dumb: unable to talk.

with milk and honey, to the place of the Canaanites, the Hittites, the Amorites, the Perizzites, the Hivites, and the Jebusites. And now, behold, the cry of the people of Israel has come to me, and I have seen the oppression with which the Egyptians oppress them. Come, I will send you to Pharaoh that you may bring forth my people, the sons of Israel, out of Egypt." But Moses said to God, "Who am I that I should go to Pharaoh, and bring the sons of Israel out of Egypt?" He said, "But I will be with you; and this shall be the sign for you, that I have sent you: when you have brought forth the people out of Egypt, you shall serve God upon this mountain."

Then Moses said to God, "If I come to the people of Israel and say to them, 'The God of your fathers has sent me to you,' and they ask me, 'What is his name?' what shall I say to them?" God said to Moses, "I AM WHO I AM." And he said, "Say this to the people of Israel, 'I AM has sent me to you.' " . . .

But Moses said to the Lord, "Oh, my Lord, I am not eloquent, either heretofore or since thou hast spoken to thy servant; but I am slow of speech and of tongue." Then the Lord said to him, "Who has made man's mouth? Who makes him dumb, or deaf, or seeing, or blind? Is it not I, the Lord? Now therefore go, and I will be with your mouth and teach you what you shall speak." But he said, "Oh, my Lord, send, I pray, some other person." Then the anger of the Lord was kindled against Moses and he said, "Is there not Aaron, your brother, the Levite? I know that he can speak well; and behold, he is coming out to meet you, and when he sees you he will be glad in his heart. And you shall speak to him and put the words in his mouth; and I will be with your mouth and with his mouth, and will teach you what you shall do. . . ."

Moses went back to Jethro his father-in-law and said to him, "Let me go back, I pray, to my kinsmen in Egypt and see whether they are still alive." And Jethro said to Moses, "Go in peace." And the Lord said to Moses in Midian, "Go back to Egypt; for all the men who were seeking your life are dead." So Moses took his wife and his sons and set them on an ass, and went back to the land of Egypt; and in his hand Moses took the rod of God.

For close reading

1 What is the result of the Egyptian policy of oppressing the Hebrews?
2 How are the Pharaoh's two orders to kill male Hebrew babies obeyed? What similarities and differences do you find in the two cases?
3 What opposite roles do women play in the stories of Moses' birth and his stay in Midian?
4 For what reasons is Moses reluctant to accept God's call to leadership?

For thought and discussion

5 Why are the Egyptians afraid of the Hebrews? Why do you think the Egyptians did not simply expel the Hebrews from the country? Can you think of other occasions when nations have reacted to "aliens" as the Egyptians do?
6 Pharaoh says that he will deal "shrewdly" with his Hebrew "problem." How wise are the measures he takes? In what ways do the Hebrew women deal "shrewdly" with Pharaoh?
7 Nowhere else in the Bible is the Hebrew word translated as "ark" or "basket" used except in the Noah and Moses stories. Assuming the words were chosen carefully, what do you suppose is the reason for connecting these two events?
8 In what ways is Moses an "outsider"? How is this indicated in the story? In your opinion, is there any connection between being an outsider and being a leader? Explain.
9 How do the following episodes relate to the assignment God later gives to Moses? *(a)* Moses rescues a Hebrew by killing an Egyptian; *(b)* he intervenes between two quarreling Hebrews; *(c)* he helps Reuel's daughters at the well.
10 Moses raises various objections at the burning bush, and God answers them in turn. From this interchange, what do you infer about the character of Moses? About God? About the meaning of the "call"?

GO
DOWN,
MOSES

Spiritual

Wh1en Israel was in Egypt's land,
    Let my people go!
Oppressed so hard they could not stand,
    Let my people go!

5   Go down, Moses,
       'Way down in Egypt's land,
       Tell old Pharaoh
       To let my people go!

    "Thus spake the Lord," bold Moses said,
10   "Let my people go!
    If not, I'll smite your firstborn dead,
       Let my people go!"

       Go down, Moses,
       'Way down in Egypt's land,
15   Tell old Pharaoh
       To let my people go!

    "No more shall they in bondage toil,
       Let my people go!
    Let them come out with Egypt's spoil,
20   Let my people go!"

       Go down, Moses,
       'Way down in Egypt's land,
       Tell old Pharaoh
       To let my people go!

For thought and discussion
_____

"Go Down, Moses" was originally sung by slaves in
America. What special meaning do you think the
Moses-Exodus story had to the singers of this song?

CHALLENGING PHARAOH

Exodus

The Lord said to Aaron, "Go into the wilderness to meet Moses." So he went, and met him at the mountain of God and kissed him. And Moses told Aaron all the words of the Lord with which he had sent him, and all the signs which he had charged him to do. Then Moses and Aaron went and gathered together all the elders of the people of Israel. And Aaron spoke all the words which the Lord had spoken to Moses, and did the signs in the sight of the people. And the people believed; and when they heard that the Lord had visited the people of Israel and that he had seen their affliction, they bowed their heads and worshiped.

Afterward Moses and Aaron went to Pharaoh and said, "Thus says the Lord, the God of Israel, 'Let my people go, that they may hold a feast to me in the wilderness.' " But Pharaoh said, "Who is the Lord, that I should heed his voice and let Israel go? I do not know the Lord, and moreover I will not let Israel go." Then they said, "The God of the Hebrews has met with us; let us go, we pray, a three days' journey into the wilderness, and sacrifice to the Lord our God, lest he fall upon us with pestilence or with sword." But the king of Egypt said to them, "Moses and Aaron, why do you take the people away from their work? Get to your burdens." . . . The same day Pharaoh commanded the taskmasters of the people and their foremen, "You shall no longer give the

mountain of God: Sinai.

signs: the Lord has told Moses of numerous miracles that will be used against the Egyptians.

pestilence: deadly disease.

Exodus 4:27–5:4; 5:6–9, 15–23; 7:14–24; 11:1–9; 12:1–13, 29–36; 14:5–14, 19–29, 31 (RSV).

idle: lazy.

people straw to make bricks, as heretofore; let them go and gather straw for themselves. But the number of bricks which they made heretofore you shall lay upon them, you shall by no means lessen it; for they are idle; therefore they cry, 'Let us go and offer sacrifice to our God.' Let heavier work be laid upon the men that they may labor at it and pay no regard to lying words.'' . . .

Then the foremen of the people of Israel came and cried to Pharaoh, "Why do you deal thus with your servants? No straw is given to your servants, yet they say to us, 'Make bricks!' And behold, your servants are beaten; but the fault is in your own people." But he said, "You are idle, you are idle; therefore you say, 'Let us go and sacrifice to the Lord.' Go now, and work; for no straw shall be given you, yet you shall deliver the same number of bricks." The foremen of the people of Israel saw that they were in evil plight, when they said, "You shall by no means lessen your daily number of bricks." They met Moses and Aaron, who were waiting for them, as they came forth from Pharaoh; and they said to them, "The Lord look upon you and judge, because you have made us offensive in the sight of Pharaoh and his servants, and have put a sword in their hand to kill us."

delivered: rescued.

Then Moses turned again to the Lord and said, "O Lord, why hast thou done evil to this people? Why didst thou ever send me? For since I came to Pharaoh to speak in thy name, he has done evil to this people, and thou hast not delivered thy people at all." . . .

rod . . . serpent: a miraculous sign given to Moses at the burning bush and repeated before Pharaoh.

Then the Lord said to Moses, "Pharaoh's heart is hardened, he refuses to let the people go. Go to Pharaoh in the morning, as he is going out to the water; wait for him by the river's brink, and take in your hand the rod which was turned into a serpent. And you shall say to him, 'The Lord, the God of the Hebrews, sent me to you, saying, "Let my people go, that they may serve me in the wilderness; and behold, you have not yet obeyed." Thus says the Lord, "By this you shall know that I am the Lord: behold, I will strike the water that is in the Nile with the rod that is in my hand, and it shall be turned to blood, and the fish in the Nile shall die, and the Nile shall become foul, and the Egyptians will loathe to

loathe: hate.

drink water from the Nile." ' " And the Lord said to Moses, "Say to Aaron, 'Take your rod and stretch out your hand over the waters of Egypt, over their rivers, their canals, and their ponds, and all their pools of water, that they may become blood; and there shall be blood throughout all the land of Egypt, both in vessels of wood and in vessels of stone.' "

vessels: containers.

Moses and Aaron did as the Lord commanded; in the sight of Pharaoh and in the sight of his servants, he lifted up the rod and struck the water that was in the Nile, and all the water that was in the Nile turned to blood. And the fish in the Nile died; and the Nile became foul, so that the Egyptians could not drink water from the Nile; and there was blood through-out all the land of Egypt. But the magicians of Egypt did the same by their secret arts; so Pharaoh's heart remained hardened, and he would not listen to them; as the Lord had said. Pharaoh turned and went into his house, and he did not lay even this to heart. And all the Egyptians dug round about the Nile for water to drink, for they could not drink the water of the Nile. . . .

lay: take.

[*Pharaoh resisted eight more increasingly harsh plagues.*]

The Lord said to Moses, "Yet one plague more I will bring upon Pharaoh and upon Egypt; afterwards he will let you go hence; when he lets you go, he will drive you away completely. Speak now in the hearing of the people, that they ask, every man of his neighbor and every woman of her neighbor, jewelry of silver and of gold." And the Lord gave the people favor in the sight of the Egyptians. Moreover, the man Moses was very great in the land of Egypt, in the sight of Pharaoh's servants and in the sight of the people.

hence: from here.

gave the people favor: made them attractive.

And Moses said, "Thus says the Lord: About midnight I will go forth in the midst of Egypt; and all the first-born in the land of Egypt shall die, from the first-born of Pharaoh who sits upon his throne, even to the first-born of the maidservant who is behind the mill; and all the first-born of the cattle. And there shall be a great cry throughout all the land of Egypt, such as there has never been, nor ever shall be again. But against any of the people of Israel,

said: to Pharaoh.

behind: working.

either man or beast, not a dog shall growl; that you may know that the Lord makes a distinction between the Egyptians and Israel. And all these your servants shall come down to me, and bow down to me, saying, 'Get you out, and all the people who follow you.' And after that I will go out." And he went out from Pharaoh in hot anger. Then the Lord said to Moses, "Pharaoh will not listen to you; that my wonders may be multiplied in the land of Egypt." . . .

The Lord said to Moses and Aaron in the land of Egypt, "This month shall be for you the beginning of months; it shall be the first month of the year for you. Tell all the congregation of Israel that on the tenth day of this month they shall take every man a lamb according to their fathers' houses, a lamb for a household; and if the household is too small for a lamb, then a man and his neighbor next to his house shall take according to the number of persons; according to what each can eat you shall make your count for the lamb. Your lamb shall be without blemish, a male a year old; you shall take it from the sheep or from the goats; and you shall keep it until the fourteenth day of this month, when the whole assembly of the congregation of Israel shall kill their lambs in the evening. Then they shall take some of the blood, and put it on the two doorposts and the lintel of the houses in which they eat them. They shall eat the flesh that night, roasted; with unleavened bread and bitter herbs they shall eat it. Do not eat any of it raw or boiled with water, but roasted, its head with its legs and its inner parts. And you shall let none of it remain until the morning, anything that remains until the morning you shall burn. In this manner you shall eat it: your loins girded, your sandals on your feet, and your staff in your hand; and you shall eat it in haste. It is the Lord's passover. For I will pass through the land of Egypt that night, and I will smite all the first-born in the land of Egypt, both man and beast; and on all the gods of Egypt I will execute judgments: I am the Lord. The blood shall be a sign for you, upon the houses where you are; and when I see the blood, I will pass over you, and no plague shall fall upon you to destroy you, when I smite the land of Egypt. . . ."

At midnight the Lord smote all the first-born in the land of Egypt, from the first-born of Pharaoh who sat

goats: a kid could take the place of a lamb.

unleavened: without yeast so that it would not rise.

loins girded: i.e., dressed for travel.
passover: movement of the Lord over Egypt.
smite: strike.

on his throne to the first-born of the captive who was in the dungeon, and all the first-born of the cattle. And Pharaoh rose up in the night, he, and all his servants, and all the Egyptians; and there was a great cry in Egypt, for there was not a house where one was not dead. And he summoned Moses and Aaron by night, and said, "Rise up, go forth from among my people, both you and the people of Israel; and go, serve the Lord, as you have said. Take your flocks and your herds, as you have said, and be gone; and bless me also!"

And the Egyptians were urgent with the people, to send them out of the land in haste; for they said, "We are all dead men." So the people took their dough before it was leavened, their kneading bowls being bound up in their mantles on their shoulders. **mantles:** cloaks, capes. The people of Israel had also done as Moses told them, for they had asked of the Egyptians jewelry of silver and of gold, and clothing; and the Lord had given the people favor in the sight of the Egyptians, so that they let them have what they asked. Thus they despoiled the Egyptians. . . . **despoiled:** stripped of possessions.

When the king of Egypt was told that the people had fled, the mind of Pharaoh and his servants was changed toward the people, and they said, "What is this we have done, that we have let Israel go from serving us?" So he made ready his chariot and took his army with him, and took six hundred picked chariots and all the other chariots of Egypt with officers over all of them. And the Lord hardened the heart of Pharaoh king of Egypt and he pursued the people of Israel as they went forth defiantly. The Egyptians pursued them, all Pharaoh's horses and chariots and his horsemen and his army, and overtook them encamped at the sea, by Pi-hahiroth, in front of Baal-zephon.

When Pharaoh drew near, the people of Israel lifted up their eyes, and behold, the Egyptians were marching after them; and they were in great fear. And the people of Israel cried out to the Lord; and they said to Moses, "Is it because there are no graves in Egypt that you have taken us away to die in the wilderness? What have you done to us, in bringing us out of Egypt? Is not this what we said to you in Egypt, 'Let us alone and let us serve the Egyptians'? For it would have been better for us to serve the Egyptians than to die in the wilderness."

And Moses said to the people, "Fear not, stand firm and see the salvation of the Lord, which he will work for you today; for the Egyptians whom you see today, you shall never see again. The Lord will fight for you, and you have only to be still." . . .

salvation: deliverance.

Then the angel of God who went before the host of Israel moved and went behind them; and the pillar of cloud moved from before them and stood behind them, coming between the host of Egypt and the host of Israel. And there was the cloud and the darkness; and the night passed without one coming near the other all night.

host: army.

Then Moses stretched out his hand over the sea; and the Lord drove the sea back by a strong east wind all night, and made the sea dry land, and the waters were divided. And the people of Israel went into the midst of the sea on dry ground, the waters being a wall to them on their right hand and on their left. The Egyptians pursued, and went in after them into the midst of the sea, all Pharaoh's horses, his chariots, and his horsemen. And in the morning watch the Lord in the pillar of fire and of cloud looked down upon the host of the Egyptians, and discomfited the host of the Egyptians, clogging their chariot wheels so that they drove heavily; and the Egyptians said, "Let us flee from before Israel; for the Lord fights for them against the Egyptians."

discomfited: threw them into panic.

Then the Lord said to Moses, "Stretch out your hand over the sea, that the water may come back upon the Egyptians, upon their chariots, and upon their horsemen." So Moses stretched forth his hand over the sea, and the sea returned to its wonted flow when the morning appeared; and the Egyptians fled into it, and the Lord routed the Egyptians in the midst of the sea. The waters returned and covered the chariots and the horsemen and all the host of Pharaoh that had followed them into the sea; not so much as one of them remained. But the people of Israel walked on dry ground through the sea, the waters being a wall to them on their right hand and on their left. . . .

wonted: normal, usual.
fled into it: i.e., tried to return.
routed: put to flight.

. . . And Israel saw the great work which the Lord did against the Egyptians, and the people feared the Lord; and they believed in the Lord and in his servant Moses.

For close reading

1 What do Moses and Aaron first ask of Pharaoh and what reasons do they give? How does Pharaoh respond?

2 By what means are the people of Israel protected when the Lord passes over Egypt?

3 When Pharaoh tells Moses and Aaron to "be gone" he concludes with what is, under the circumstances, an extraordinary request. What is the request and what does it imply?

4 What specific actions does the Lord perform during the escape?

For thought and discussion

5 Why is Pharaoh unconvinced when the water of the Nile is "turned to blood"? What do you think is the difference between magic and miracles?

6 The Lord gives detailed instructions regarding the Hebrew feast. For what reasons do you think they are to dress for travel and eat "in haste"? In what ways do people attach religious meaning to food and eating today? Why do you think this is done?

7 At one point Moses asks, "O Lord, why hast thou done evil to this people?" Do you think this is a fair question for Moses to ask? Why or why not?

Activities

1 The Passover remains to this day a vital holiday for Jews. Invite a rabbi to the class to explain the celebration of Passover.

2 Write a monologue expressing Pharaoh's thoughts at his moment of greatest despair.

MOSES

Lucille Clifton

i walk on bones
snakes twisting
in my hand
locusts breaking my mouth
5 an old man
leaving slavery.
home is burning in me
like a bush
God got his eye on.

For thought and discussic _____

1 Who is speaking in this poem?
2 In what way is the last figure of speech particularly appropriate?
3 The poem contains one capital, short phrases, and little punctuation. What do these elements of style contribute to the poem?

From *Good News About the Earth*, by Lucille Clifton. Copyright © 1970, 1971, 1972 by Lucille Clifton. Reprinted by permission of Random House, Inc. and Curtis Brown, Ltd.

RUNAGATE
RUNAGATE

Robert Hayden

I.

Runs falls rises stumbles on from darkness into darkness
and the darkness thicketed with shapes of terror
and the hunters pursuing and the hounds pursuing
and the night cold and the night long and the river
5   to cross and the jack-muh-lanterns beckoning beckoning
and blackness ahead and when shall I reach that somewhere
morning and keep on going and never turn back and keep on going

       Runagate
           Runagate
10   Runagate   **Runagate:** a runaway;
                                           here, a runaway slave.

Many thousands rise and go
many thousands crossing over

                  O mythic North
             O star-shaped yonder Bible city

15 Some go weeping and some rejoicing
some in coffins and some in carriages
some in silks and some in shackles

       Rise and go or fare you well

No more auction block for me
20 no more driver's lash for me

    If you see my Pompey, 30 yrs of age,   **Pompey:** name of a
    new breeches, plain stockings, negro shoes;   slave.
    if you see my Anna, likely young mulatto

branded E on the right cheek, R on the left,
25   catch them if you can and notify subscriber.
Catch them if you can, but it won't be easy.
They'll dart underground when you try to catch
    them,
plunge into quicksand, whirlpools, mazes,
turn into scorpions when you try to catch them.

30   And before I'll be a slave
I'll be buried in my grave

North star and bonanza gold
I'm bound for the freedom, freedom-bound
and oh Susyanna don't you cry for me

35   Runagate

                                Runagate

    II.

Rises from their anguish and their power,

                                Harriet Tubman,

                                woman of earth, whipscarred,
40   a summoning, a shining

                                Mean to be free

And this was the way of it, brethren brethren,
way we journeyed from Can't to Can.
Moon so bright and no place to hide,
45   the cry up and the patterollers riding,
hound dogs belling in bladed air.
And fear starts a-murbling, Never make it,
we'll never make it. *Hush that now,*
and she's turned upon us, levelled pistol
50   glinting in the moonlight:
Dead folks can't jaybird-talk, she says;
you keep on going now or die, she says.

Wanted   Harriet Tubman   alias The General
alias Moses   Stealer of Slaves

55   In league with Garrison   Alcott   Emerson
Garrett   Douglass   Thoreau   John Brown
Armed and known to be Dangerous

Wanted   Reward   Dead or Alive

   Tell me, Ezekiel, oh tell me do you see
60   mailed Jehovah coming to deliver me?

Hoot-owl calling in the ghosted air,
five times calling to the hants in the air.
Shadow of a face in the scary leaves,
shadow of a voice in the talking leaves:

65   Come ride-a my train

   Oh that train, ghost-story train
   through swamp and savanna movering movering,
   over trestles of dew, through caves of the wish,
   Midnight Special on a sabre track movering movering,
70   *first stop Mercy and the last Hallelujah.*

   Come ride-a my train

   Mean mean mean to be free.

For thought and discussion

1 What does the use of present tense, the lack of punctuation, and the frequent use of "and" suggest about how the first seven lines should be read?
2 Who is speaking in lines 21–29? Why do you think this section is included in the poem?
3 The poem is in two parts. What seems to be the main content of each part?
4 Who says "Hush that now" in line 48? How is this person like Moses?
5 This poem is more effective when read aloud. With the help of several class members, prepare an oral reading. There is no clear-cut distinction among speakers in many cases, so you and your readers should work out the most effective presentation. You may want to experiment with dramatic lighting, music, and taped sound effects as well.

IN
THE
WILDERNESS

Exodus, Deuteronomy

Sin: Hebrew place
name; not related to
"sin."

murmured: complained.

fleshpots: containers
of meat.

Then they came to Elim, where there were twelve
springs of water and seventy palm trees; and they
encamped there by the water.

They set out from Elim, and all the congregation of
the people of Israel came to the wilderness of Sin,
which is between Elim and Sinai, on the fifteenth day
of the second month after they had departed from
the land of Egypt. And the whole congregation of
the people of Israel murmured against Moses and
Aaron in the wilderness, and said to them, "Would
that we had died by the hand of the Lord in the land
of Egypt, when we sat by the fleshpots and ate bread
to the full; for you have brought us out into this
wilderness to kill this whole assembly with
hunger." . . .

And Moses said to Aaron, "Say to the whole
congregation of the people of Israel, 'Come near before the Lord, for he has heard your murmurings.' "
And as Aaron spoke to the whole congregation of
the people of Israel, they looked toward the wilderness, and behold, the glory of the Lord appeared in
the cloud. And the Lord said to Moses, "I have heard
the murmurings of the people of Israel; say to them,
'At twilight you shall eat flesh, and in the morning
you shall be filled with bread; then you shall know
that I am the Lord your God.' "

In the evening quails came up and covered the

Exodus 15:27; 16:1–3, 9–15, 31, 35; 19:1–6a, 16–19; 20:1–21; 31:18; 32:1–7,
15–20, 30–34; 33:7–11a, 12–13, 17–20; 34:4–5, 27–35. Deuteronomy 31:14–
18; 34:1–12 (RSV).

camp; and in the morning dew lay round about the camp. And when the dew had gone up, there was on the face of the wilderness a fine, flakelike thing, fine as hoarfrost on the ground. When the people of Israel saw it, they said to one another, "What is it?" For they did not know what it was. And Moses said to them, "It is the bread which the Lord has given you to eat. . . ."

Now the house of Israel called its name manna; it was like coriander seed, white, and the taste of it was like wafers made with honey. . . . And the people of Israel ate the manna forty years, till they came to a habitable land; they ate the manna, till they came to the border of the land of Canaan. . . .

> [Before you read the passage below, briefly summarize as many commandments as you can remember.]

On the third new moon after the people of Israel had gone forth out of the land of Egypt, on that day they came into the wilderness of Sinai. And when they set out from Rephidim and came into the wilderness of Sinai, they encamped in the wilderness; and there Israel encamped before the mountain. And Moses went up to God, and the Lord called to him out of the mountain, saying, "Thus you shall say to the house of Jacob, and tell the people of Israel: You have seen what I did to the Egyptians, and how I bore you on eagles' wings and brought you to myself. Now therefore, if you will obey my voice and keep my covenant, you shall be my own possession among all peoples; for all the earth is mine, and you shall be to me a kingdom of priests and a holy nation. . . ."

On the morning of the third day there were thunders and lightnings, and a thick cloud upon the mountain, and a very loud trumpet blast, so that all the people who were in the camp trembled. Then Moses brought the people out of the camp to meet God; and they took their stand at the foot of the mountain. And Mount Sinai was wrapped in smoke, because the Lord descended upon it in fire; and the smoke of it went up like the smoke of a kiln, and the whole mountain quaked greatly. And as the sound of the trumpet grew louder and louder, Moses spoke, and God answered him in thunder. . . .

what is it: in Hebrew: *man hu.* The Hebrew word for manna is *man* meaning "what."

coriander seed: a flavorful fruit.

The commandments are divided and numbered in different ways by various religious groups.

And God spoke all these words, saying,

"I am the Lord your God, who brought you out of the land of Egypt, out of the house of bondage.

"You shall have no other gods before me.

graven: carved.

"You shall not make for yourself a graven image, or any likeness of anything that is in heaven above, or that is in the earth beneath, or that is in the water under the earth; you shall not bow down to them or serve them; for I the Lord your God am a jealous God, visiting the iniquity of the fathers upon the children to the third and the fourth generation of those who hate me, but showing steadfast love to thousands of those who love me and keep my commandments.

visiting the iniquity: punishing the sins.

take . . . in vain: use without respect.

"You shall not take the name of the Lord your God in vain; for the Lord will not hold him guiltless who takes his name in vain.

"Remember the sabbath day, to keep it holy. Six days you shall labor, and do all your work; but the seventh day is a sabbath to the Lord your God; in it you shall not do any work, you, or your son, or your daughter, your manservant, or your maidservant, or your cattle, or the sojourner who is within your gates; for in six days the Lord made heaven and earth, the sea, and all that is in them, and rested the seventh day; therefore the Lord blessed the sabbath day and hallowed it.

sojourner: visitor.

hallowed: made it holy.

"Honor your father and your mother, that your days may be long in the land which the Lord your God gives you.

kill: in other translations, "murder."

"You shall not kill.

"You shall not commit adultery.

"You shall not steal.

bear false witness: tell lies under oath.

"You shall not bear false witness against your neighbor.

covet: envy and desire.

"You shall not covet your neighbor's house; you shall not covet your neighbor's wife, or his manservant, or his maidservant, or his ox, or his ass, or anything that is your neighbor's."

Now when all the people perceived the thunderings and the lightnings and the sound of the trumpet and the mountain smoking, the people were afraid and trembled; and they stood afar off, and said to Moses, "You speak to us, and we will hear; but let not God speak to us, lest we die." And Moses said to the people, "Do not fear; for God has come to prove you, and that the fear of him may be before your eyes, that you may not sin."

And the people stood afar off, while Moses drew near to the thick darkness where God was. . . .

And he gave to Moses, when he had made an end of speaking with him upon Mount Sinai, the two tables of the testimony, tables of stone, written with the finger of God.

tables: tablets.
testimony: command-ments.

When the people saw that Moses delayed to come down from the mountain, the people gathered themselves together to Aaron, and said to him, "Up, make us gods, who shall go before us; as for this Moses, the man who brought us up out of the land of Egypt, we do not know what has become of him." And Aaron said to them, "Take off the rings of gold which are in the ears of your wives, your sons, and your daughters, and bring them to me." So all the people took off the rings of gold which were in their ears, and brought them to Aaron. And he received the gold at their hand, and fashioned it with a graving tool, and made a molten calf; and they said, "These are your gods, O Israel, who brought you up out of the land of Egypt!" When Aaron saw this, he built an altar before it; and Aaron made proclamation and said, "Tomorrow shall be a feast to the Lord." And they rose up early on the morrow, and offered burnt offerings and brought peace offerings; and the people sat down to eat and drink, and rose up to play.

molten: produced by melting and casting.

And the Lord said to Moses, "Go down; for your people, whom you brought up out of the land of Egypt, have corrupted themselves . . . ."

And Moses turned, and went down from the mountain with the two tables of the testimony in his hands, tables that were written on both sides; on the one side and on the other were they written. And the tables were the work of God, and the writing was the writing of God, graven upon the tables. When Joshua heard the noise of the people as they shouted, he said to Moses, "There is a noise of war in the camp." But he said, "It is not the sound of shouting for victory, or the sound of the cry of defeat, but the sound of singing that I hear." And as soon as he came near the camp and saw the calf and the dancing, Moses' anger burned hot, and he threw the tables out of his hands and broke them at the

Joshua: Moses' assistant, who had gone part way up the mountain with him.

foot of the mountain. And he took the calf which they had made, and burnt it with fire, and ground it to powder, and scattered it upon the water, and made the people of Israel drink it. . . .

On the morrow Moses said to the people, "You have sinned a great sin. And now I will go up to the Lord; perhaps I can make atonement for your sin." So Moses returned to the Lord and said, "Alas, this people have sinned a great sin; they have made for themselves gods of gold. But now, if thou wilt forgive their sin—and if not, blot me, I pray thee, out of thy book which thou hast written." But the Lord said to Moses, "Whoever has sinned against me, him will I blot out of my book. But now go, lead the people to the place of which I have spoken to you; behold, my angel shall go before you. Nevertheless, in the day when I visit, I will visit their sin upon them." . . .

Now Moses used to take the tent and pitch it outside the camp, far off from the camp; and he called it the tent of meeting. And every one who sought the Lord would go out to the tent of meeting, which was outside the camp. Whenever Moses went out to the tent, all the people rose up, and every man stood at his tent door, and looked after Moses, until he had gone into the tent. When Moses entered the tent, the pillar of cloud would descend and stand at the door of the tent, and the Lord would speak with Moses. And when all the people saw the pillar of cloud standing at the door of the tent, all the people would rise up and worship, every man at his tent door. Thus the Lord used to speak to Moses face to face, as a man speaks to his friend . . . .

Moses said to the Lord, "See, thou sayest to me, 'Bring up this people'; but thou hast not let me know whom thou wilt send with me. Yet thou hast said, 'I know you by name, and you have also found favor in my sight.' Now therefore, I pray thee, if I have found favor in thy sight, show me now thy ways, that I may know thee and find favor in thy sight. Consider too that this nation is thy people." . . .

And the Lord said to Moses, "This very thing that you have spoken I will do; for you have found favor in my sight, and I know you by name." Moses said, "I pray thee, show me thy glory." And he said, "I will make all my goodness pass before you, and will

make atonement: get forgiveness.

book: i.e., list of righteous people.

I will visit . . . upon them: at the appropriate time I will punish them for their sin.

meeting: i.e., meeting God.

proclaim before you my name 'The LORD'; and I will be gracious to whom I will be gracious, and will show mercy on whom I will show mercy. But," he said, "you cannot see my face; for man shall not see me and live." . . .

. . . So Moses cut two tables of stone like the first; and he rose early in the morning and went up on Mount Sinai, as the Lord had commanded him, and took in his hand two tables of stone. And the Lord descended in the cloud and stood with him there, and proclaimed the name of the Lord. . . .

And the Lord said to Moses, "Write these words; in accordance with these words I have made a covenant with you and with Israel." And he was there with the Lord forty days and forty nights; he neither ate bread nor drank water. And he wrote upon the tables the words of the covenant, the ten commandments.

When Moses came down from Mount Sinai, with the two tables of the testimony in his hand as he came down from the mountain, Moses did not know that the skin of his face shone because he had been talking with God. And when Aaron and all the people of Israel saw Moses, behold, the skin of his face shone, and they were afraid to come near him. But Moses called to them; and Aaron and all the leaders of the congregation returned to him, and Moses talked with them. And afterward all the people of Israel came near, and he gave them in commandment all that the Lord had spoken with him in Mount Sinai. And when Moses had finished speaking with them, he put a veil on his face; but whenever Moses went in before the Lord to speak with him, he took the veil off, until he came out; and when he came out, and told the people of Israel what he was commanded, the people of Israel saw the face of Moses, that the skin of Moses' face shone; and Moses would put the veil upon his face again, until he went in to speak with him. . . .

[*The people of Israel remained in the wilderness for forty years—an entire generation.*]

And the Lord said to Moses, "Behold, the days approach when you must die; call Joshua, and present yourselves in the tent of meeting, that I may

'The LORD': i.e., a name of God so holy that most Jews today will not speak it. Also translated "Yahweh."

be gracious: show favor.

Deut. 31:14.

commission him: instruct him in his duties.

commission him." And Moses and Joshua went and presented themselves in the tent of meeting. And the Lord appeared in the tent in a pillar of cloud; and the pillar of cloud stood by the door of the tent.

And the Lord said to Moses, "Behold, you are about to sleep with your fathers; then this people will rise and play the harlot after the strange gods of the land, where they go to be among them, and they will forsake me and break my covenant which I have made with them. Then my anger will be kindled against them in that day, and I will forsake them and hide my face from them, and they will be devoured; and many evils and troubles will come upon them, so that they will say in that day, 'Have not these evils come upon us because our God is not among us?' And I will surely hide my face in that day on account of all the evil which they have done, because they have turned to other gods. . . ."

And Moses went up from the plains of Moab to Mount Nebo, to the top of Pisgah, which is opposite Jericho. And the Lord showed him all the land, Gilead as far as Dan, all Naphtali, the land of Ephraim and Manasseh, all the land of Judah as far as the western sea, the Negeb, and the Plain, that is, the valley of Jericho the city of palm trees, as far as Zoar. And the Lord said to him, "This is the land of which I swore to Abraham, to Isaac, and to Jacob, 'I

you shall not go: this was a punishment for an episode in the wilderness when Moses disobeyed God.

will give it to your descendants.' I have let you see it with your eyes, but you shall not go over there." So Moses the servant of the Lord died there in the land of Moab, according to the word of the Lord, and he buried him in the valley in the land of Moab opposite Beth-peor; but no man knows the place of his burial to this day. Moses was a hundred and twenty years old when he died; his eye was not dim, nor his

natural force abated: vigor weakened.

natural force abated. And the people of Israel wept for Moses in the plains of Moab thirty days; then the days of weeping and mourning for Moses were ended.

And Joshua the son of Nun was full of the spirit of wisdom, for Moses had laid his hands upon him; so the people of Israel obeyed him, and did as the Lord had commanded Moses. And there has not arisen a prophet since in Israel like Moses, whom the Lord knew face to face, none like him for all the signs and the wonders which the Lord sent him to do in the land of Egypt, to Pharaoh and to all his servants and to all his land, and for all the mighty power and all the great and terrible deeds which Moses wrought in the sight of all Israel.

wrought: did.

For close reading

1 How long were the Hebrews in the wilderness?
2 How did the Lord first answer the "murmurings" of the people against Moses?
3 God appears in "thick darkness" at Mount Sinai. In what earlier stories has darkness been connected with important events?
4 Which of the commandments did the people violate at the foot of Sinai?
5 What finally happened to the golden calf?
6 Moses was not permitted to see God's "glory." What other disappointments did he have at the end of his life?

For thought and discussion

7 Considering their circumstances as the Hebrews emerge from Egypt, in what ways might they benefit from an extended period in the wilderness? How do they initially respond to this situation? In what various ways do people respond to "wilderness" today?
8 Examine the brief list of the ten commandments you made from memory. Which ones did everyone in class remember? What were the ones the class tended to forget? Why do you think this was so?
9 Why do you think the Lord prohibited the construction of "graven images"? Some people today regard money and material possessions as modern graven images. Explain your agreement or disagreement with that opinion.
10 The presence of the Lord on the mountain is made dramatically evident. Compare and contrast

this moment with two or three appearances of the Lord in earlier passages. Do you think a mountain is an appropriate meeting place? Why or why not?

11 Beginning with Moses' early youth, how does the story prepare the reader for the people's lack of trust in Moses and the Lord at the foot of Mount Sinai?

12 If the Lord will not forgive the people for their sin, Moses asks that he himself be blotted out. What does this response indicate about Moses? His relation to God? To his people?

13 Water plays an important part at many points in the Moses-Exodus story. Find as many "water episodes" as you can in the three Bible passages included in this chapter. Do you see any similarities between the episodes? What symbolic meaning does water seem to have? Is fire also used in a symbolic way in the Moses stories? If so, where?

14 What heroic qualities does Moses possess? In your opinion, what is his greatest achievement as a leader? What do you think is his greatest disappointment?

Activities

1 Draw a map of the wanderings in the wilderness.

2 Write a newspaper account of the hardships and complaints of the Hebrews in the wilderness.

3 Imagine that you are Moses and nearing death. Write your thoughts as you look over your life. How was your understanding of your life's purpose changed by certain key events? Are there any things you regret?

THE LATEST DECALOGUE

Arthur Hugh Clough

Thou shalt have one God only; who
Would be at the expense of two?
No graven images may be
Worshiped, except the currency.
5   Swear not at all; for, for thy curse
Thine enemy is none the worse.
At church on Sunday to attend
Will serve to keep the world thy friend.
Honor thy parents; that is, all
10 From whom advancement may befall.
Thou shalt not kill; but need'st not strive
Officiously to keep alive.
Do not adultery commit;
Advantage rarely comes of it.
15 Thou shalt not steal; an empty feat,
When it's so lucrative to cheat.
Bear not false witness; let the lie
Have time on its own wings to fly.
Thou shalt not covet, but tradition
20 Approves all forms of competition.

Decalogue: the ten commandments.

officiously: excessively forward in offering help.

lucrative: profitable.

For thought and discussion

1 The poem suggests reasons for obeying the commandments. What do these various reasons seem to have in common? Can you summarize them in one or two sentences?
2 What is the tone of the poem? How does the poet feel about society's response to the ten commandments?
3 In your opinion, how do people today respond to the commandments?

THE
MURDER
OF
MOSES

Karl Shapiro

By reason of despair we set forth behind you
And followed the pillar of fire like a doubt,
To hold to belief wanted a sign,
Called the miracle of the staff and the plagues
5 Natural phenomena.

expediency: usefulness,
desirability.

We questioned the expediency of the march,
Gossiped about you. What was escape
To the fear of going forward and Pharaoh's wheels?
When the chariots mired and the army flooded
10 Our cry of horror was one with theirs.

You always went alone, a little ahead,
Prophecy disturbed you, you were not a fanatic.
The women said you were meek, the men
Regarded you as a typical leader.
15 You and your black wife might have been
    foreigners.

We even discussed your parentage; were you
    really a Jew?
We remembered how Joseph had made himself a
    prince,
All of us shared in the recognition
Of his skill of management, sense of propriety,
20 Devotion to his brothers and Israel.

We hated you daily. Our children died. The water
  spilled.
It was as if you were trying to lose us one by one.
Our wandering seemed the wandering of your
  mind,
The cloud believed we were tireless,
25 We expressed our contempt and our boredom
  openly.

At last you ascended the rock; at last returned.
Your anger that day was probably His.
When we saw you come down from the mountain,
  your skin alight
And the stones of our law flashing,
30 We fled like animals and the dancers scattered.

We watched where you overturned the calf on the
  fire,
We hid when you broke the tablets on the rock,
We wept when we drank the mixture of gold and
  water.
We had hoped you were lost or had left us.
35 This was the day of our greatest defilement.

defilement: dishonor.

You were simple of heart; you were sorry for
  Miriam,

Miriam: Moses' sister,
who was afflicted with
leprosy by God.

You reasoned with Aaron, who was your enemy.
However often you cheered us with songs and
    prayers
We cursed you again. The serpent bit us,
40 And mouth to mouth you entreated the Lord for
    our sake.

At the end of it all we gave you the gift of death.
Invasion and generalship were spared you.
The hand of our direction, resignedly you fell,
And while officers prepared for the river-crossing
45 The One God blessed you and covered you with
    earth.

Though you were mortal and once committed
    murder
You assumed the burden of the covenant,
Spoke for the world and for our understanding.

converse: conversation.   Converse with God made you a thinker,
50 Taught us all early justice, made us a race.

For thought and discussion

1 Is the title of this poem in keeping with the biblical
story of Moses? What does it mean, and why do you
think Shapiro chose it?
2 The speaker says "the men/Regarded you as a
typical leader." What does this mean to you?
3 Choose one of the following lines from the poem,
and try to briefly explain what you think it means:
line 23, line 40, or line 50.
4 What does this poem say about the difficulties of
being a leader? About the difficulties of being a
follower?

Moses Crossing the Red Sea, detail from a miniature in an illuminated Haggadah. The British Library Board.

ABOVE: *Moses and the Tables of the Law* by Shalom of Safed. After 1957. The Israel Museum, Jerusalem.
BELOW: *Moses Breaking the Tables of the Law,* detail from an illustration by Gustave Doré, 1866.

Deborah Riding into Battle with Barak, detail from a French illuminated miniature in the Psalter of St. Louis, 1252-1270. The Bibliothèque Nationale, Paris.

Samson and the Lion, bronze engraved aquamanile (ewer), Lorraine or Upper Rhine, thirteenth century. Courtesy of the Museum of Fine Arts, Boston, Benjamin Shelton Fund.

Thomas Mann
Translated by H. T. Lowe-Porter

[*This excerpt from a novella describes
Moses' experiences on Mount Sinai.*]

Accordingly Moses crossed the wilderness on his
staff, his wide-set eyes bent on the mount of God,
which was smoking like a chimney and often spew-
ing out fire. It had an odd shape, the mountain:
cracks and ridges ran round it, seeming to divide it
into several stories. They looked like paths running
round it, but they were not: only terracelike grada-
tions with yellow rear walls. By the third day the
pilgrim had crossed the foothills to the rugged base;
now he began to climb, his fist closed round his
staff, which he set before him as he mounted the
pathless, trackless, blackened, scalded waste. Hours
and hours he mounted, pace by pace, higher and
higher into the nearness of God; as far as ever a
human being could. For after a while the sulphurous
vapors, smelling like hot metal, so filled the air that
he gasped for breath and began to cough. Yet he got
up to the topmost ridge just below the peak, where
there was an extended view on both sides over the

bare desert range and beyond the wilderness toward Kadesh. He could even see the little tribal encampment, closer in and far down in the depths.

Here Moses, coughing, found a cavity in the mountain wall, with a roof formed by a ledge of rock that should protect him from flying stones and molten streams. Here he set up his rest and took time to get his breath. And now he prepared to embark upon the task which God had laid upon him. Under all the difficulties (the metallic vapors oppressed his chest and even made the water taste of sulphur), the work was to take him forty days and forty nights.

But why so long? The question is an idle one. God's whole moral law, in permanently compact and compendious form, binding to all time, had to be composed and graven on the stone of His own mountain, in order that Moses might carry it down to his father's crude, confused, bewildered folk, down to the enclosure where they were waiting. It should be among them, from generation to generation inviolably graven as well in their minds and hearts and their flesh and blood, the quintessence of human good behavior. God commanded him loudly from out of his own breast to hew two tables from the living rock and write the decrees on them, five on one and five on the other—in all, ten decrees. To make the tablets, to smooth them and shape them to be adequate bearers of the eternal law—that in itself was no small thing. One man alone, even though he had broad wrists and had drunk the milk of a stone-mason's daughter, might not for many days accomplish it. Actually the making of the tables took a quarter of the forty days. But the writing itself, when he came to it, was a problem that might well bring Moses' stay on the hilltop to more than forty days. For how was he to write? In his Theban boarding school he had learned the decorative picture writing of the Egyptians and its cursive adaptation; also the cramped cuneiform of the formal script practiced in the region of the Euphrates and employed by the kings of the earth to exchange ideas on earthen shards. And among the Midianites he had got acquainted with a third kind of semantic magic expressed in symbols, such as eyes, crosses, beetles, rings, and various kinds of wavy lines. This

compendious: concise.

inviolably graven: sacredly carved.

quintessence: most perfect example.

cursive: written with letters joined together.
cuneiform (kyü nēʹə form): wedge-shaped characters.
earthen shards: broken pieces of pottery.
semantic: having to do with the meaning of words.

kind of writing was used in the land of Sinai; it was a clumsy attempt to imitate Egyptian picture writing, but it did not manage to symbolize whole words and things—only syllables to be read together. Moses saw that no one of these three methods of putting down ideas would serve in the present case, for the simple reason that all of them depended on the language they expressed by signs. Not in Babylonian or Egyptian or the jargon of the Bedouins of Sinai— not in any one of these could he possibly write down the ten decrees. No, they must and could only be written in the tongue of the fathers' seed—the idiom it spoke, the dialect he himself used in his formative task; and that no matter whether they could read it or not. Indeed, how should they read it, when it could scarcely be written and there did not yet exist any semantic magic whatever for the tongue they talked in?

Bedouins (bed′ü ən): desert wanderers; nomads.

Fervently, with all his heart, Moses wished for it: for a kind of simple writing that they would be able to read quite quickly; one that they, children as they were, could learn in a few days—and it followed that such a one, God's help being nigh, could also be thought out and invented in no longer time. For thought out and invented a kind of writing had got to be, since it did not exist.

What a pressing, oppressive task! He had not measured it beforehand. He had thought only of "writing"—not at all of the fact that one could not just "write." His head glowed and steamed like a furnace; it was like the top of the peak itself, on fire with the fervor of his hopes for his people. He felt as though rays streamed from his head; as though horns came out on his brow for very strain of desire and pure inspiration. He could not invent signs for all the words his people used, nor for the syllables which composed them. The vocabulary of the people down there in the camp was small enough. But even so it would need so many symbols that they could not be invented in the limited number of days at his command; much less could the people learn to read them. So Moses contrived something else— and horns stood forth from his head out of sheer pride of his god-invention. He classified the sounds of the language: those made with the lips, with the tongue and palate, and with the throat; and he

horns: There was a tradition in art of depicting Moses with horns on his head, because early translators did not know that the same Hebrew word can mean both "horns" and "rays of light."

divided off from them the smaller group of open sounds which became words only when they were included in combinations with the others. Of those others there were not so very many—a bare twenty; and if you gave them signs which regularly obliged anyone pronouncing them to buzz or hiss, to huff or puff, or mumble or rumble, then you might adapt your sounds and combine them into words and pictures of things, paying no heed to those in the other group, which came in automatically anyhow. You could make as many combinations as you liked, and that not only in the language spoken by his father's people, but in any language whatever. You could even write Egyptian and Babylonian with them.

A god-inspiration! An inspiration with horns to it! It was like to its source, to the Invisible and Spiritual whence it came, who possessed all the world, and who, though He had especially elected the stock down below for His own, yet He was Lord everywhere and all over on earth. But it was also an inspiration peculiarly apt for Moses' immediate and urgent purpose and for the necessity out of which it was born—for the brief and binding text of the law. Of course, this was first to be impressed upon the seed which Moses had led out of Egypt, because God and he had a common love to it. But just as the handful of arbitrary signs might be used to write down all the words of all the tongues of all the people on earth, and just as Jahwe was omnipotent over all these, so also the text which Moses intended to set down by means of those signs should likewise be universal. It should be a compendium of such a kind as to serve everywhere on earth and to all the peoples on it as a foundation stone of morality and good conduct.

So, then, Moses—his head on fire—began by scratching his signs on the rocky wall in loose imitation of the sounds the Sinai people made, conjuring them up in his mind as he went. With his graving tool he scratched on the rock the signs he had made to represent the burrs and purrs and whirrs, the hisses and buzzes, the humming and gurgling of his father's native tongue. He set them down in an order that pleased his ear—and lo, with them one could set down the whole world in writ-

arbitrary: determined by chance.

Jahwe (yä′wä): a name of God; also *Yahweh* or *Jehovah*.

conjuring them: causing them to appear.

ing: the signs that took up space and those that took none, the derived and the contrived—in short, everything on earth.

And he wrote; I mean, he drilled and chiseled and scooped at the splintery stone of the tables; for these he had prepared beforehand with great pains, during the time he had spent cogitating his script. The whole took him rather more than forty days— and no wonder!

cogitating: thinking over.

Young Joshua came up to him a few times, to fetch water and bread. The people did not need to know this: they believed that Moses sojourned up there sustained solely by God's presence and His words, and Joshua for strategic reasons preferred them to remain in this belief.

Moses rose with the dawn and labored till the sun set back in the desert. We must picture him there, sitting bare to the waist, his breast hairy, with the strong arms bequeathed him by his father the slain water-bearer; with wide-set eyes, flattened nose, and parted grizzling beard; chewing a pancake, coughing now and then from the metallic vapors, and in the sweat of his brow hewing at the tables, filing and planing. Squatting before them as he leaned against the rocky wall, he toiled away with great attention to detail; first drawing his pothooks, his magic runes, with the graver and then drilling them into the stone.

magic runes: marks or characters with mysterious or magic meaning.

He wrote on the first table:

I, Jahwe, am thy God; thou shalt have no other gods before me.

Thou shalt not make unto thyself any graven image.

Thou shalt not take my name in vain.

Be mindful of my day to keep it holy.

Honor thy father and thy mother.

And on the other table he wrote:

Thou shalt not kill.

Thou shalt not commit adultery.

Thou shalt not steal.

Thou shalt not affront thy neighbor by bearing false witness.

Thou shalt not cast a covetous eye upon thy neighbor's goods.

This was what he wrote, leaving out the vowels, which were taken for granted. And while he worked it seemed to him as though rays like a pair of horns stood out from the hair of his brow.

When Joshua came up for the last time he stayed a little longer than before, in fact, two whole days, for Moses was not done with his work, and they wanted to go down together. The youth admired and warmly praised what his master had done, consoling him in the matter of a few letters which, despite all Moses' loving care and greatly to his distress, had got splintered and were illegible. Joshua assured him that the general effect was unharmed.

As a finishing touch in Joshua's presence Moses colored the letters he had engraved. He did it with his own blood, that they might stand out better. No other coloring matter was at hand; so he pricked his strong arm with the tool and carefully let the drops of blood run into the outlines of the letters, so that they showed red against the stone. When the script was dry, Moses took a table under each arm, handed to the young man the staff which had supported him on his climb; and so they went down together from the mountain of God to the tribal encampment opposite in the desert.

For close reading

1 According to this account, what does Moses invent before he begins to write on the tablets?
2 What part does Joshua play in this story?
3 What details of this account emphasize the conditions under which Moses worked? What details focus on the mental work involved? The physical work?

For thought and discussion

4 God speaks to Moses in the Bible story; in this passage God is not directly quoted. What other differences do you find between the two accounts?
5 In this account, the Tables of the Law have a double importance; they give a system of writing as well as a code of law to the Hebrews. Why do you suppose the author so strongly emphasizes the creation of a written language?

4

israel's
youthful
days

DEBORAH AND JAEL: VICTORY FOR ISRAEL

Judges

[The Book of Judges *is a series of stories that follows a pattern. In each story the Israelites stray from righteousness, God sends a foreign power to oppress them, they cry to God for help, a God-appointed leader—a "judge"—arises in Israel to deliver them and they return to God and his law. The most prominent of these successive leaders are Ehud, Deborah, Gideon, Jephthah, and Samson. This chapter includes the stories of Deborah and Samson.]*

And the people of Israel again did what was evil in the sight of the Lord, after Ehud died. And the Lord sold them into the hand of Jabin king of Canaan, who reigned in Hazor; the commander of his army was Sisera, who dwelt in Harosheth-ha-goiim. Then the people of Israel cried to the Lord for help; for he had nine hundred chariots of iron, and oppressed the people of Israel cruelly for twenty years.

Now Deborah, a prophetess, the wife of Lappidoth, was judging Israel at that time. She used to sit under the palm of Deborah between Ramah and Bethel in the hill country of Ephraim; and the people of Israel came up to her for judgment. She sent and

iron: the Israelites had only the softer bronze metal.

prophetess: Deborah is the only prophet (one who speaks for God) and only woman among the judges.

Judges 4:1–9, 12–22; 5:1, 3–5, 11d, 19–31 (RSV).
LEFT: *Ruth Brings Gleanings to Naomi*, detail from a full-page illuminated miniature in an Old Testament, French, about 1250. The Pierpont Morgan Library.

summoned Barak the son of Abinoam from Kedesh in Naphtali, and said to him, "The Lord, the God of Israel, commands you, 'Go, gather your men at Mount Tabor, taking ten thousand from the tribe of Naphtali and the tribe of Zebulun. And I will draw out Sisera, the general of Jabin's army, to meet you by the river Kishon with his chariots and his troops; and I will give him into your hand.' " Barak said to her, "If you will go with me, I will go; but if you will not go with me, I will not go." And she said, "I will surely go with you; nevertheless, the road on which you are going will not lead to your glory, for the Lord will sell Sisera into the hand of a woman." Then Deborah arose, and went with Barak to Kedesh . . . .

When Sisera was told that Barak the son of Abinoam had gone up to Mount Tabor, Sisera called out all his chariots, nine hundred chariots of iron, and all the men who were with him, from Harosheth-ha-goiim to the river Kishon. And Deborah said to Barak, "Up! For this is the day in which the Lord has given Sisera into your hand. Does not the Lord go out before you?" So Barak went down from Mount Tabor with ten thousand men following him. And the Lord routed Sisera and all his chariots and all his army before Barak at the edge of the sword; and Sisera alighted from his chariot and fled away on foot. And Barak pursued the chariots and the army to Harosheth-ha-goiim, and all the army of Sisera fell by the edge of the sword; not a man was left.

But Sisera fled away on foot to the tent of Jael, the wife of Heber the Kenite; for there was peace between Jabin the king of Hazor and the house of Heber the Kenite. And Jael came out to meet Sisera, and said to him, "Turn aside, my lord, turn aside to me; have no fear." So he turned aside to her into the tent, and she covered him with a rug. And he said to her, "Pray, give me a little water to drink; for I am thirsty." So she opened a skin of milk and gave him a drink and covered him. And he said to her, "Stand at the door of the tent, and if any man comes and asks you, 'Is any one here?' say, No." But Jael the wife of Heber took a tent peg, and took a hammer in her hand, and went softly to him and drove the peg into his temple, till it went down into the ground, as he was lying fast asleep from weari-

Jael (jā'əl).
Kenites: sheep herding people distantly related to the Israelites.

ness. So he died. And behold, as Barak pursued Sisera, Jael went out to meet him, and said to him, "Come, and I will show you the man whom you are seeking." So he went in to her tent; and there lay Sisera dead, with the tent peg in his temple. . . .

Then sang Deborah and Barak the son of Abinoam on that day: . . .

The song of Deborah and Barak retells the story in poetic and slightly different form.

"Hear, O kings; give ear, O princes;
to the Lord I will sing,
I will make melody to the Lord, the God of
Israel.

Lord, when thou didst go forth from Seir,
when thou didst march from the region of
Edom,
the earth trembled, and the heavens dropped,
yea, the clouds dropped water.
The mountains quaked before the Lord,
yon Sinai before the Lord, the God of
Israel. . . .

Seir, Edom: regions south of Israel.

Then down to the gates marched the people of
the Lord. . . .

The kings came, they fought;
then fought the kings of Canaan,
at Taanach, by the waters of Megiddo;
they got no spoils of silver.
From heaven fought the stars,
from their courses they fought against Sisera.
The torrent Kishon swept them away,
the onrushing torrent, the torrent Kishon.
March on, my soul, with might!

Then loud beat the horses' hoofs
with the galloping, galloping of his steeds.

Curse Meroz, says the angel of the Lord,
curse bitterly its inhabitants,
because they came not to the help of the Lord,
to the help of the Lord against the mighty.

Meroz: probably a nearby Israelite village.

Most blessed of women be Jael,
the wife of Heber the Kenite,
of tent-dwelling women most blessed.
He asked water and she gave him milk,

she brought him curds in a lordly bowl.
She put her hand to the tent peg
and her right hand to the workmen's mallet;
she struck Sisera a blow,
she crushed his head,
she shattered and pierced his temple.
He sank, he fell,
he lay still at her feet;
at her feet he sank, he fell;
where he sank, there he fell dead.

Out of the window she peered,
the mother of Sisera gazed through the lattice:
'Why is his chariot so long in coming?
Why tarry the hoofbeats of his chariots?'
Her wisest ladies make answer,
nay, she gives answer to herself,
'Are they not finding and dividing the spoil?——
A maiden or two for every man;
stuffs: fabrics; cloth.   spoil of dyed stuffs for Sisera,
spoil of dyed stuffs embroidered,
two pieces of dyed work embroidered for my
    neck as spoil?'

So perish all thine enemies, O Lord!
But thy friends be like the sun as he rises in his
    might."

For close reading

1 What weapon of the enemy casts particular fear
into the Israelites?
2 What part does Barak play in this story?
3 How does God show his power?
4 In the poem, how is nature shown to be on the
side of the Israelites?

For thought and discussion

5 What part do women play in this story? What difference does it make to the story that they are women rather than men?

6 What would you say are the main differences between the prose and the poetic accounts of events? What are the advantages of each way of telling the story? Of including both?

7 Though the Bible generally includes few details, the poetic description of the killing of Sisera is extremely detailed. Why do you think this is so?

8 Why do you suppose the last part of the victory song concentrates on the Canaanite women?

Activities

1 Many songs commemorate events in the history of a people; "The Star-Spangled Banner" is one example. Some ballads, such as "John Henry," tell the stories of folk heroes. Think of some other examples. What characteristics do they seem to have in common? You may wish to sing or play recordings of several of these songs and ballads in class.

2 Aesop and James Thurber used to add "moral" statements to the ends of their stories. For example, "The Fox and the Crow" has as its moral, "Don't be greedy." Invent a "moral" for the Deborah-Jael story.

3 Create a picture of "stormy nature" or some other feature of the story, using whatever medium you wish.

SISERA

Muriel Spark

Sisera, dead by hammer and nail, fared worst
Where he fared well; the woman had fed him first.
After the kill Deborah came,
A holy kite to claim the heathen viscera.
5 Is not her song impressive? All the same,
I am for Sisera

Whose ruin had rhetoric enough and fitness
For Deborah's prophecy, so are God's enemies
   supplanted.
She needed no polemic, as God was her witness
10 Gloriously to publish the story condensed:
'The stars in their courses fought against
Sisera,' she descanted.

The hostess it was, who pinned the villain mute;
But Deborah whittled her fine art, the keener to
   spike him
15 On a final point: 'His women wait for the loot.'
So, from God's poets may God perfectly defend
Sisera and all the rest of us like him,
With whom the stars contend.

For thought and discussion

1 With what does the poet compare Deborah? How does Deborah "spike" Sisera?
2 In what lines does the poet link herself with Sisera? Why do you think she feels this bond? What are your feelings about Sisera and his death?
3 If "the stars in their courses" fight against you, what are your chances of winning?

THE STORY OF SAMSON

Judges

And there was a certain man of Zorah, of the tribe of the Danites, whose name was Manoah; and his wife was barren and had no children. And the angel of the Lord appeared to the woman and said to her, "Behold, you are barren and have no children; but you shall conceive and bear a son. Therefore beware, and drink no wine or strong drink, and eat nothing unclean, for lo, you shall conceive and bear a son. No razor shall come upon his head, for the boy shall be a Nazirite to God from birth; and he shall begin to deliver Israel from the hand of the Philistines." . . .

. . . And the woman bore a son, and called his name Samson; and the boy grew, and the Lord blessed him. And the Spirit of the Lord began to stir him in Mahaneh-dan, between Zorah and Eshtaol.

Samson went down to Timnah, and at Timnah he saw one of the daughters of the Philistines. Then he came up, and told his father and mother, "I saw one of the daughters of the Philistines at Timnah; now get her for me as my wife." But his father and mother said to him, "Is there not a woman among the daughters of your kinsmen, or among all our

unclean: meat of animals forbidden as food by the Lord.

Nazirite: holy person. One of the vows of a Nazirite was not to cut his hair. (Not to be confused with Nazarene, a person from Nazareth.)

Philistines: traditional enemies of the Israelites. They invaded south Canaan from the sea.

Judges 13:2–5, 24–25; 14:1–15:16; 16:1–23, 25–31 (RSV).

people, that you must go to take a wife from the uncircumcised Philistines?" But Samson said to his father, "Get her for me; for she pleases me well."

His father and mother did not know that it was from the Lord; for he was seeking an occasion against the Philistines. At that time the Philistines had dominion over Israel.

Then Samson went down with his father and mother to Timnah, and he came to the vineyards of Timnah. And behold, a young lion roared against him; and the Spirit of the Lord came mightily upon him, and he tore the lion asunder as one tears a kid; and he had nothing in his hand. But he did not tell his father or his mother what he had done. Then he went down and talked with the woman; and she pleased Samson well. And after a while he returned to take her; and he turned aside to see the carcass of the lion, and behold, there was a swarm of bees in the body of the lion, and honey. He scraped it out into his hands, and went on, eating as he went; and he came to his father and mother, and gave some to them, and they ate. But he did not tell them that he had taken the honey from the carcass of the lion.

And his father went down to the woman, and Samson made a feast there; for so the young men used to do. And when the people saw him, they brought thirty companions to be with him. And Samson said to them, "Let me now put a riddle to you; if you can tell me what it is, within the seven days of the feast, and find it out, then I will give you thirty linen garments and thirty festal garments; but if you cannot tell me what it is, then you shall give me thirty linen garments and thirty festal garments." And they said to him, "Put your riddle, that we may hear it." And he said to them,

> "Out of the eater came something to eat.
> Out of the strong came something sweet."

And they could not in three days tell what the riddle was.

On the fourth day they said to Samson's wife, "Entice your husband to tell us what the riddle is, lest we burn you and your father's house with fire. Have you invited us here to impoverish us?" And Samson's wife wept before him, and said, "You only hate me, you do not love me; you have put a riddle

asunder: apart.
kid: a young goat.

festal garments: clothing worn to celebrations.

entice: coax.

impoverish us: make us poor.

to my countrymen, and you have not told me what it is." And he said to her, "Behold, I have not told my father nor my mother, and shall I tell you?" She wept before him the seven days that their feast lasted; and on the seventh day he told her, because she pressed him hard. Then she told the riddle to her countrymen. And the men of the city said to him on the seventh day before the sun went down.

> "What is sweeter than honey?
> What is stronger than a lion?"

And he said to them,

> "If you had not plowed with my heifer,
> you would not have found out my riddle."

And the Spirit of the Lord came mightily upon him, and he went down to Ashkelon and killed thirty men of the town, and took their spoil and gave the festal garments to those who had told the riddle. In hot anger he went back to his father's house. And Samson's wife was given to his companion, who had been his best man.

After a while, at the time of wheat harvest, Samson went to visit his wife with a kid; and he said, "I will go in to my wife in the chamber." But her father would not allow him to go in. And her father said, "I really thought that you utterly hated her; so I gave her to your companion. Is not her younger sister fairer than she? Pray take her instead." And Samson said to them, "This time I shall be blameless in regard to the Philistines, when I do them mischief." So Samson went and caught three hundred foxes, and took torches; and he turned them tail to tail, and put a torch between each pair of tails. And when he had set fire to the torches, he let the foxes go into the standing grain of the Philistines, and burned up the shocks and standing grain, as well as the olive orchards. Then the Philistines said, "Who has done this?" And they said, "Samson, the son-in-law of the Timnite, because he has taken his wife and given her to his companion." And the Philistines came up, and burned her and her father with fire. And Samson said to them, "If this is what you do, I swear I will be avenged upon you, and after that I will quit." And he smote them hip and thigh with great slaughter; and

shocks: piles of cut grain stalks.

smote . . . thigh: i.e., attacked them unmercifully.

cleft: cave.

he went down and stayed in the cleft of the rock of Etam.

Then the Philistines came up and encamped in Judah, and made a raid on Lehi. And the men of Judah said, "Why have you come up against us?" They said, "We have come up to bind Samson, to do to him as he did to us." Then three thousand men of Judah went down to the cleft of the rock of Etam, and said to Samson, "Do you not know that the Philistines are rulers over us? What then is this that you have done to us?" And he said to them, "As they did to me, so have I done to them." And they said to him, "We have come down to bind you, that we may give you into the hands of the Philistines." And Samson said to them, "Swear to me that you will not fall upon me yourselves." They said to him, "No; we will only bind you and give you into their hands; we will not kill you." So they bound him with two new ropes, and brought him up from the rock.

When he came to Lehi, the Philistines came shouting to meet him; and the Spirit of the Lord came mightily upon him, and the ropes which were on his arms became as flax that has caught fire, and his bonds melted off his hands. And he found a fresh jawbone of an ass, and put out his hand and seized it, and with it he slew a thousand men. And Samson said,

flax: a plant fiber which is spun into thread and woven into linen.

> "With the jawbone of an ass,
> heaps upon heaps,
> With the jawbone of an ass
> have I slain a thousand men." . . .

harlot: a prostitute.

Samson went to Gaza, and there he saw a harlot, and he went in to her. The Gazites were told, "Samson has come here," and they surrounded the place and lay in wait for him all night at the gate of the city. They kept quiet all night, saying, "Let us wait till the light of the morning; then we will kill him." But Samson lay till midnight, and at midnight he arose and took hold of the doors of the gate of the city and the two posts, and pulled them up, bar and all, and put them on his shoulders and carried them to the top of the hill that is before Hebron.

before: in front of.

After this he loved a woman in the valley of Sorek, whose name was Delilah. And the lords of the Philistines came to her and said to her, "Entice him, and see wherein his great strength lies, and by what means we may overpower him, that we may bind him to subdue him; and we will each give you eleven hundred pieces of silver." And Delilah said to Samson, "Please tell me wherein your great strength lies, and how you might be bound, that one could subdue you." And Samson said to her, "If they bind me with seven fresh bowstrings which have not been dried, then I shall become weak, and be like any other man." Then the lords of the Philistines brought her seven fresh bowstrings which had not been dried, and she bound him with them. Now she had men lying in wait in an inner chamber. And she said to him, "The Philistines are upon you, Samson!" But he snapped the bowstrings, as a string of tow snaps when it touches the fire. So the secret of his strength was not known.

tow (tō): coarse, broken fibers of flax.

And Delilah said to Samson, "Behold, you have mocked me, and told me lies; please tell me how you might be bound." And he said to her, "If they bind me with new ropes that have not been used, then I shall become weak, and be like any other man." So Delilah took new ropes and bound him with them, and said to him, "The Philistines are upon you, Samson!" And the men lying in wait were in an inner chamber. But he snapped the ropes off his arms like a thread.

And Delilah said to Samson, "Until now you have mocked me, and told me lies; tell me how you might be bound." And he said to her, "If you weave the seven locks of my head with the web and make it tight with the pin, then I shall become weak, and be like any other man." So while he slept, Delilah took the seven locks of his head and wove them into the web. And she made them tight with the pin, and said to him, "The Philistines are upon you, Samson!" But he awoke from his sleep, and pulled away the pin, the loom, and the web.

web: warp; the yarns placed lengthwise in a loom.

And she said to him, "How can you say, 'I love you,' when your heart is not with me? You have mocked me these three times, and you have not told me wherein your great strength lies." And when she pressed him hard with her words day after day, and urged him, his soul was vexed to death. And he told her all his mind, and said to her, "A razor has never come upon my head; for I have been a Nazirite to God from my mother's womb. If I be shaved, then my strength will leave me, and I shall become weak, and be like any other man."

When Delilah saw that he had told her all his mind, she sent and called the lords of the Philistines, saying, "Come up this once, for he has told me all his mind." Then the lords of the Philistines came up to her, and brought the money in their hands. She made him sleep upon her knees; and she called a man, and had him shave off the seven locks of his head. Then she began to torment him, and his strength left him. And she said, "The Philistines are upon you, Samson!" And he awoke from his sleep, and said, "I will go out as at other times, and shake myself free." And he did not know that the Lord had left him. And the Philistines seized him and gouged out his eyes, and brought him down to Gaza, and bound him with bronze fetters; and he ground at the mill in the prison. But the hair of his head began to grow again after it had been shaved.

Now the lords of the Philistines gathered to offer a great sacrifice to Dagon their god, and to rejoice; for they said, "Our god has given Samson our enemy into our hand." . . . And when their hearts were merry, they said, "Call Samson, that he may make sport for us." So they called Samson out of the prison, and he made sport before them. They made him stand between the pillars; and Samson said to the lad who held him by the hand, "Let me feel the pillars on which the house rests, that I may lean against them." Now the house was full of men and women; all the lords of the Philistines were there, and on the roof there were about three thousand men and women, who looked on while Samson made sport.

Then Samson called to the Lord and said, "O Lord God, remember me, I pray thee, and strengthen me, I pray thee, only this once, O God, that I may be avenged upon the Philistines for one of my two eyes." And Samson grasped the two middle pillars upon which the house rested, and he leaned his weight upon them, his right hand on the one and his left hand on the other. And Samson said, "Let me die with the Philistines." Then he bowed with all his might; and the house fell upon the lords and upon all the people that were in it. So the dead whom he slew at his death were more than those whom he had slain during his life. Then his brothers and all his

knees: lap.

fetters: chains.
ground at the
mill: turned a heavy
stone used to grind
grain.

bowed (boud): bent
forward.

family came down and took him and brought him up and buried him between Zorah and Eshtaol in the tomb of Manoah his father. He had judged Israel twenty years.

For close reading

1 List the occasions and the reasons Samson does harm to the Philistines. Which of his feats are clever tricks? Which are acts of sheer strength?
2 Describe the methods Delilah and the daughter of Timnah use to get what they want from Samson.
3 Write down as many of Samson's characteristics as you can.
4 Where in the story are the following verbs used: *entice, bind,* and *avenge?*
5 After he is blinded by the Philistines, what is the first task Samson is given to do?

For thought and discussion

6 Samson's characteristics seem both good and bad. Why do you suppose such a person is chosen to save Israel from the Philistines?
7 What is the effect on the story of the repetition of the words *entice, bind,* and *avenge?* How do these words apply to Samson? To Israel?
8 Are Samson's character and behavior consistent throughout the story? Does he develop or mature as a result of his experiences? Explain.
9 Samson asks the Lord that he "be avenged upon

the Philistines for one" of his eyes. Why do you think he does not ask to be avenged for both eyes? **10** Samson's actions are never directly commanded or condemned by the Lord, who plays an important part only at the beginning and end of Samson's life. Why do you think this is so?

Activities

1 Make a cartoon strip which illustrates the episodes of Samson's life.
2 Look up the stories of Hercules in Greek mythology, and Paul Bunyan of American folklore. Describe the similarities and differences you see among Samson, Hercules, and Paul Bunyan. What other "mighty men" do you know of?

HOW SAMSON BORE AWAY THE GATES OF GAZA

Vachel Lindsay

Once, in a night as black as ink,
She drove him out when he would not drink.
Round the house there were men in wait
Asleep in rows by the Gaza gate.
5   But the Holy Spirit was in this man.
Like a gentle wind he crept and ran.
("It is midnight," said the big town clock.)

He lifted the gates up, post and lock.
The hole in the wall was high and wide
10 When he bore away old Gaza's pride
Into the deep of the night:—
The bold Jack Johnson Israelite,—
Samson—
The Judge,
15 The Nazarite.

> **Jack Johnson:** first black man to be heavyweight boxing champion.

The air was black, like the smoke of a dragon.
Samson's heart was as big as a wagon.
He sang like a shining golden fountain.
He sweated up to the top of the mountain.
20 He threw down the gates with a noise like
      judgment.
And the quails all ran with the big arousement.

But he wept—"I must not love tough queens,
And spend on them my hard earned means.
I told that girl I would drink no more.
25 Therefore she drove me from her door.
Oh sorrow!
Sorrow!
I cannot hide.
Oh Lord look down from your chariot side.
30 You made me Judge, and I am not wise.
I am weak as a sheep for all my size."

*Let Samson
Be coming
Into your mind.*

35 The moon shone out, the stars were gay.
He saw the foxes run and play.

rent: tore.

He rent his garments, he rolled around
In deep repentance on the ground.
Then he felt a honey in his soul.

grace abounding: great
amounts of mercy or
favor.

40 Grace abounding made him whole.
Then he saw the Lord in a chariot blue.
The gorgeous stallions whinnied and flew.
The iron wheels hummed an old hymn-tune
And crunched in thunder over the moon.
45 And Samson shouted to the sky:
"My Lord, my Lord is riding high."

Like a steed, he pawed the gates with his hoof.
He rattled the gates like rocks on the roof,
And danced in the night
50 On the mountain-top,
Danced in the deep of the night:
The Judge, the holy Nazarite,
Whom ropes and chains could never bind.

*Let Samson
55 Be coming
Into your mind.*

Whirling his arms, like a top he sped.
His long black hair flew round his head
Like an outstretched net of silky cord,
60 Like a wheel of the chariot of the Lord.

Let Samson
Be coming
Into your mind.

Samson saw the sun anew.
65 He left the gates in the grass and dew.
He went to a county-seat a-nigh   **a-nigh:** nearby.
Found a harlot proud and high:
Philistine that no man could tame—
Delilah was her lady-name.
70 Oh sorrow,
Sorrow,
She was too wise.
She cut off his hair,
She put out his eyes.

75 *Let Samson*
Be coming
Into your mind.

For thought and discussion

1 Though the poem concentrates on the "gates of
Gaza" episode, several words and phrases hint at
other events in Samson's life. How many of these
"hints" can you find?
2 What emotions does Samson express in this
poem?
3 What do you think the poet means by "Let Sam-
son/Be coming/Into your mind"?

THE
STORY
OF
RUTH

Ruth

Moab (mō′ab): a
country east of the
Dead Sea. Its people
were often unfriendly
to Israel.

In the days when the judges ruled there was a famine in the land, and a certain man of Bethlehem in Judah went to sojourn in the country of Moab, he and his wife and his two sons. The name of the man was Elimelech and the name of his wife Naomi, and the names of his two sons were Mahlon and Chilion; they were Ephrathites from Bethlehem in Judah. They went into the country of Moab and remained there. But Elimelech, the husband of Naomi, died, and she was left with her two sons. These took Moabite wives; the name of the one was Orpah and the name of the other Ruth. They lived there about ten years; and both Mahlon and Chilion died, so that the woman was bereft of her two sons and her husband.

bereft of: left without.

Then she started with her daughters-in-law to return from the country of Moab, for she had heard in the country of Moab that the Lord had visited his people and given them food. So she set out from the place where she was, with her two daughters-in-law, and they went on the way to return to the land of Judah. But Naomi said to her two daughters-in-law, "Go, return each of you to her mother's house. May the Lord deal kindly with you, as you have dealt with the dead and with me. The Lord grant that you may find a home, each of you in the house of her husband!" Then she kissed them, and they lifted up their voices and wept. And they said to her, "No, we will return with you to your people." But Naomi said, "Turn back, my daughters, why will you go

Ruth 1:1–4:17 (RSV).

with me? Have I yet sons in my womb that they may become your husbands? Turn back, my daughters, go your way, for I am too old to have a husband. If I should say I have hope, even if I should have a husband this night and should bear sons, would you therefore wait till they were grown? Would you therefore refrain from marrying? No, my daughters, for it is exceedingly bitter to me for your sake that the hand of the Lord has gone forth against me." Then they lifted up their voices and wept again; and Orpah kissed her mother-in-law, but Ruth clung to her.

And she said, "See, your sister-in-law has gone back to her people and to her gods; return after your sister-in-law." But Ruth said, "Entreat me not to leave you or to return from following you; for where you go I will go, and where you lodge I will lodge; your people shall be my people, and your God my God; where you die I will die, and there will I be buried. May the Lord do so to me and more also if even death parts me from you." And when Naomi saw that she was determined to go with her, she said no more.

So the two of them went on until they came to Bethlehem. And when they came to Bethlehem, the whole town was stirred because of them; and the women said, "Is this Naomi?" She said to them, "Do not call me Naomi, call me Mara, for the Almighty has dealt very bitterly with me. I went away full, and the Lord has brought me back empty. Why call me Naomi, when the Lord has afflicted me and the Almighty has brought calamity upon me?"

So Naomi returned, and Ruth the Moabitess her daughter-in-law with her, who returned from the country of Moab. And they came to Bethlehem at the beginning of barley harvest.

Now Naomi had a kinsman of her husband's, a man of wealth, of the family of Elimelech, whose name was Boaz. And Ruth the Moabitess said to Naomi, "Let me go to the field, and glean among the ears of grain after him in whose sight I shall find favor." And she said to her, "Go, my daughter." So she set forth and went and gleaned in the field after the reapers; and she happened to come to the part of the field belonging to Boaz, who was of the family of Elimelech. And behold, Boaz came from Bethlehem; and he said to the reapers, "The Lord be with

sons . . . your husbands: according to Israelite law, an unmarried man must wed his dead brother's widow if she is childless.

entreat: urge.

do so to: punish.

Naomi: in Hebrew, "pleasant."
Mara: in Hebrew, "bitter."

Boaz (bō′az).
glean: gather fallen grains which, according to Israelite law, were left by the reapers for the poor.

you!" And they answered, "The Lord bless you."
Then Boaz said to his servant who was in charge of
the reapers, "Whose maiden is this?" And the servant who was in charge of the reapers answered, "It
is the Moabite maiden, who came back with Naomi
from the country of Moab. She said, 'Pray, let me
glean and gather among the sheaves after the reapers.' So she came, and she has continued from early
morning until now, without resting even for a moment."

Then Boaz said to Ruth, "Now, listen, my daughter, do not go to glean in another field or leave this
one, but keep close to my maidens. Let your eyes be
upon the field which they are reaping, and go after
them. Have I not charged the young men not to
molest you? And when you are thirsty, go to the

vessels: jars.

vessels and drink what the young men have drawn."
Then she fell on her face, bowing to the ground, and
said to him, "Why have I found favor in your eyes,
that you should take notice of me, when I am a
foreigner?" But Boaz answered her, "All that you
have done for your mother-in-law since the death of
your husband has been fully told me, and how you
left your father and mother and your native land and
came to a people that you did not know before. The

recompense: repay, reward.

Lord recompense you for what you have done, and a
full reward be given you by the Lord, the God of
Israel, under whose wings you have come to take
refuge!" Then she said, "You are most gracious to
me, my lord, for you have comforted me and spoken
kindly to your maidservant, though I am not one of
your maidservants."

And at mealtime Boaz said to her, "Come here,
and eat some bread, and dip your morsel in the
wine." So she sat beside the reapers, and he passed
to her parched grain; and she ate until she was
satisfied, and she had some left over. When she rose
to glean, Boaz instructed his young men, saying,
"Let her glean even among the sheaves, and do not
reproach her. And also pull out some from the
bundles for her, and leave it for her to glean, and do

rebuke: criticize.

not rebuke her."

So she gleaned in the field until evening; then she
beat out what she had gleaned, and it was about an

ephah (ē′fə): about a bushel.

ephah of barley. And she took it up and went into
the city; she showed her mother-in-law what she
had gleaned, and she also brought out and gave her

what food she had left over after being satisfied. And her mother-in-law said to her, "Where did you glean today? And where have you worked? Blessed be the man who took notice of you." So she told her mother-in-law with whom she had worked, and said, "The man's name with whom I worked today is Boaz." And Naomi said to her daughter-in-law, "Blessed be he by the Lord, whose kindness has not forsaken the living or the dead!" Naomi also said to her, "The man is a relative of ours, one of our nearest kin." And Ruth the Moabitess said, "Besides, he said to me, 'You shall keep close by my servants, till they have finished all my harvest.' " And Naomi said to Ruth, her daughter-in-law, "It is well, my daughter, that you go out with his maidens, lest in another field you be molested." So she kept close to the maidens of Boaz, gleaning until the end of the barley and wheat harvests; and she lived with her mother-in-law.

Then Naomi her mother-in-law said to her, "My daughter, should I not seek a home for you, that it may be well with you? Now is not Boaz our kinsman, with whose maidens you were? See, he is winnowing barley tonight at the threshing floor. Wash therefore and anoint yourself, and put on your best clothes and go down to the threshing floor; but do not make yourself known to the man until he has finished eating and drinking. But when he lies down, observe the place where he lies; then, go and uncover his feet and lie down; and he will tell you what to do." And she replied, "All that you say I will do."

Since Ruth's husband left no brother to marry her, the law required his nearest unmarried relative to wed her. Naomi is advising Ruth to make her claim to Boaz in this unusual and symbolic way.

So she went down to the threshing floor and did just as her mother-in-law had told her. And when Boaz had eaten and drunk, and his heart was merry, he went to lie down at the end of the heap of grain. Then she came softly, and uncovered his feet, and lay down. At midnight the man was startled, and turned over, and behold, a woman lay at his feet! He said, "Who are you?" And she answered, "I am Ruth, your maidservant; spread your skirt over your maidservant, for you are next of kin." And he said, "May you be blessed by the Lord, my daughter; you have made this last kindness greater than the first, in that you have not gone after young men, whether poor or rich. And now, my daughter, do not fear, I will do for you all that you ask, for all my fellow

kindness: i.e., act of family loyalty.

townsmen know that you are a woman of worth. And now it is true that I am a near kinsman, yet there is a kinsman nearer than I. Remain this night, and in the morning, if he will do the part of the next of kin for you, well; let him do it; but if he is not willing to do the part of the next of kin for you, then, as the Lord lives, I will do the part of the next of kin for you. Lie down until the morning."

So she lay at his feet until the morning, but arose before one could recognize another; and he said, "Let it not be known that the woman came to the threshing floor." And he said, "Bring the mantle you are wearing and hold it out." So she held it, and he measured out six measures of barley, and laid it upon her; then she went into the city. And when she came to her mother-in-law, she said, "How did you fare, my daughter?" Then she told her all that the man had done for her, saying, "These six measures of barley he gave to me, for he said, 'You must not go back empty-handed to your mother-in-law.' " She replied, "Wait, my daughter, until you learn how the matter turns out, for the man will not rest, but will settle the matter today."

And Boaz went up to the gate and sat down there; and behold, the next of kin, of whom Boaz had spoken, came by. So Boaz said, "Turn aside, friend; sit down here"; and he turned aside and sat down. And he took ten men of the elders of the city, and said, "Sit down here"; so they sat down. Then he said to the next of kin, "Naomi, who has come back from the country of Moab, is selling the parcel of land which belonged to our kinsman Elimelech. So I thought I would tell you of it, and say, Buy it in the presence of those sitting here, and in the presence of the elders of my people. If you will redeem it, redeem it; but if you will not, tell me, that I may know, for there is no one besides you to redeem it, and I come after you." And he said, "I will redeem it." Then Boaz said, "The day you buy the field from the hand of Naomi, you are also buying Ruth the Moabitess, the widow of the dead, in order to restore the name of the dead to his inheritance." Then the next of kin said, "I cannot redeem it for myself, lest I impair my own inheritance. Take my right of redemption yourself, for I cannot redeem it."

Now this was the custom in former times in Israel

gate: where legal agreements were made before witnesses.

concerning redeeming and exchanging: to confirm a transaction, the one drew off his sandal and gave it to the other, and this was the manner of attesting in Israel. So when the next of kin said to Boaz, "Buy it for yourself," he drew off his sandal. Then Boaz said to the elders and all the people, "You are witnesses this day that I have bought from the hand of Naomi all that belonged to Elimelech and all that belonged to Chilion and to Mahlon. Also Ruth the Moabitess, the widow of Mahlon, I have bought to be my wife, to perpetuate the name of the dead in his inheritance, that the name of the dead may not be cut off from among his brethren and from the gate of his native place; you are witnesses this day." Then all the people who were at the gate, and the elders, said, "We are witnesses. May the Lord make the woman, who is coming into your house, like Rachel and Leah, who together built up the house of Israel. May you prosper in Ephrathah and be renowned in Bethlehem; and may your house be like the house of Perez, whom Tamar bore to Judah, because of the children that the Lord will give you by this young woman."

So Boaz took Ruth and she became his wife; and he went in to her, and the Lord gave her conception, and she bore a son. Then the women said to Naomi, "Blessed be the Lord, who has not left you this day without next of kin; and may his name be renowned in Israel! He shall be to you a restorer of life and a nourisher of your old age; for your daughter-in-law who loves you, who is more to you than seven sons, has borne him." Then Naomi took the child and laid him in her bosom, and became his nurse. And the women of the neighborhood gave him a name, saying, "A son has been born to Naomi." They named him Obed; he was the father of Jesse, the father of David.

Ruth . . . I have bought: i.e., bought the right to marry Ruth.

Rachel and Leah: wives of Jacob, "mothers of Israel."

Perez: Judah's son Perez was an ancestor of Boaz, born to a widow who, like Ruth, claimed the right of kinship.

For close reading

1 What are the conditions in Bethlehem when Naomi first leaves for Moab? When she returns with Ruth?

2 "I went away full, and the Lord has brought me

back empty." What does Naomi mean? How many times in the story does Ruth bring something to Naomi to overcome her emptiness?

3 What references to widowhood, childlessness, and famine can you find in this story? What references to abundant harvest and fruitful marriage?

For thought and discussion

4 How does the story link personal loss and emptiness with famine in the land? What connections can you find between abundant harvest and fruitful marriage? How do these motifs relate to the overall theme of the story?

5 What obligations and responsibilities do relatives have for each other today? Do you think kinship is as important now as it was in Ruth's time? Why or why not?

6 The concept of the proxy (substitute or "stand in") is important to the story of Ruth. In what ways is Ruth a proxy for Naomi? In what way is Boaz a proxy? The baby Obed?

7 What is your opinion of the law concerning gleaning as a way of providing for the needy? Can you think of any modern equivalents to this system? Explain.

8 What does Ruth "glean" besides grain? What does Naomi glean—personally and through Ruth? In what sense does Boaz glean?

9 What do you think is the moment of greatest suspense in this story? What techniques are used to increase the tension of this moment?

Activities

1 Ruth speaks once with great beauty, but for the most part we must interpret her character from her actions, and from the things which are said to her and about her. Choose one point in the story and write Ruth's thoughts at that moment.

2 Write a song lyric telling Ruth's story. Find or compose appropriate music and, if possible, tape record your song.

Louise Bogan

Women have no wilderness in them,
They are provident instead,
Content in the tight hot cell of their hearts
To eat dusty bread.

provident: careful in providing for the future.

5 They do not see cattle cropping red winter grass,
They do not hear
Snow water going down under culverts
Shallow and clear.

They wait, when they should turn to journeys,
10 They stiffen, when they should bend.
They use against themselves that benevolence
To which no man is friend.

benevolence: good will; kindly feeling.

They cannot think of so many crops to a field
Or of clean wood cleft by an ax.
15 Their love is an eager meaninglessness
Too tense, or too lax.

They hear in every whisper that speaks to them
A shout and a cry.
As like as not, when they take life over their door-
sills
20 They should let it go by.

For thought and discussion

1 One of the most interesting discussions people have concerns the differences in outlooks or attitudes between men and women. What does the poet think some of those differences are? Do you agree or disagree?
2 The Bible passages in this chapter have featured several women. Do any of these women fit Bogan's description? Explain.

5

anointed
kings

SAUL:
THE MIGHTY
ARE
FALLEN

1 & 2 Samuel

There was a man of Benjamin whose name was Kish, the son of Abiel, son of Zeror, son of Becorath, son of Aphiah, a Benjaminite, a man of wealth; and he had a son whose name was Saul, a handsome young man. There was not a man among the people of Israel more handsome than he; from his shoulders upward he was taller than any of the people.

from . . . taller: he was a head taller.

Now the asses of Kish, Saul's father, were lost. So Kish said to Saul his son, "Take one of the servants with you, and arise, go and look for the asses." And they passed through the hill country of Ephraim and passed through the land of Shalishah, but they did not find them. . . .

When they came to the land of Zuph, Saul said to his servant who was with him, "Come, let us go back, lest my father cease to care about the asses and become anxious about us." But he said to him, "Behold, there is a man of God in this city, and he is a man that is held in honor; all that he says comes

1 Samuel 9:1–4a, 5–6, 11–12a, 15–19, 26–27; 10:1a, 9a; 11:1–11, 15a; 15:1–3, 5, 7–9a, 13–16, 22–28, 35a; 16:14; 18:6–8a, 9; 28:3–15a, 18–19b; 31:1–5. 2 Samuel 1:17, 19–20, 23–27 (RSV).
LEFT: *David,* detail from a stained-glass window, twelfth century Augsburg. Courtesy The Cathedral of Augsburg, Germany.

true. Let us go there; perhaps he can tell us about the journey on which we have set out." . . .

As they went up the hill to the city, they met young maidens coming out to draw water, and said to them, "Is the seer here?" They answered, "He is; behold, he is just ahead of you. . . ."

seer: prophet, one who spoke for God.

Now the day before Saul came, the Lord had revealed to Samuel: "Tomorrow about this time I will send to you a man from the land of Benjamin, and you shall anoint him to be prince over my people Israel. He shall save my people from the hand of the Philistines; for I have seen the affliction of my people, because their cry has come to me." When Samuel saw Saul, the Lord told him, "Here is the man of whom I spoke to you! He it is who shall rule over my people." Then Saul approached Samuel in the gate, and said, "Tell me where is the house of the seer?" Samuel answered Saul, "I am the seer; go up before me to the high place, for today you shall eat with me, and in the morning I will let you go and will tell you all that is on your mind. . . ."

anoint: sprinkle his head with oil (as a sign that God appointed him king).

high place: At that time there were shrines to God on certain hills in Israel.

. . . Then at the break of dawn Samuel called to Saul upon the roof, "Up, that I may send you on your way." So Saul arose, and both he and Samuel went out into the street.

As they were going down to the outskirts of the city, Samuel said to Saul, "Tell the servant to pass on before us, and when he has passed on stop here yourself for a while, that I may make known to you the word of God."

vial: small bottle.

Then Samuel took a vial of oil and poured it on his head, and kissed him and said, "Has not the Lord anointed you to be prince over his people Israel? And you shall reign over the people of the Lord and you will save them from the hand of their enemies round about. . . ."

When he turned his back to leave Samuel, God gave him another heart . . . .

Ammonites: enemies to the east of Israel.

Then Nahash the Ammonite went up and besieged Jabesh-gilead; and all the men of Jabesh said to Nahash, "Make a treaty with us, and we will serve you." But Nahash the Ammonite said to them, "On this condition I will make a treaty with you, that I gouge out all your right eyes, and thus put disgrace upon all Israel." The elders of Jabesh said to him, "Give us seven days respite that we may send

respite: delay.

messengers through all the territory of Israel. Then, if there is no one to save us, we will give ourselves up to you." When the messengers came to Gibeah of Saul, they reported the matter in the ears of the people; and all the people wept aloud.

of Saul: i.e., where he lived.

Now Saul was coming from the field behind the oxen; and Saul said, "What ails the people, that they are weeping?" So they told him the tidings of the men of Jabesh. And the spirit of God came mightily upon Saul when he heard these words, and his anger was greatly kindled. He took a yoke of oxen, and cut them in pieces and sent them throughout all the territory of Israel by the hand of messengers, saying, "Whoever does not come out after Saul and Samuel, so shall it be done to his oxen!" Then the dread of the Lord fell upon the people, and they came out as one man. When he mustered them at Bezek, the men of Israel were three hundred thousand, and the men of Judah thirty thousand. And they said to the messengers who had come, "Thus shall you say to the men of Jabesh-gilead: 'Tomorrow, by the time the sun is hot, you shall have deliverance.' " When the messengers came and told the men of Jabesh, they were glad. Therefore the men of Jabesh said, "Tomorrow we will give ourselves up to you, and you may do to us whatever seems good to you." And on the morrow Saul put the people in three companies; and they came into the midst of the camp in the morning watch, and cut down the Ammonites until the heat of the day; and those who survived were scattered, so that no two of them were left together.

tidings: news.

mustered: assembled.
Israel, Judah: names for the ten northern tribes and for the two southern tribes.

said: i.e., to Nahash, the enemy king.

. . . So all the people went to Gilgal, and there they made Saul king before the Lord in Gilgal.

And Samuel said to Saul, "The Lord sent me to anoint you king over his people Israel; now therefore hearken to the words of the Lord. Thus says the Lord of hosts, 'I will punish what Amalek did to Israel in opposing them on the way, when they came up out of Egypt. Now go and smite Amalek, and utterly destroy all that they have; do not spare them, but kill both man and woman, infant and suckling, ox and sheep, camel and ass.' "

Amalek: the Amalekites, southern enemies.
suckling: nursing infant.

. . . And Saul came to the city of Amalek, and lay in wait in the valley. . . . And Saul defeated the Amalekites, from Havilah as far as Shur, which is east

of Egypt. And he took Agag the king of the Amalekites alive, and utterly destroyed all the people with
the edge of the sword. But Saul and the people
spared Agag, and the best of the sheep and of the
oxen and of the fatlings, and the lambs, and all that
was good, and would not utterly destroy them . . . .

fatlings: fattened
young animals.

. . . And Samuel came to Saul, and Saul said to
him, "Blessed be you to the Lord; I have performed
the commandment of the Lord." And Samuel said,
"What then is this bleating of the sheep in my ears,
and the lowing of the oxen which I hear?" Saul
said, "They have brought them from the Amalekites;
for the people spared the best of the sheep and of
the oxen, to sacrifice to the Lord your God; and the
rest we have utterly destroyed." Then Samuel said to
Saul, "Stop! I will tell you what the Lord said to me
this night." And he said to him, "Say on." . . . And
Samuel said,

lowing (lō′ing):
mooing.

> "Has the Lord as great delight in burnt offerings
>   and sacrifices,
> as in obeying the voice of the Lord?
> Behold, to obey is better than sacrifice,
> and to hearken than the fat of rams.
> For rebellion is as the sin of divination,
> and stubbornness is as iniquity and idolatry.
> Because you have rejected the word of the
>   Lord,
> he has also rejected you from being king."

hearken: listen.
divination: witchcraft.
iniquity: wickedness.
idolatry: worshiping
idols.

And Saul said to Samuel, "I have sinned; for I have
transgressed the commandment of the Lord and
your words, because I feared the people and obeyed
their voice. Now therefore, I pray, pardon my sin,
and return with me, that I may worship the Lord."
And Samuel said to Saul, "I will not return with you;
for you have rejected the word of the Lord, and the
Lord has rejected you from being king over Israel."
As Samuel turned to go away, Saul laid hold upon
the skirt of his robe, and it tore. And Samuel said to
him, "The Lord has torn the kingdom of Israel from
you this day, and has given it to a neighbor of yours,
who is better than you. . . ."

transgressed: dis-
obeyed.

. . . And Samuel did not see Saul again until the
day of his death, but Samuel grieved over Saul. . . .

Now the Spirit of the Lord departed from Saul,
and an evil spirit from the Lord tormented him. . . .

[*A stalemate between Saul's army and the Philistines is ended when a young shepherd, David, kills the enemy champion, Goliath. But this victory brings Saul no peace of mind.*]

As they were coming home, when David returned from slaying the Philistine, the women came out of all the cities of Israel, singing and dancing, to meet King Saul, with timbrels, with songs of joy, and with instruments of music. And the women sang to one another as they made merry,

timbrels: tambourines, hand drums that jingle when shaken.

"Saul has slain his thousands,
And David his ten thousands."

And Saul was very angry, and this saying displeased him; he said, "They have ascribed to David ten thousands, and to me they have ascribed thousands; and what more can he have but the kingdom?" And Saul eyed David from that day on.

[*Saul's anger turns to hatred; though David is now his son-in-law and close friends with his son Jonathan, Saul tries to kill him. While he is pursuing David, the Philistines again invade Israel.*]

Now Samuel had died, and all Israel had mourned for him and buried him in Ramah, his own city. And Saul had put the mediums and the wizards out of the land. The Philistines assembled, and came and encamped at Shunem; and Saul gathered all Israel, and they encamped at Gilboa. When Saul saw the army of the Philistines, he was afraid, and his heart trembled greatly. And when Saul inquired of the Lord, the Lord did not answer him, either by dreams, or by Urim, or by prophets. Then Saul said to his servants, "Seek out for me a woman who is a medium, that I may go to her and inquire of her." And his servants said to him, "Behold, there is a medium at Endor."

put . . . land: banned and driven out people who dealt with spirits.

Urim (ûr′im): holy objects used to tell the will of God.

So Saul disguised himself and put on other garments, and went, he and two men with him; and they came to the woman by night. And he said, "Divine for me by a spirit, and bring up for me whomever I shall name to you." The woman said to

divine for me: tell my fortune.

snare: trap.

him, "Surely you know what Saul has done, how he has cut off the mediums and the wizards from the land. Why then are you laying a snare for my life to bring about my death?" But Saul swore to her by the Lord, "As the Lord lives, no punishment shall come upon you for this thing." Then the woman said, "Whom shall I bring up for you?" He said, "Bring up Samuel for me." When the woman saw Samuel, she cried out with a loud voice; and the woman said to Saul, "Why have you deceived me? You are Saul." The king said to her, "Have no fear; what do you

god: i.e., a spirit, a supernatural being.

see?" And the woman said to Saul, "I see a god coming up out of the earth." He said to her, "What is his appearance?" And she said, "An old man is coming up; and he is wrapped in a robe." And Saul knew that it was Samuel, and he bowed with his face

and did obeisance: on his knees.

to the ground, and did obeisance.

Then Samuel said to Saul, "Why have you disturbed me by bringing me up?" . . . "Because you did not obey the voice of the Lord, and did not carry out his fierce wrath against Amalek, therefore the Lord has done this thing to you this day. Moreover the Lord will give Israel also with you into the hand of the Philistines; and tomorrow you and your sons shall be with me . . . . "

Now the Philistines fought against Israel; and the men of Israel fled before the Philistines, and fell slain on Mount Gilboa. And the Philistines overtook Saul and his sons; and the Philistines slew Jonathan and Abinadab and Malchishua, the sons of Saul. The battle pressed hard upon Saul, and the archers found him; and he was badly wounded by the archers. Then Saul said to his armor-bearer, "Draw

armor-bearer: a sort of military "caddy."
uncircumcized: i.e., pagans.

your sword, and thrust me through with it, lest these uncircumcised come and thrust me through, and make sport of me." But his armor-bearer would not; for he feared greatly. Therefore Saul took his own sword, and fell upon it. And when his armor-bearer saw that Saul was dead, he also fell upon his sword, and died with him. . . .

2 Sam. 1:17.

lamented with this lamentation: (created and) sang this song of sorrow.

And David lamented with this lamentation over Saul and Jonathan his son, . . .

"Thy glory, O Israel, is slain upon thy high places!

How are the mighty fallen!
Tell it not in Gath,
publish it not in the streets of Ashkelon;
lest the daughters of the Philistines rejoice,
lest the daughters of the uncircumcised
   exult. . . .

Gath, Ashkelon: two of the main Philistine cities.

exult: rejoice.

Saul and Jonathan, beloved and lovely!
In life and in death they were not divided;
they were swifter than eagles,
they were stronger than lions.

lovely: lovable.

Ye daughters of Israel, weep over Saul,
who clothed you daintily in scarlet,
who put ornaments of gold upon your apparel.

daintily: beautifully.

How are the mighty fallen
in the midst of the battle!

Jonathan lies slain upon thy high places.
I am distressed for you, my brother Jonathan;
very pleasant have you been to me;
your love to me was wonderful,
passing the love of women.

How are the mighty fallen,
and the weapons of war perished!"

For close reading

1 What method does Saul use to raise an army to break the siege of Jabesh-gilead?
2 Saul is named ruler twice. Describe the two occasions, and tell who is present, and what reason is given for his being named king.
3 After the Amalekite battle, how does Samuel know immediately that Saul has disobeyed the Lord?
4 What excuse does Saul offer when Samuel accuses him?
5 Why is Saul angry at what the women sang about David and himself?
6 What does the spirit of Samuel at Endor foretell to Saul?

For thought and discussion

7 Saul could have been anointed by Samuel *after* the battle of Jabesh-gilead. What difference would that shift have made in the story?

8 Saul is named leader by God; later the people "made Saul king." This double approval suggests two responsibilities: to God and to his people's needs. Do you think Saul felt a conflict between these two responsibilities? Explain.

9 Why do you think Saul disguises himself for his visit to the medium at Endor? What do you suppose there is about the approaching spirit that makes the medium realize that her visitor is Saul?

10 What is a "tragedy"? A "tragic hero"? In what ways does the story of Saul fit your definitions? In what ways does it not? Compare and contrast the story of Saul with that of some tragic hero you have studied.

Activities

1 Act out, or pantomime, Saul's visit to the medium at Endor.

2 Saul is in his tent on the evening before his final battle with the Philistines. Express his thoughts in his letter home to his wife.

3 Write an account of Saul's death as it might be reported in a modern newspaper.

4 Find or compose some music to serve as introduction and background to David's lament for Saul and Jonathan, and read the passage aloud to the music. You might make a recording of the performance.

THE DEATH OF KINGS

William Shakespeare

Let's talk of graves, of worms and epitaphs;
Make dust our paper and with rainy eyes
Write sorrow on the bosom of the earth,

.   .   .

For God's sake, let us sit upon the ground
5   And tell sad stories of the death of kings:
How some have been depos'd; some slain in war;   **depos'd:** removed from power.
Some haunted by the ghosts they have depos'd;
Some poisoned by their wives; some sleeping
     kill'd;
All murdered: for within the hollow crown
10 That rounds the mortal temples of a king
Keeps Death his court and there the antic sits,   **antic:** clown, jester.
Scoffing his state and grinning at his pomp,
Allowing him a breath, a little scene,
To monarchize, be fear'd and kill with looks,
15 Infusing him with self and vain conceit,   **infusing:** i.e., filling.
As if this flesh which walls about our life
Were brass impregnable, and humour'd thus   **impregnable:** able to resist attack.
Comes at the last and with a little pin   **humour'd thus:** having been amused (referring to Death).
Bores through his castle wall, and farewell king!

Richard II, Act 3, Scene 2

For thought and discussion

1 According to this passage, what are the various ways in which kings are "removed"?
2 Why do you think the speaker used the expression "the hollow crown"?
3 What seems to be the speaker's attitude about "the death of kings"? How do his feelings differ from David's feelings after the deaths of Saul and Jonathan?

DAVID:
YOUNG CHAMPION
OF
ISRAEL

1 Samuel

[This chapter includes three episodes from the life of David. The first occurs while Saul is still king.]

horn: container made of an animal's horn.

before him: here, this one.

The Lord said to Samuel, "How long will you grieve over Saul, seeing I have rejected him from being king over Israel? Fill your horn with oil, and go; I will send you to Jesse the Bethlehemite, for I have provided for myself a king among his sons." . . . Samuel did what the Lord commanded, and came to Bethlehem. . . . And he consecrated Jesse and his sons, and invited them to the sacrifice.

When they came, he looked on Eliab and thought, "Surely the Lord's anointed is before him." But the Lord said to Samuel, "Do not look on his appearance or on the height of his stature, because I have rejected him; for the Lord sees not as man sees; man looks on the outward appearance, but the Lord looks on the heart." Then Jesse called Abinadab, and made him pass before Samuel. And he said, "Neither has the Lord chosen this one." Then Jesse made Shammah pass by. And he said, "Neither has the Lord chosen this one." And Jesse made seven of his sons pass before Samuel. And Samuel said to Jesse, "The Lord has not chosen these." And Samuel said to Jesse, "Are all your sons here?" And he said, "There remains yet the youngest, but behold, he is keeping the sheep." And Samuel said to Jesse, "Send and fetch him; for we will not sit down till he comes here." And he sent, and brought him in. Now

1 Samuel 16:1, 4, 5d–13; 17:1–9, 11a, 13a, 15–16a, 17–51 (RSV).

he was ruddy, and had beautiful eyes, and was handsome. And the Lord said, "Arise, anoint him; for this is he." Then Samuel took the horn of oil, and anointed him in the midst of his brothers; and the Spirit of the Lord came mightily upon David from that day forward. And Samuel rose up, and went to Ramah. . . .

Now the Philistines gathered their armies for battle; and they were gathered at Socoh, which belongs to Judah, and encamped between Socoh and Azekah, in Ephes-dammim. And Saul and the men of Israel were gathered, and encamped in the valley of Elah, and drew up in line of battle against the Philistines. And the Philistines stood on the mountain on the one side, and Israel stood on the mountain on the other side, with a valley between them. And there came out from the camp of the Philistines a champion named Goliath, of Gath, whose height was six cubits and a span. He had a helmet of bronze on his head, and he was armed with a coat of mail, and the weight of the coat was five thousand shekels of bronze. And he had greaves of bronze upon his legs, and a javelin of bronze slung between his shoulders. And the shaft of his spear was like a weaver's beam, and his spear's head weighed six hundred shekels of iron; and his shield-bearer went before him. He stood and shouted to the ranks of Israel, "Why have you come out to draw up for battle? Am I not a Philistine, and are you not servants of Saul? Choose a man for yourselves, and let him come down to me. If he is able to fight with me and kill me, then we will be your servants; but if I prevail against him and kill him, then you shall be our servants and serve us." . . . When Saul and all Israel heard these words of the Philistine, they were dismayed and greatly afraid.

. . . The three eldest sons of Jesse had followed Saul to the battle . . . but David went back and forth from Saul to feed his father's sheep at Bethlehem. For forty days the Philistine came forward and took his stand, morning and evening.

And Jesse said to David his son, "Take for your brothers an ephah of this parched grain, and these ten loaves, and carry them quickly to the camp to your brothers; also take these ten cheeses to the

ruddy: healthy in color; pink-cheeked.

Philistines: enemy invaders who entered south Canaan from the sea.

six cubits . . . span: Goliath is between nine and ten feet tall.

five thousand shekels: about one hundred sixty pounds.

greaves: leg guards.
weaver's beam: i.e., about three inches thick.

six hundred shekels: about twenty pounds.

prevail against: defeat.

ephah (ē′fə): about a bushel.

commander of their thousand. See how your brothers fare, and bring some token from them."

Now Saul, and they, and all the men of Israel, were in the valley of Elah, fighting with the Philistines. And David rose early in the morning, and left the sheep with a keeper, and took the provisions, and went, as Jesse had commanded him; and he came to the encampment as the host was going forth to the battle line, shouting the war cry. And Israel and the Philistines drew up for battle, army against army. And David left the things in charge of the keeper of the baggage, and ran to the ranks, and went and greeted his brothers. As he talked with them, behold, the champion, the Philistine of Gath, Goliath by name, came up out of the ranks of the Philistines, and spoke the same words as before. And David heard him.

All the men of Israel, when they saw the man, fled from him, and were much afraid. And the men of Israel said, "Have you seen this man who has come up? Surely he has come up to defy Israel; and the man who kills him, the king will enrich with great riches, and will give him his daughter, and make his father's house free in Israel." And David said to the men who stood by him, "What shall be done for the man who kills this Philistine, and takes away the reproach from Israel? For who is this uncircumcised Philistine, that he should defy the armies of the living God?" And the people answered him in the same way, "So shall it be done to the man who kills him."

Now Eliab his eldest brother heard when he spoke to the men; and Eliab's anger was kindled against David, and he said, "Why have you come down? And with whom have you left those few sheep in the wilderness? I know your presumption, and the evil of your heart; for you have come down to see the battle." And David said, "What have I done now? Was it not but a word?" And he turned away from him toward another, and spoke in the same way; and the people answered him again as before.

When the words which David spoke were heard, they repeated them before Saul; and he sent for him. And David said to Saul, "Let no man's heart fail because of him; your servant will go and fight with this Philistine." And Saul said to David, "You are not able to go against this Philistine to fight with him; for

host: army.

free: from paying taxes.

you are but a youth, and he has been a man of war from his youth." But David said to Saul, "Your servant used to keep sheep for his father; and when there came a lion, or a bear, and took a lamb from the flock, I went after him and smote him and delivered it out of his mouth; and if he arose against me, I caught him by his beard, and smote him and killed him. Your servant has killed both lions and bears; and this uncircumcised Philistine shall be one of them, seeing he has defied the armies of the living God." And David said, "The Lord who delivered me from the paw of the lion and from the paw of the bear, will deliver me from the hand of this Philistine." And Saul said to David, "Go, and the Lord be with you!" Then Saul clothed David with his armor; he put a helmet of bronze on his head, and clothed him with a coat of mail. And David girded his sword over his armor, and he tried in vain to go, for he was not used to them. Then David said to Saul, "I cannot go with these; for I am not used to them." And David put them off. Then he took his staff in his hand, and chose five smooth stones from the brook, and put them in his shepherd's bag, in his wallet; his sling was in his hand, and he drew near to the Philistine.

And the Philistine came on and drew near to David, with his shield-bearer in front of him. And when the Philistine looked, and saw David, he disdained him; for he was but a youth, ruddy and comely in appearance. And the Philistine said to David, "Am I a dog, that you come to me with sticks?" And the Philistine cursed David by his gods. The Philistine said to David, "Come to me, and I will give your flesh to the birds of the air and to the beasts of the field." Then David said to the Philistine, "You come to me with a sword and with a spear and with a javelin; but I come to you in the name of the Lord of hosts, the God of the armies of Israel, whom you have defied. This day the Lord will deliver you into my hand, and I will strike you down, and cut off your head; and I will give the dead bodies of the host of the Philistines this day to the birds of the air and to the wild beasts of the earth; that all the earth may know that there is a God in Israel, and that all this assembly may know that the Lord saves not with sword and spear; for the battle is the Lord's and he will give you into our hand."

your servant: i.e., David.

sling: a weapon consisting of a pouch with two cords. It is whirled over the head to throw a stone with great force when one of the cords is released.

When the Philistine arose and came and drew near to meet David, David ran quickly toward the battle line to meet the Philistine. And David put his hand in his bag and took out a stone, and slung it, and struck the Philistine on his forehead; the stone sank into his forehead, and he fell on his face to the ground.

So David prevailed over the Philistine with a sling and with a stone, and struck the Philistine, and killed him; there was no sword in the hand of David. Then David ran and stood over the Philistine, and took his sword and drew it out of its sheath, and killed him, and cut off his head with it. When the Philistines saw that their champion was dead, they fled.

For close reading

1 How many sons of Jesse does Samuel inspect before he discovers David?
2 Samuel is told that "the Lord sees not as man sees." How is this explained?
3 Why does David decide to fight Goliath? Why is he confident of victory?
4 Why does David decide not to wear Saul's armor?
5 What is Goliath's "outward appearance" before the combat? David's? List as many differences as you can between the two.

For thought and discussion

6 Eliab resents his favored younger brother. Where has this situation occurred in other Bible stories you have read? What is there about stories of younger children triumphing over their older brothers or sisters that so appeals to or interests readers?
7 In what ways do "outward appearances" reveal a person's character? In what ways do they mislead? Do you think it is ever possible for a person to "look

on the heart" of another, almost as the Lord does? Explain.

8 Descriptions of important characters in the Bible usually have few details, and adjectives are used sparingly. Goliath, by contrast, is described in specific detail. What dramatic effects result from this description?

9 What is your impression of David as a young man? Try to describe him in a single sentence.

10 The story of David and Goliath is one of the best-known Bible stories. What aspects of the story make it so appealing?

Activities

1 Using whatever medium you wish (paint, sculpture, needlepoint, etc.) try to suggest the battle of David and Goliath *without depicting human figures* (use colors, sizes, and shapes to indicate the characters).

2 Describe the "match" between David and Goliath as if you were a sportscaster.

3 Act out or pantomime the confrontation between David and Goliath.

AFTER GOLIATH

Kingsley Amis

The first shot out of that sling
Was enough to finish the thing:
The champion laid out cold
Before half the programs were sold.
5 And then, what howls of dismay
From his fans in their dense array:
From aldermen, adjutants, aunts,
Administrators of grants,
Assurance-men, auctioneers,
10 Advisers about careers,
And advertisers, of course,
Plus the obvious b——s in force—
The whole reprehensible throng
Ten times an alphabet strong.
15 But such an auspicious debut
Was a little too good to be true,
Our victor sensed; the applause
From those who supported his cause
Sounded shrill and excessive now,
20 And who were they, anyhow?
Academics, actors who lecture,
Apostles of architecture,
Ancient-gods-of-the-abdomen men,
Angst-pushers, adherents of Zen,
25 Alastors, austenites, A-test
Abolishers—even the straightest
Of issues looks pretty oblique

array: formation.
adjutants: military administrative officers.

assurance: insurance.

reprehensible: deserving blame.

auspicious: favorable.

angst: anxiety.
alastors: avengers.
austenites: admirers of the novelist Jane Austen.
oblique (ə blēk′): not straightforward; unclear.

"After Goliath" by Kingsley Amis. Reprinted by permission of A.D. Peters and Co.

When a movement turns into a clique,
The conqueror mused, as he stopped
30 By the sword his opponent had dropped:
Trophy, or means of attack
On the rapturous crowd at his back?
He shrugged and left it, resigned
To a new battle, fought in the mind,
35 For faith that his quarrel was just,
That the right man lay in the dust.

clique (klēk): a small,
exclusive group.

For thought and discussion

1 Have you ever accomplished something or won a victory "too good to be true"? If so, how were you affected by that experience?

2 Goliath's "fans" are described in lines 6-14; they include businessmen, politicans, and military men. David's fans are described in lines 21-26, and include professors, reformers, and followers of various causes. Why do you think the poet sets these groups on opposite sides?

3 Amis has said that this poem ". . . is something I had been trying to get said for a long time: that there is a disappointing lack of contrast between the enemies of progress . . . and those theoretically on the side of progress." How does the poem suggest "disappointment"? How does it suggest the "lack of contrast" between the two opposing groups?

4 What does David consider doing with Goliath's sword?

DAVID
AND
BATHSHEBA

2 Samuel

[*David has now been king for many years and has led his armies to many victories. He has established Jerusalem as his capital and built a palace there.*]

Joab (jō′ab): the commander of David's army.

In the spring of the year, the time when kings go forth to battle, David sent Joab, and his servants with him, and all Israel; and they ravaged the Ammonites, and besieged Rabbah. But David remained at Jerusalem.

It happened, late one afternoon, when David arose from his couch and was walking upon the roof of the king's house, that he saw from the roof a woman bathing; and the woman was very beautiful. And David sent and inquired about the woman. And one said, "Is not this Bathsheba, the daughter of Eliam, the wife of Uriah the Hittite?" So David sent messengers, and took her; and she came to him, and he lay with her. . . . Then she returned to her house. And the woman conceived; and she sent and told David, "I am with child."

So David sent word to Joab, "Send me Uriah the Hittite." And Joab sent Uriah to David. When Uriah came to him, David asked how Joab was doing, and how the people fared, and how the war prospered. Then David said to Uriah, "Go down to your house, and wash your feet." And Uriah went out of the king's house, and there followed him a present from

wash your feet: i.e., clean up after the trip.

2 Samuel 11:1–4b, 4d–11, 14–18, 23–27; 12:1–10, 13–15a (RSV).

the king. But Uriah slept at the door of the king's house, with all the servants of his lord, and did not go down to his house. When they told David, "Uriah did not go down to his house," David said to Uriah, "Have you not come from a journey? Why did you not go down to your house?" Uriah said to David, "The ark and Israel and Judah dwell in booths; and my lord Joab and the servants of my lord are camping in the open field; shall I then go to my house, to eat and to drink, and to lie with my wife? As you live, and as your soul lives, I will not do this thing." . . .

In the morning David wrote a letter to Joab, and sent it by the hand of Uriah. In the letter he wrote, "Set Uriah in the forefront of the hardest fighting, and then draw back from him, that he may be struck down, and die." And as Joab was besieging the city, he assigned Uriah to the place where he knew there were valiant men. And the men of the city came out and fought with Joab; and some of the servants of David among the people fell. Uriah the Hittite was slain also. Then Joab sent and told David all the news about the fighting . . . .

The messenger said to David, "The men gained an advantage over us, and came out against us in the field; but we drove them back to the entrance of the gate. Then the archers shot at your servants from the wall; some of the king's servants are dead; and your servant Uriah the Hittite is dead also." David said to the messenger, "Thus shall you say to Joab, 'Do not let this matter trouble you, for the sword devours now one and now another; strengthen your attack upon the city, and overthrow it.' And encourage him."

When the wife of Uriah heard that Uriah her husband was dead, she made lamentation for her husband. And when the mourning was over, David sent and brought her to his house, and she became his wife, and bore him a son. But the thing that David had done displeased the Lord.

And the Lord sent Nathan to David. He came to him, and said to him, "There were two men in a certain city, the one rich and the other poor. The rich man had very many flocks and herds; but the poor man had nothing but one little ewe lamb, which he had bought. And he brought it up, and it grew up with him and with his children; it used to

ark: the Ark of the Covenant, the sacred chest probably containing the tablets of the law given to Moses. The ark symbolized the presence of the Lord.
booths: temporary shelters (on the battlefield).

devours: i.e., kills.

Nathan: a prophet.

morsel: bit of food.

kindled: fired up.

smitten: struck.

eat of his morsel, and drink from his cup, and lie in his bosom, and it was like a daughter to him. Now there came a traveler to the rich man, and he was unwilling to take one of his own flock or herd to prepare for the wayfarer who had come to him, but he took the poor man's lamb, and prepared it for the man who had come to him." Then David's anger was greatly kindled against the man; and he said to Nathan, "As the Lord lives, the man who has done this deserves to die; and he shall restore the lamb fourfold, because he did this thing, and because he had no pity."

Nathan said to David, "You are the man. Thus says the Lord, the God of Israel, 'I anointed you king over Israel, and I delivered you out of the hand of Saul; and I gave you your master's house, and your master's wives into your bosom, and gave you the house of Israel and of Judah; and if this were too little, I would add to you as much more. Why have you despised the word of the Lord, to do what is evil in his sight? You have smitten Uriah the Hittite with the sword, and have taken his wife to be your wife, and have slain him with the sword of the Ammonites. Now therefore the sword shall never depart from your house, because you have despised me, and have taken the wife of Uriah the Hittite to be your wife.' . . . 'Behold, I will raise up evil against you out of your own house . . . .' " David said to Nathan, "I have sinned against the Lord." And Nathan said to David, "The Lord also has put away your sin; you shall not die. Nevertheless, because by this deed you have utterly scorned the Lord, the child that is born to you shall die." Then Nathan went to his house.

For close reading

1 How many occasions can you find where David "sent" someone or some message?
2 What reason does Uriah give for not returning to his home?
3 How does David respond when he learns of Uriah's death?
4 List the links in David's "chain" of wrongdoing.

For thought and discussion

5 Examine closely the opening paragraph of this passage, then think of David's other actions in this story. How does David the king compare with the David who fought Goliath? In what ways has he changed? How would you account for the changes?

6 What differences in character and actions are there between David and Uriah? What other hints are there in the story that prepare us for the statement that the Lord is displeased?

7 Why do you suppose Nathan begins with a story rather than a direct accusation of David? Do you think a direct accusation would have been more effective? Why or why not? Given David's early career, why is it significant that Nathan speaks of a cherished lamb? What other details of Nathan's parable are especially fitting for David's actions?

8 Compare David's reaction to Nathan's story with his response to Uriah's death. Are David's responses in any way typical of human nature? Explain.

9 Compare the sins and the punishments of Saul and David. Why do you think David's life and throne are spared? In what ways might his punishment be at least as severe as Saul's?

Activities

1 You are Bathsheba. What are your thoughts after learning of Uriah's death? How would your thoughts change if you don't know who is truly responsible for the death?

2 Draw a plot line of the action of this story. Where would you put the turning point?

3 From history or current events, choose a person (or a government) that you feel has been guilty of some wrong. Using Nathan's as a model, write a brief "story" that will indirectly accuse that person of the wrong.

THE
REBELLION
OF
ABSALOM

2 Samuel

*[Now an old man,
David is challenged by his
ambitious son.]*

Now in all Israel there was no one so much to be praised for his beauty as Absalom; from the sole of his foot to the crown of his head there was no blemish in him. And when he cut the hair of his head (for at the end of every year he used to cut it; when it was heavy on him, he cut it), he weighed the hair of his head, two hundred shekels by the king's weight. There were born to Absalom three sons, and one daughter whose name was Tamar; she was a beautiful woman. . . .

two hundred shekels: about five pounds.

After this Absalom got himself a chariot and horses, and fifty men to run before him. And Absalom used to rise early and stand beside the way of the gate; and when any man had a suit to come before the king for judgment, Absalom would call to him, and say, "From what city are you?" And when he said, "Your servant is of such and such a tribe in Israel," Absalom would say to him, "See, your claims are good and right; but there is no man deputed by the king to hear you." Absalom said moreover, "Oh that I were judge in the land! Then every man with a suit or cause might come to me, and I would give him justice." And whenever a man came near to do obeisance to him, he would put out

a suit to come: a case to bring.

deputed: appointed.

2 Samuel 14:25–27; 15:1–16a, 23; 18:1–5, 9–15, 31–33 (RSV).

his hand, and take hold of him, and kiss him. Thus Absalom did to all of Israel who came to the king for judgment; so Absalom stole the hearts of the men of Israel.

And at the end of four years Absalom said to the king, "Pray let me go and pay my vow, which I have vowed to the Lord, in Hebron. For your servant vowed a vow while I dwelt at Geshur in Aram, saying, 'If the Lord will indeed bring me back to Jerusalem, then I will offer worship to the Lord.' " The king said to him, "Go in peace." So he arose, and went to Hebron. But Absalom sent secret messengers throughout all the tribes of Israel saying, "As soon as you hear the sound of the trumpet, then say, 'Absalom is king at Hebron!' " With Absalom went two hundred men from Jerusalem who were invited guests, and they went in their simplicity, and knew nothing. And while Absalom was offering the sacrifices, he sent for Ahithophel the Gilonite, David's counselor, from his city Giloh. And the conspiracy grew strong, and the people with Absalom kept increasing.

Hebron (hē′brən): David's capital city before he moved to Jerusalem. Absalom was born here.

And a messenger came to David, saying, "The hearts of the men of Israel have gone after Absalom." Then David said to all his servants who were with him at Jerusalem, "Arise, and let us flee; or else there will be no escape for us from Absalom; go in haste, lest he overtake us quickly, and bring down evil upon us, and smite the city with the edge of the sword." And the king's servants said to the king, "Behold, your servants are ready to do whatever my lord the king decides." So the king went forth, and all his household after him. . . .

. . . And all the country wept aloud as all the people passed by, and the king crossed the brook Kidron, and all the people passed on toward the wilderness. . . .

brook Kidron (kē′drən): the city boundary.

Then David mustered the men who were with him, and set over them commanders of thousands and commanders of hundreds. And David sent forth the army, one third under the command of Joab, one third under the command of Abishai the son of Zeruiah, Joab's brother, and one third under the command of Ittai the Gittite. And the king said to the men, "I myself will also go out with you." But the men said, "You shall not go out. For if we flee,

mustered: assembled.

they will not care about us. If half of us die, they will not care about us. But you are worth ten thousand of us; therefore it is better that you send us help from the city." The king said to them, "Whatever seems best to you I will do." So the king stood at the side of the gate, while all the army marched out by hundreds and by thousands. And the king ordered Joab and Abishai and Ittai, "Deal gently for my sake with the young man Absalom." And all the people heard when the king gave orders to all the commanders about Absalom. . . .

And Absalom chanced to meet the servants of David. Absalom was riding upon his mule, and the mule went under the thick branches of a great oak, and his head caught fast in the oak, and he was left hanging between heaven and earth, while the mule that was under him went on. And a certain man saw it, and told Joab, "Behold, I saw Absalom hanging in an oak." Joab said to the man who told him, "What, you saw him! Why then did you not strike him there to the ground? I would have been glad to give you ten pieces of silver and a girdle." But the man said to Joab, "Even if I felt in my hand the weight of a thousand pieces of silver, I would not put forth my hand against the king's son; for in our hearing the king commanded you and Abishai and Ittai, 'For my sake protect the young man Absalom.' On the other hand, if I had dealt treacherously against his life (and there is nothing hidden from the king), then you yourself would have stood aloof." Joab said, "I will not waste time like this with you." And he took three darts in his hand, and thrust them into the heart of Absalom, while he was still alive in the oak. And ten young men, Joab's armor-bearers, surrounded Absalom and struck him, and killed him. . . .

And behold, the Cushite came; and the Cushite said, "Good tidings for my lord the king! For the Lord has delivered you this day from the power of all who rose up against you." The king said to the Cushite, "Is it well with the young man Absalom?" And the Cushite answered, "May the enemies of my lord the king, and all who rise up against you for evil, be like that young man." And the king was deeply moved, and went up to the chamber over the gate, and wept; and as he went, he said, "O my son Absalom, my son, my son Absalom! Would I had died instead of you, O Absalom, my son, my son!"

the city: David's headquarters.

head: some translations say "hair."

stood aloof: kept out of it.

Cushite: Ethiopian slave.

chamber: room.

For close reading

1 How does Absalom go about gaining power for himself?
2 What instructions does David give his generals before the battle against the rebels?
3 Retell in your own words how Absalom met his death.

For thought and discussion

4 Whose story is being told in this passage: David's or Absalom's? How does Absalom compare with the young David portrayed earlier—in appearance? In character?
5 What similarities and what differences do you find between this story and the killing of Uriah the Hittite?
6 Why do you think Joab insists on killing Absalom? What do the words spoken by Joab and his soldier reveal about the relation between officers and common soldiers?
7 The three David stories give us radically different pictures of the man at crucial moments of his life. Which story did you find most appealing? Most moving? Why?
8 Compare David's public life as soldier and king with his personal life. What differences do you find? How does the Absalom episode symbolize the conflict between the two areas of David's life?

Activities

1 You are David at the end of your long life. An interviewer asks you what you think was the turning point of your life. What is your answer and explanation? Or, you are David weeping over the death of Absalom. What other regrets come to mind to increase your grief?
2 Sketch or paint a portrait of Absalom.

6

spokesmen
of
god

ELIJAH: THE ONLY ONE LEFT

1 Kings

[*Approximately forty years after the death of David, the nation of Israel was divided. The Northern Kingdom retained the name Israel; the Southern Kingdom, ruled by descendants of David, was called Judah. The rulers of the two kingdoms often "did evil in the sight of the Lord," which led to greater activity by a series of prophets—God's spokesmen.*

Elijah was a prophet in the Northern Kingdom during the reign of Ahab, a king who was strongly influenced by his foreign wife, Jezebel. Ahab angered the Lord by introducing the worship of Baal (bā/əl), a pagan god of storm and rain.]

Now Elijah the Tishbite, of Tishbe in Gilead, said to Ahab, "As the Lord the God of Israel lives, before whom I stand, there shall be neither dew nor rain these years, except by my word." And the word of the Lord came to him, "Depart from here and turn eastward, and hide yourself by the brook Cherith, that is east of the Jordan. You shall drink from the brook, and I have commanded the ravens to feed you there." So he went and did according to the word of the Lord; he went and dwelt by the brook Cherith that is east of the Jordan. And the ravens brought him bread and meat in the morning, and

Gilead (gil/ē əd): region east of the Jordan River.

1 Kings 17:1–24; 18:1–2, 17–46; 19:1–18; 21:1–11, 15–24 (RSV).
LEFT: Marble bust of a prophet by Giovanni Pisano. Museo Civico, Pisa.

bread and meat in the evening; and he drank from the brook. And after a while the brook dried up, because there was no rain in the land.

Then the word of the Lord came to him, "Arise, go to Zarephath, which belongs to Sidon, and dwell there. Behold, I have commanded a widow there to feed you." So he arose and went to Zarephath; and when he came to the gate of the city, behold, a widow was there gathering sticks; and he called to her and said, "Bring me a little water in a vessel, that I may drink." And as she was going to bring it, he called to her and said, "Bring me a morsel of bread in your hand." And she said, "As the Lord your God lives, I have nothing baked, only a handful of meal in a jar, and a little oil in a cruse; and now, I am gathering a couple of sticks, that I may go in and prepare it for myself and my son, that we may eat it, and die." And Elijah said to her, "Fear not; go and do as you have said; but first make me a little cake of it and bring it to me, and afterward make for yourself and your son. For thus says the Lord the God of Israel, 'The jar of meal shall not be spent, and the cruse of oil shall not fail, until the day that the Lord sends rain upon the earth.' " And she went and did as Elijah said; and she, and he, and her household ate for many days. The jar of meal was not spent, neither did the cruse of oil fail, according to the word of the Lord which he spoke by Elijah.

After this the son of the woman, the mistress of the house, became ill; and his illness was so severe that there was no breath left in him. And she said to Elijah, "What have you against me, O man of God? You have come to me to bring my sin to remembrance, and to cause the death of my son!" And he said to her, "Give me your son." And he took him from her bosom, and carried him up into the upper chamber, where he lodged, and laid him upon his own bed. And he cried to the Lord, "O Lord my God, hast thou brought calamity even upon the widow with whom I sojourn, by slaying her son?" Then he stretched himself upon the child three times, and cried to the Lord, "O Lord my God, let this child's soul come into him again." And the Lord hearkened to the voice of Elijah; and the soul of the child came into him again, and he revived. And Elijah took the child, and brought him down from the upper chamber into the house, and delivered

meal: coarsely ground grain.
cruse (krüz): jar.

sojourn (sō'jėrn): stay.

hearkened: listened.

him to his mother; and Elijah said, "See, your son lives." And the woman said to Elijah, "Now I know that you are a man of God, and that the word of the Lord in your mouth is truth."

After many days the word of the Lord came to Elijah, in the third year, saying, "Go, show yourself to Ahab; and I will send rain upon the earth." So Elijah went to show himself to Ahab. Now the famine was severe in Samaria. . . .

Samaria: the capital city of the Northern Kingdom.

When Ahab saw Elijah, Ahab said to him, "Is it you, you troubler of Israel?" And he answered, "I have not troubled Israel; but you have, and your father's house, because you have forsaken the commandments of the Lord and followed the Baals. Now therefore send and gather all Israel to me at Mount Carmel, and the four hundred and fifty prophets of Baal and the four hundred prophets of Asherah, who eat at Jezebel's table."

Asherah (ə shir′ə): pagan goddess associated with the worship of Baal.

So Ahab sent to all the people of Israel, and gathered the prophets together at Mount Carmel. And Elijah came near to all the people, and said, "How long will you go limping with two different opinions? If the Lord is God, follow him; but if Baal, then follow him." And the people did not answer him a word. Then Elijah said to the people, "I, even I only, am left a prophet of the Lord; but Baal's prophets are four hundred and fifty men. Let two bulls be given to us; and let them choose one bull for themselves, and cut it in pieces and lay it on the wood, but put no fire to it; and I will prepare the other bull and lay it on the wood, and put no fire to it. And you call on the name of your god and I will call on the name of the Lord; and the God who answers by fire, he is God." And all the people answered, "It is well spoken." Then Elijah said to the prophets of Baal, "Choose for yourselves one bull and prepare it first, for you are many; and call on the name of your god, but put no fire to it." And they took the bull which was given them, and they prepared it, and called on the name of Baal from morning until noon, saying, "O Baal, answer us!" But there was no voice, and no one answered. And they limped about the altar which they had made. And at noon Elijah mocked them, saying, "Cry aloud, for he is a god; either he is musing, or he has gone aside, or he is on a journey, or perhaps he is

musing: meditating, thinking.

raved: shouted wildly.

time . . . oblation: i.e.,
midafternoon.

asleep and must be awakened." And they cried aloud, and cut themselves after their custom with swords and lances, until the blood gushed out upon them. And as midday passed, they raved on until the time of the offering of the oblation, but there was no voice; no one answered, no one heeded.

Then Elijah said to all the people, "Come near to me"; and all the people came near to him. And he repaired the altar of the Lord that had been thrown down; Elijah took twelve stones, according to the number of the tribes of the sons of Jacob, to whom the word of the Lord came, saying, "Israel shall be your name"; and with the stones he built an altar in the name of the Lord. And he made a trench about the altar, as great as would contain two measures of seed. And he put the wood in order, and cut the bull in pieces and laid it on the wood. And he said, "Fill four jars with water, and pour it on the burnt offering, and on the wood." And he said, "Do it a second time"; and they did it a second time. And he said, "Do it a third time"; and they did it a third time. And the water ran round about the altar, and filled the trench also with water.

And at the time of the offering of the oblation, Elijah the prophet came near and said, "O Lord, God of Abraham, Isaac, and Israel, let it be known this day that thou art God in Israel, and that I am thy servant, and that I have done all these things at thy word. Answer me, O Lord, answer me, that this people may know that thou, O Lord, art God, and that thou hast turned their hearts back." Then the fire of the Lord fell, and consumed the burnt offering, and the wood, and the stones, and the dust, and licked up the water that was in the trench. And when all the people saw it, they fell on their faces; and they said, "The Lord, he is God; the Lord, he is

RIGHT: *The Sorrows of the King,* cut-out gouache by Henri Matisse, 1952. Courtesy of the Musée National d'Art Moderne, Paris. © SPADEM, Paris 1975.
David, detail from marble statue by Michelangelo, 1501-1504. Galleria della Accademia, Florence.
Page 198: *The Prophet* by Julio Gonzalez, pen and ink, ink wash, and pencil, 1941. The Rijksmuseum Kröller-Müller, Otterlo, The Netherlands.
Page 199: *Jonah Cast Up,* marble, eastern Mediterranean, mid-third century. The Cleveland Museum of Art, John L. Severance Fund.

God." And Elijah said to them, "Seize the prophets
of Baal; let not one of them escape." And they
seized them; and Elijah brought them down to the
brook Kishon, and killed them there.

And Elijah said to Ahab, "Go up, eat and drink; for
there is a sound of the rushing of rain." So Ahab
went up to eat and to drink. And Elijah went up to
the top of Carmel; and he bowed himself down
upon the earth, and put his face between his knees.
And he said to his servant, "Go up now, look toward
the sea." And he went up and looked, and said,
"There is nothing." And he said, "Go again seven
times." And at the seventh time he said, "Behold, a
little cloud like a man's hand is rising out of the sea."
And he said, "Go up, say to Ahab, 'Prepare your
chariot and go down, lest the rain stop you.' " And
in a little while the heavens grew black with clouds
and wind, and there was a great rain. And Ahab rode
and went to Jezreel. And the hand of the Lord was
on Elijah; and he girded up his loins and ran before
Ahab to the entrance of Jezreel.

**girded up his
loins:** i.e., got ready
for action.
Jezreel: Ahab's
summer home.

Ahab told Jezebel all that Elijah had done, and
how he had slain all the prophets with the sword.
Then Jezebel sent a messenger to Elijah, saying, "So
may the gods do to me and more also, if I do not
make your life as the life of one of them by this time
tomorrow." Then he was afraid, and he arose and
went for his life, and came to Beersheba, which
belongs to Judah, and left his servant there.

But he himself went a day's journey into the
wilderness, and came and sat down under a broom
tree; and he asked that he might die, saying, "It is
enough; now, O Lord, take away my life; for I am no
better than my fathers." And he lay down and slept
under a broom tree; and behold, an angel touched
him, and said to him, "Arise and eat." And he
looked, and behold, there was at his head a cake
baked on hot stones and a jar of water. And he ate
and drank, and lay down again. And the angel of the
Lord came again a second time, and touched him,
and said, "Arise and eat, else the journey will be too
great for you." And he arose, and ate and drank, and
went in the strength of that food forty days and forty
nights to Horeb the mount of God.

Horeb: also, Mount
Sinai, on which Moses
received the
commandments.

And there he came to a cave, and lodged there; and behold, the word of the Lord came to him, and he said to him, "What are you doing here, Elijah?" He said, "I have been very jealous for the Lord, the God of hosts; for the people of Israel have forsaken thy covenant, thrown down thy altars, and slain thy prophets with the sword; and I, even I only, am left; and they seek my life, to take it away." And he said, "Go forth, and stand upon the mount before the Lord." And behold, the Lord passed by, and a great and strong wind rent the mountains, and broke in pieces the rocks before the Lord, but the Lord was not in the wind; and after the wind an earthquake, but the Lord was not in the earthquake; and after the earthquake a fire, but the Lord was not in the fire; and after the fire a still small voice. And when Elijah heard it, he wrapped his face in his mantle and went out and stood at the entrance of the cave. And behold, there came a voice to him, and said, "What are you doing here, Elijah?" He said, "I have been very jealous for the Lord, the God of hosts; for the people of Israel have forsaken thy covenant, thrown down thy altars, and slain thy prophets with the sword; and I, even I only, am left; and they seek my life, to take it away." And the Lord said to him, "Go, return on your way to the wilderness of Damascus; and when you arrive, you shall anoint Hazael to be king over Syria; and Jehu the son of Nimshi you shall anoint to be king over Israel; and Elisha the son of Shaphat of Abel-meholah you shall anoint to be prophet in your place. And him who escapes from the sword of Hazael shall Jehu slay; and him who escapes from the sword of Jehu shall Elisha slay. Yet I will leave seven thousand in Israel, all the knees that have not bowed to Baal, and every mouth that has not kissed him." . . .

Now Naboth the Jezreelite had a vineyard in Jezreel, beside the palace of Ahab king of Samaria. And after this Ahab said to Naboth, "Give me your vineyard, that I may have it for a vegetable garden, because it is near my house; and I will give you a better vineyard for it; or, if it seems good to you, I will give you its value in money." But Naboth said to Ahab, "The Lord forbid that I should give you the inheritance of my fathers." And Ahab went into his house vexed and sullen because of what Naboth the

covenant: agreement.

anoint: pour oil upon as a sign of God's blessing.

Naboth (nā′both).

vexed and sullen: angry and moody.

Jezreelite had said to him; for he had said, "I will not give you the inheritance of my fathers." And he lay down on his bed, and turned away his face, and would eat no food.

But Jezebel his wife came to him, and said to him, "Why is your spirit so vexed that you eat no food?" And he said to her, "Because I spoke to Naboth the Jezreelite, and said to him, 'Give me your vineyard for money; or else, if it please you, I will give you another vineyard for it'; and he answered, 'I will not give you my vineyard.' " And Jezebel his wife said to him, "Do you now govern Israel? Arise, and eat bread, and let your heart be cheerful; I will give you the vineyard of Naboth the Jezreelite."

So she wrote letters in Ahab's name and sealed them with his seal, and she sent the letters to the elders and the nobles who dwelt with Naboth in his city. And she wrote in the letters, "Proclaim a fast, and set Naboth on high among the people; and set two base fellows opposite him, and let them bring a charge against him, saying, 'You have cursed God and the king.' Then take him out, and stone him to death." And the men of his city, the elders and the nobles who dwelt in his city, did as Jezebel had sent word to them. . . .

As soon as Jezebel heard that Naboth had been stoned and was dead, Jezebel said to Ahab, "Arise, take possession of the vineyard of Naboth the Jezreelite, which he refused to give you for money; for Naboth is not alive, but dead." And as soon as Ahab heard that Naboth was dead, Ahab arose to go down to the vineyard of Naboth the Jezreelite, to take possession of it.

Then the word of the Lord came to Elijah the Tishbite, saying, "Arise, go down to meet Ahab king of Israel, who is in Samaria; behold, he is in the vineyard of Naboth, where he has gone to take possession. And you shall say to him, 'Thus says the Lord, "Have you killed, and also taken possession?" ' And you shall say to him, 'Thus says the Lord: "In the place where dogs licked up the blood of Naboth shall dogs lick your own blood." ' "

Ahab said to Elijah, "Have you found me, O my enemy?" He answered, "I have found you, because you have sold yourself to do what is evil in the sight of the Lord. Behold, I will bring evil upon you; I will utterly sweep you away, and will cut off from Ahab

Jeroboam . . . Baasha:
former kings of Israel
whose families had
been destroyed by
prophet-led
revolutions.

every male, bond or free, in Israel; and I will make your house like the house of Jeroboam the son of Nebat, and like the house of Baasha the son of Ahijah, for the anger to which you have provoked me, and because you have made Israel to sin. And of Jezebel the Lord also said, 'The dogs shall eat Jezebel within the bounds of Jezreel.' Any one belonging to Ahab who dies in the city the dogs shall eat; and any one of his who dies in the open country the birds of the air shall eat."

For close reading

1 How many journeys does Elijah make? From where to where?
2 In their contest with Elijah, how do the prophets of Baal appeal to their god? How does Elijah make the Lord's demonstration of power more dramatic?
3 List the miracles which Elijah performs through the power of the Lord. How do the people who witness or benefit from these miracles respond to them?
4 How does Ahab get the vineyard of Naboth?

For thought and discussion

5 Consider Elijah's experiences on Mount Carmel (the contest with the prophets of Baal) and his experiences on Mount Horeb (in the cave). On both occasions Elijah says "I, even I only am left." Are his feelings the same in each case? Explain. The Lord responds to Elijah in both episodes. How does the story in each case "build up" to this moment? In your opinion, which response is more dramatic? Why?

6 Would you say that Elijah's low spirits on Mount Horeb are caused mainly by: *(a)* Fear for his life? *(b)* A sense of personal failure? *(c)* Disappointment that Israel has forsaken the Lord? Support your choice with details from the story.

7 What does the episode of Naboth's vineyard reveal about Ahab's character? About Jezebel's?

8 The hero of Henrik Ibsen's play *The Enemy of the People* states: "The strongest man in the world is he who stands most alone." Do you think Elijah would have agreed? Do you agree with this statement? Explain.

Activities

1 Act out or pantomime the contest between Elijah and the prophets of Baal.

2 Listen to a recording of Mendelssohn's oratorio *Elijah*. How does this experience affect your feeling about the story?

3 You are Jezebel. Write an entry in your diary that expresses your feelings about Elijah and your husband after the episode of Naboth's vineyard.

4 Suppose that Elijah, in his lowest moment, appeared in the office of a psychiatrist. Write the advice which the psychiatrist might have given.

AMOS:
LET JUSTICE
ROLL
DOWN

Amos

[*A migrant worker, harvesting or herding from place to place, Amos spoke out in the Northern Kingdom approximately a century after Elijah. For the rich in Israel, this was a time of peace and prosperity; for the poor, it was a time of hardship.*

In the passage below, Amos begins by telling his audience in Israel how their enemies have sinned— the Syrians (whose capital is Damascus) to the north- east, the Ammonites and the Moabites to the south and east. As a climax Amos shocks the people of Israel with their own injustices to the poor.]

Tekoa (tə kō′ə): city in Judah. Amos was born in the Southern Kingdom.

The words of Amos, who was among the shep- herds of Tekoa, which he saw concerning Israel in the days of Uzziah king of Judah and in the days of Jeroboam the son of Joash, king of Israel, two years before the earthquake. And he said:

Zion: hill in Jerusalem on which the temple of the Lord stood.

"The Lord roars from Zion,
 and utters his voice from Jerusalem;
the pastures of the shepherds mourn,
 and the top of Carmel withers."

Thus says the Lord:

transgressions: sins.
revoke: cancel, take back.

"For three transgressions of Damascus,
 and for four, I will not revoke the punishment;
because they have threshed Gilead
 with threshing sledges of iron.
So I will send a fire upon the house of Hazael,

threshed . . . iron: this may refer to a means of executing prisoners by running horse-drawn sledges over them.

Amos 1:1–5, 13–15; 2:1–3, 6–7, 13, 15–16; 5:18–24; 7:10–15; 3:3–8 (RSV).

and it shall devour the strongholds of Ben-
   hadad.
I will break the bar of Damascus,
   and cut off the inhabitants from the Valley
   of Aven,
and him that holds the scepter from Beth-
   eden;
   and the people of Syria shall go into exile to
   Kir,"

says the Lord. . . .

bar: the great beam
which holds shut the
city gate.

Thus says the Lord:
"For three transgressions of the Ammonites,
   and for four, I will not revoke the punishment;
because they have ripped up women with
   child in Gilead,
   that they might enlarge their border.
So I will kindle a fire in the wall of Rabbah,
   and it shall devour her strongholds,
with shouting in the day of battle,
   with a tempest in the day of the whirlwind;
and their king shall go into exile,
   he and his princes together,"

says the Lord. . . .

Thus says the Lord:
"For three transgressions of Moab,
   and for four, I will not revoke the punishment;
because he burned to lime
   the bones of the king of Edom.
So I will send a fire upon Moab,
   and it shall devour the strongholds of
   Kerioth,
and Moab shall die amid uproar,
   amid shouting and the sound of the trumpet;
I will cut off the ruler from its midst,
   and will slay all its princes with him,"

says the Lord. . . .

he: i.e., the kingdom
of Moab.

burned . . . bones: it
was a great sin not to
give a body proper
burial.

Thus says the Lord:
"For three transgressions of Israel,
   and for four, I will not revoke the punishment;
because they sell the righteous for silver,
   and the needy for a pair of shoes——

they that trample the head of the poor into
    the dust of the earth,
  and turn aside the way of the afflicted; . . .
Behold, I will press you down in your place,
  as a cart full of sheaves presses down. . . .
he who handles the bow shall not stand,
  and he who is swift of foot shall not save
    himself,
    nor shall he who rides the horse save
    his life;
and he who is stout of heart among the
  mighty shall flee away naked in that day,"
                   says the Lord. . . .

Woe to you who desire the day of the Lord!
  Why would you have the day of the Lord?
It is darkness, and not light;
  as if a man fled from a lion,
  and a bear met him;
or went into the house and leaned with his
    hand against the wall,
  and a serpent bit him.
Is not the day of the Lord darkness, and not
    light,
  and gloom with no brightness in it?

"I hate, I despise your feasts,
  and I take no delight in your solemn assem-
    blies.
Even though you offer me your burnt offerings
    and cereal offerings,
  I will not accept them,
and the peace offerings of your fatted beasts
  I will not look upon.
Take away from me the noise of your songs;
  to the melody of your harps I will not listen.
But let justice roll down like waters,
  and righteousness like an ever-flowing
    stream. . . . "

cereal: grain.

Then Amaziah the priest of Bethel sent to Jeroboam king of Israel, saying, "Amos has conspired
against you in the midst of the house of Israel; the
land is not able to bear all his words. For thus Amos
has said,

    'Jeroboam shall die by the sword,

and Israel must go into exile
away from his land.' "

And Amaziah said to Amos, "O seer, go, flee away
to the land of Judah, and eat bread there, and
prophesy there; but never again prophesy at Bethel,
for it is the king's sanctuary, and it is a temple of the
kingdom."

seer: prophet.

Then Amos answered Amaziah, "I am no prophet,
nor a prophet's son; but I am a herdsman, and a
dresser of sycamore trees, and the Lord took me
from following the flock, and the Lord said to me,
'Go, prophesy to my people Israel.' "

dresser . . . trees: in
the Middle East, the
sycamore is a type of
fig tree. Amos tended
the blossoms so that
the figs could ripen
properly.

"Do two walk together,
    unless they have made an appointment?
Does a lion roar in the forest,
    when he has no prey?
Does a young lion cry out from his den,
    if he has taken nothing?
Does a bird fall in a snare on the earth,
    when there is no trap for it?
Does a snare spring up from the ground,
    when it has taken nothing?
Is a trumpet blown in a city,
    and the people are not afraid?
Does evil befall a city,
    unless the Lord has done it?
Surely the Lord God does nothing,
    without revealing his secret
    to his servants the prophets.
The lion has roared;
    who will not fear?
The Lord God has spoken;
    who can but prophesy?" . . .

For close reading

1 What four countries are condemned in this passage? What differences do you find between the
offenses of Israel and the offenses of the first three
countries?

2 What country is Amos from? What country does he mainly speak against? What is his occupation?

3 How do the people in power respond to Amos's message? Where is this shown?

For thought and discussion

4 Do you think Amos's way of making a living had anything to do with his view of the world or might anyone have seen what he saw and condemned it? Explain.

5 How does Amos emphasize and dramatize his message? Why do you think he begins by accusing Israel's enemies?

6 For what reasons might people in Israel be likely to object to Amos as a prophet?

7 What do you think Amos means when he says he is "no prophet"?

8 A Turkish proverb says "He who tells the truth should have one foot in the stirrup." Do you think people generally do not prefer to hear the truth? Explain.

Activities

1 Using Amos's method ("For three transgressions of . . .") write an essay against some injustice you see in today's world.

2 Collect photographs and create a collage, a scrapbook, or posters which will illustrate your views on a modern injustice.

3 Choose a public figure of this century that you regard as a modern Amos. In a brief essay, compare this person with Amos.

4 "Prophets" have been a favorite subject of cartoonists. Usually the prophets are shown carrying a sign which bears some startling message. As a class project, you might make a collection of such cartoons.

PROPHETS FOR A NEW DAY

Margaret Walker

1.

As the Word came to prophets of old,
As the burning bush spoke to Moses,
And the fiery coals cleansed the lips of Isaiah;
As the wheeling cloud in the sky
Clothed the message of Ezekiel;
So the Word of fire burns today
On the lips of our prophets in an evil age——
Our sooth-sayers and doom-tellers and doers
    of the Word.
So the Word of the Lord stirs again
These passionate people toward deliverance.
As Amos, Shepherd of Tekoa, spoke
To the captive children of Judah,
Preaching to the dispossessed and the poor,
So today in the pulpits and the jails,
On the highways and in the byways,
A fearless shepherd speaks at last
To his suffering weary sheep.

dispossessed: people who have lost their home or land.

2.

So, kneeling by the river bank
Comes the vision to a valley of believers
So in flaming flags of stars in the sky
And in the breaking dawn of a blinding sun

The lamp of truth is lighted in the Temple
And the oil of devotion is burning at midnight
So the glittering censer in the Temple

25 Trembles in the presence of the priests
And the pillars of the doorposts move
And the incense rises in smoke
And the dark faces of the sufferers
Gleam in the new morning
30 The complaining faces glow
And the winds of freedom begin to blow
While the Word descends on the waiting
    World below.

3.

A beast is among us.
His mark is on the land.
35 His horns and his hands and his lips are gory
    with our blood.

He is War and Famine and Pestilence
He is Death and Destruction and Trouble
And he walks in our houses at noonday
And devours our defenders at midnight.
40 He is the demon who drives us with whips of fear
And in his cowardice
He cries out against liberty
He cries out against humanity
Against all dignity of green valleys and high hills
45 Against clean winds blowing through our living;
Against the broken bodies of our brothers.
He has crushed them with a stone.
He drinks our tears for water
And he drinks our blood for wine;
50 He eats our flesh like a ravenous lion
And he drives us out of the city
To be stabbed on a lonely hill.

For thought and discussion

1 In a poem filled with biblical references and images, what lines suggest modern times?
2 In the Bible, prophets frequently brought bad news to their people. What kind of news is being prophesied here?
3 According to the poem, what kind of people are the prophets for a new day?
4 What do you think is the "beast" among us?
5 Sum up the three parts of the poem in one sentence each. How does the tone or feeling of the last section differ from the rest of the poem?

JONAH: A RELUCTANT PROPHET

Jonah

Nineveh (nin′ə və): the capital of one of Israel's most hated enemies, this city was a symbol of corruption and evil.

Now the word of the Lord came to Jonah the son of Amittai, saying, "Arise, go to Nineveh, that great city, and cry against it; for their wickedness has come up before me." But Jonah rose to flee to Tarshish from the presence of the Lord. He went down to Joppa and found a ship going to Tarshish; so he paid the fare, and went on board, to go with them to Tarshish, away from the presence of the Lord.

But the Lord hurled a great wind upon the sea, and there was a mighty tempest on the sea, so that the ship threatened to break up. Then the mariners were afraid, and each cried to his god; and they threw the wares that were in the ship into the sea, to lighten it for them. But Jonah had gone down into the inner part of the ship and had lain down, and was fast asleep. So the captain came and said to him, "What do you mean, you sleeper? Arise, call upon your god! Perhaps the god will give a thought to us, that we do not perish."

cast lots: i.e., choose by chance (probably using marked stones).

And they said to one another, "Come, let us cast lots, that we may know on whose account this evil has come upon us." So they cast lots, and the lot fell upon Jonah. Then they said to him, "Tell us, on whose account this evil has come upon us? What is your occupation? And whence do you come? What is your country? And of what people are you?" And he said to them, "I am a Hebrew; and I fear the Lord, the God of heaven, who made the sea and the dry

Jonah 1:1–2:6, 10; 3:1–4:11 (RSV).

land." Then the men were exceedingly afraid, and said to him, "What is this that you have done!" For the men knew that he was fleeing from the presence of the Lord, because he had told them.

Then they said to him, "What shall we do to you, that the sea may quiet down for us?" For the sea grew more and more tempestuous. He said to them, "Take me up and throw me into the sea; then the sea will quiet down for you; for I know it is because of me that this great tempest has come upon you." Nevertheless the men rowed hard to bring the ship back to land, but they could not, for the sea grew more and more tempestuous against them. Therefore they cried to the Lord, "We beseech thee, O Lord, let us not perish for this man's life, and lay not on us innocent blood; for thou, O Lord, hast done as it pleased thee." So they took up Jonah and threw him into the sea; and the sea ceased from its raging. Then the men feared the Lord exceedingly, and they offered a sacrifice to the Lord and made vows.

And the Lord appointed a great fish to swallow up Jonah; and Jonah was in the belly of the fish three days and three nights.

Then Jonah prayed to the Lord his God from the belly of the fish, saying,

> "I called to the Lord, out of my distress,
>   and he answered me;
> out of the belly of Sheol I cried,
>   and thou didst hear my voice.
> For thou didst cast me into the deep,
>   into the heart of the seas,
>   and the flood was round about me;
> all thy waves and thy billows passed over me.
> Then I said, 'I am cast out from thy presence;
> how shall I again look upon thy holy temple?'
> The waters closed in over me,
>   the deep was round about me;
> weeds were wrapped about my head
>   at the roots of the mountains.
> I went down to the land
>   whose bars closed upon me for ever;
> yet thou didst bring up my life from the Pit,
> O Lord my God. . . . "

Sheol: place of the dead; the underworld.

And the Lord spoke to the fish, and it vomited out Jonah upon the dry land.

Then the word of the Lord came to Jonah the second time, saying, "Arise, go to Nineveh, that great city, and proclaim to it the message that I tell you." So Jonah arose and went to Nineveh, according to the word of the Lord. Now Nineveh was an exceedingly great city, three days' journey in breadth. Jonah began to go into the city, going a day's journey. And he cried, "Yet forty days, and Nineveh shall be overthrown!" And the people of Nineveh believed God; they proclaimed a fast, and put on sackcloth, from the greatest of them to the least of them.

Then tidings reached the king of Nineveh, and he arose from his throne, removed his robe, and covered himself with sackcloth, and sat in ashes. And he made proclamation and published through Nineveh, "By the decree of the king and his nobles: Let neither man nor beast, herd nor flock, taste anything; let them not feed, or drink water, but let man and beast be covered with sackcloth, and let them cry mightily to God; yea, let everyone turn from his evil way and from the violence which is in his hands. Who knows, God may yet repent and turn from his fierce anger, so that we perish not?"

When God saw what they did, how they turned from their evil way, God repented of the evil which he had said he would do to them; and he did not do it.

But it displeased Jonah exceedingly, and he was angry. And he prayed to the Lord and said, "I pray thee, Lord, is not this what I said when I was yet in my country? That is why I made haste to flee to Tarshish; for I knew that thou art a gracious God and merciful, slow to anger, and abounding in steadfast love, and repentest of evil. Therefore now, O Lord, take my life from me, I beseech thee, for it is better for me to die than to live." And the Lord said, "Do you do well to be angry?" Then Jonah went out of the city and sat to the east of the city, and made a booth for himself there. He sat under it in the shade, till he should see what would become of the city.

And the Lord God appointed a plant, and made it come up over Jonah, that it might be a shade over his head, to save him from his discomfort. So Jonah was exceedingly glad because of the plant. But when dawn came up the next day, God appointed a worm which attacked the plant, so that it withered. When

sackcloth: rough cloth worn as a sign of mourning or penitence for a sin.

sat in ashes: another sign of mourning or penitence.

booth: shelter.

the sun rose, God appointed a sultry east wind, and the sun beat upon the head of Jonah so that he was faint; and he asked that he might die, and said, "It is better for me to die than to live." But God said to Jonah, "Do you do well to be angry for the plant?" And he said, "I do well to be angry, angry enough to die." And the Lord said, "You pity the plant, for which you did not labor, nor did you make it grow, which came into being in a night, and perished in a night. And should not I pity Nineveh, that great city, in which there are more than a hundred and twenty thousand persons who do not know their right hand from their left, and also much cattle?"

For close reading

1 What suggestion does Jonah make to the sailors to end the storm?
2 At what two times does the Lord show sympathy and mercy to Jonah? How does Jonah react in each case?
3 How do the sailors react when they find that God has spared them? How do the Ninevites react when they hear Jonah's message?
4 What is Jonah's message to the Ninevites?

For thought and discussion

5 Compare Jonah's reactions to the Lord with the reactions of the "pagan" sailors and Ninevites. Why do you suppose this contrast is made so clearly?
6 Some have called the story of Jonah a satire

making fun of Jonah. Do you agree that there are moments of satire and humor in the story? If so, why do you think the story uses satire?

7 What "lesson" do you think the Lord is teaching Jonah? How does each episode in the story relate to that lesson?

8 Why do you think Jonah is angry when he hears that the Lord has spared Nineveh?

9 The story ends with the Lord's question. Would the story have been more, or less, effective if it had been a statement? If Jonah's answer were given? How might Jonah have answered?

10 Think of Elijah, Amos, and Jonah as prophets of the Lord. Which man, in your opinion, had the most difficult job? Who was the most successful? Which prophet did you feel closest to? Why?

Activities

1 Illustrate the story of Jonah as a cartoon strip.

2 Using whatever medium you wish (painting, collage, sculpture, needlework, etc.) show Jonah in the belly of the fish.

3 You are Jonah. Describe your experiences in a letter to your family.

4 Look up *Jonah* in a dictionary. What does it mean to say that someone is "a Jonah"? What other expressions can you think of that use biblical names in that way?

JONAH

Enrique Lihn
Translated by Miller Williams

I could damn all things equally. Don't ask me
in the name of what.
In the name of Isaiah, the prophet,
but with the gesture
5 grotesque and incomplete
of his cohort Jonah
who was never able to finish his petty commission
given to the lows and highs of good and evil,
the shifting circumstances of history,
10 that left him lost in the uncertainty
of a whale's belly.
Like Jonah, the clown of heaven,
obstinate always
in finishing his minor assignments,
15 the incendiary briefcase under the sweaty armpit,
the umbrella worn down to a lightning rod.
Above him, the uncertainty of Jehovah,
swaying between forgiveness and fury,
between taking him up and flinging him down
20 an old tool of uncertain usefulness
fallen at last into perfect disuse.

I will end also under a tree
but like those old drunken bums
who despise all things equally,
25 don't ask me anything,

grotesque: odd or
unnatural.
cohort (kō′hôrt):
associate or follower.
commission: assign-
ment.

incendiary: causing
fires, violence, or
rebellion.

all I know is we will be destroyed.
I see as a blind man
the hand of the lord whose name I don't
    remember,
the delicate fingers twisted and clumsy.
30 And something else, that has nothing to do
with this. I remember something
like that—
no, no it was more. A thing,
it doesn't matter.
35 I don't know again where I'm going

Lord, in thy abandonment, attend me.

For thought and discussion

1 What words and phrases reveal the poet's opinion of Jonah?
2 How does the poet link his own life to Jonah's? Why do you suppose he does so?
3 In line 7, the poet says Jonah "was never able to finish his petty commission." What do you think the poet means?
4 What is the effect of lines 30-35?
5 How would you describe the poet's mood up to the last line of the poem? What are the poet's feelings in the last line?

IT SHOULD HAPPEN TO A DOG

Wolf Mankowitz

Author's Note

It Should Happen to a Dog is a serio-comic strip, which, those who know the story of Jonah will see, is faithful to the original. If the characters speak as people we know personally, it is because there is no other way for us to know characters. If Jonah is somewhat familiar in his manner of address to the Almighty—it is because one may assume that a greater intimacy exists between Prophets and their source of instruction than does for the rest of us.

In the staging of *It Should Happen to a Dog,* a coatstand is required from which the rope of the ship is hung, and upon which any practical props may also hang. The coatstand becomes the tree in the last scene, and should be placed behind Jonah's back in full view of the audience by the Angel or by a property man who may be written in at the director's discretion. A thunder-sheet will be found useful. The characters should be dressed in an anachronistic selection of garments suggestive of our own time and of biblical times, and the piece should be played at a fast tempo.

As to the message of the story—"Why should I not spare Nineveh?" This is, one hopes, how God feels about Man—unlike Man, who is less tolerant of himself.

From *Expresso Bongo, A Wolf Mankowitz Reader.* © 1961 by A.S. Barnes and Company, Inc. Reprinted by permission.

Characters

**JONAH
A MAN**

SCENE I

JONAH. Please, please, what do you want from my life? He won't leave me alone. All these years I've been running—a traveler—Jonah, the traveler, representing Top Hat; Braces For The Trousers; Fair Lady Fancy Buttons; Hold Tight Hair Grips— only good brands in the suitcase. Ask them in Tarshish, ask them in Aleppo, in Carthage even; they all know Jonah ben Amittai, regular call once a month for more than thirty years. I don't complain only I'm tired of running, that's all. Now at last I'm tired. I get this good pitch here—at last—so I shouldn't have to run with a suitcase any more. And still he nags me. All right. I heard. I'm going. What happens to me shouldn't happen to a dog.

(A man stands in his way.)

MAN. It's a nice pitch you got here.

JONAH. It's nice.

MAN. So what are you looking so down in the mouth for?

JONAH. What's the use of talking? It has to happen to me.

MAN. What happens?

JONAH. This dream.

MAN. Dream?

JONAH. I tell you, this is a most terrible dream. The voice comes like the voice of a bird. In the middle hours of the night it comes chirping, chirping, "The end of the world is at hand. The end of the world is at hand."

MAN. Could be right. It wouldn't be the first time.

JONAH. So all right then, let it be the end of the world. Is it my business? Am I to blame?

MAN. And this is *all* the voice says?

JONAH *(lying).* Certainly that's all. Isn't it enough? What else should it say?

MAN. Nothing. Only if that is all the voice says you got nothing to worry about. Look—if it *is* the end

braces: suspenders. (This play contains many British expressions.)

pitch: situation, place of business.

of the world, what can you do? On the other hand—if it isn't—you got nothing to worry about. I'll take a quarter ounce Archangel Gabriel tobacco.

JONAH *(handing him a small packet of tobacco)*. That's a good brand. I opened up the Tarshish territory for Archangel Gabriel.

MAN. I never smoke nothing else. *(Starts to go out)*

JONAH. Ay, ay.

MAN. Oh. *(Giving coin)* Chirp, chirp? Chirp, chirp, heh, heh. *(As he goes)*

JONAH. I hate birds. You know what it says? "Arise, Jonah, arise. Go to Nineveh, that great city, and cry against it." I ask you. Why pick on me? Why sort me out? Chirp, chirp. It's in my head the whole time. Once I could sleep fifteen hours— like a short course of death. No more. I don't sleep that good no more. I hate birds. *(To God)* All right, I'm going—to the docks—for a ship—I'm going. *(He walks into the next area and set-up.)*

SCENE II

(The same man as before, as a sailor, is untying a rope from a capstan as JONAH enters.)

JONAH *(to God)*. Certainly I'm on my way. By ship. You expect me to fly? If you are so clever and in such a hurry, make me sprout a couple of wings so I'll take off. It's quicker by air. But so far is only invented the ship. *(To the SAILOR)* Which way you going, shipmate?

SAILOR. Tarshish.

JONAH. You don't say. I got a lot of friends there. It's a beautiful place. In Tarshish they got more people over a hundred years old than anywhere else.

SAILOR. Who wants to live so long?

JONAH. In some circumstances, chirp, chirp, who gets a chance to live so long? Tarshish, eh? *(Aside)* It seems silly, if I'm going all this way to Nineveh (where I am certainly eventually going) why don't I break my journey and look up a few old friends in Tarshish. Why not? *(To the SAILOR)* It's a crime? You can take passengers?

SAILOR. First class or tourist?

JONAH. In the old days when I was traveling for

myself, nothing but first class for J. B. Amittai. But in these circumstances, one tourist.

SAILOR. Single or return?

JONAH. What's the matter with you? Return, of course. I got a wonderful little business waiting for me when I come back.

SAILOR *(shouts).* One more tourist coming up. Tarshish return.

JONAH *(aside, as he begins to board ship).* I'll spend a couple of days there to build my strength up and then I'll give such a shout against Nineveh. After all, it's a tough territory, and what difference can a couple of days make? Thank you. *(Sits)* Oh, it's a beautiful day for sailing. Any more for the *Skylark?*

(Black out)

SCENE III

(JONAH asleep on some bales of goods. The SAILOR wakes him.)

JONAH. Chirp, chirp. The end of the world is at hand. *(He wakes up.)*

SAILOR. If it isn't troubling you.

JONAH. The weather's come over black all of a sudden.

SAILOR. In all my years I never knew a storm this time of the year.

JONAH. Are we far from Tarshish?

barmy: mad, crazy.

SAILOR. Are you barmy? We been stuck out here the past five hours, and all the wind does is try to blow us back. In all my years I never see anything like it.

JONAH. Very interesting phenomena. Like St. Ermin's fire; caused by electricity in the atmosphere, you understand? And take the sea serpent, for example.

St. Ermin's fire: Jonah means *St. Elmo's fire,* a glowing light sometimes seen during storms at sea.

SAILOR. I will.

JONAH. The sea serpent is really a very big eel. Science proves it.

SAILOR. I don't take any chances. After I tried every trick I know, I pray. *(He prays for a few moments. Then he looks at JONAH.)* You too, guv'ner.

JONAH. I already said my prayers today. To duplicate is just silly. When it comes to the evening I'll say my evening prayers.

SAILOR. Don't take no chances. Pray now.

JONAH. It should happen to a dog what happens to me. Listen, God. Stop messing me about. Didn't I give you my word of honor I will go to Nineveh? Ask anybody anywhere in these territories. Jonah's word is his bond. *(A gale begins to blow.)* Do me a favor just this once. I will catch the first boat from Tarshish to Nineveh. The very first boat. *(The gale blows stronger.)*

SAILOR. Did you make a sacrifice yet? We got all the passengers making sacrifices to all the different gods. That way we must hit the right god sooner or later and he'll stop the storm. Guv'ner, did you make a sacrifice yet?

JONAH. Here. I sacrifice this beautiful meat pie. I only ate a small portion of it.

SAILOR. Right. Throw it overboard with an appropriate prayer.

JONAH. Here, God. And remember I'm catching the first boat from Tarshish. All right? *(He throws the pie overboard. The pie is thrown straight back, and* **JONAH** *catches it. The* **SAILOR** *looks at him significantly, then calls out.)*

SAILOR. Aye, aye. This is it folks.

JONAH. It's a perfectly natural phenomena.

SAILOR. This man is the troublemaker.

JONAH. It's got a perfectly natural explanation.

SAILOR. His sacrifice was definitely refused. He's the one. Overboard with him—overboard. *(He advances on* **JONAH***.)*

JONAH. You can't do this to me. I am on very important business. I can drown in there. What happens to me should happen to a dog. *(He backs away from the influence of the* **SAILOR** *till he falls overboard and the gale stops and the sun comes out.)*

SAILOR. I never did like the look of that fella. To me, he always looked a troublemaker. Uh? What? *(He follows the progress of* **JONAH** *in the water.)* You could live a thousand years, you wouldn't see a man swallowed by a whale. But who would believe such a story.

(Black out)

SCENE IV

*(***JONAH** *gropes in the dark, then strikes a match.)*

JONAH. Faugh—it smells like Billingsgate in here. All right. Now what am I supposed to do. Now I can't go to Nineveh. All I wanted to do was to go to Nineveh and cry against it, and look at me. Maybe I'm dead. I must be dead. Who would have thought that being dead was a blackout in a fish shop? Maybe *this is* the end of the world. But if it isn't, if, for example, don't laugh, I happen to have been swallowed by a whale, tee-hee, I categorically put it on record that if I could go to Nineveh at this moment I would definitely and unconditionally go to Nineveh at this moment. *(A crash of thunder; lightning.* JONAH *executes a double somersault into the light. Looks round, amazed)* Honestly, God, sometimes I can't make you out. You've got such a mysterious way of carrying on. *(He stretches himself.)* So where's Tarshish? Tarshish. *(Disgusted)* If I'm not dead and if I'm not mistaken and if my memory serves me right that great city in the distance is— Nineveh. It should happen to a dog. *(Exit, towards Nineveh)*

SCENE V

KING *(enters, sits, sorts papers, looks up).* Jonah B. Amittai.

JONAH. Yes, Your Majesty.

KING. You are up on a charge of vagrancy.

JONAH. Uh?

KING. Vagrancy.

JONAH. Oh.

KING. Also it seems you have been talking a lot of seditious nonsense about the end of the world is at hand. Also—what's this? Also you keep saying "chirp, chirp." This official work is beginning to get me down. All night long I get the most terrible dreams. Mmm—what have you got to say for yourself?

JONAH. Just a minute. *(He mounts the throne and sings.)* The Lord saith: Cry out against Nineveh, that great city, for their wickedness is come up before me. Stop. Yet forty days and Nineveh shall be overthrown. Stop. The end of the world is at hand. Stop. Repent lest ye perish. End of message. And that, Your Majesty, in short, is what I am instructed to tell you. *(Sits)* Personally it makes

Billingsgate: formerly, a fish market in London.

vagrancy: wandering about without ability to earn a living.

seditious: stirring up discontent or rebellion.

no difference to me. I should be just as pleased for Nineveh not to be destroyed. For my part it can go on being as wicked as you like, though, if you was to ask my opinion, as a businessman of some experience, I'll tell you straight out that honesty is always the best policy. A satisfied client is better than government consols. Especially as, I am instructed to tell you, the government is not going to last too long, anyway.

consols: bonds, securities (British).

KING. What's the source of your information?

JONAH. A little bird tells me every night.

KING *(alarmed).* A bird?

JONAH. A little bird. Chirp, chirp. It makes just like that.

KING. What color the feathers?

JONAH. The feathers! One wing is blue, the other wing white, the breast red, the tail purple, but the funny thing is, this bird has one brown eye and——

KING.—and the other a blue!

JONAH. You are familiar with it?

KING. I have been getting the same dream.

JONAH. Oh. So *your* little bird tells *me* one hundred times nightly to come to Nineveh and inform *you* that in forty days from now *you* are completely in liquidation. And that's what *I'm* telling *you?* It's a madhouse here!

you . . . liquidation: i.e., your business will be ended; you will be dead.

KING *(stands up and tears his robe).* Let neither man nor beast, herd nor flock, taste anything. Let them not eat food nor drink water; but let man and beast be covered with sackcloth and cry mightily unto God. Yea, let them turn every one from his evil way, and from the violence that is in their hands. Let them turn from the violence that is in their hands for the sake of the smallest bird, for the bird also is God. *(To* **JONAH***)* Who can tell if God will turn and repent, and turn away from his fierce anger, that we perish not?

JONAH. Who can tell? But if you ask my opinion, I don't think so. Otherwise he doesn't go to all this trouble. No, king, this is the end. Still, you can always try. There's no charge for trying.

(Exeunt)

SCENE VI

(**JONAH** *is sitting on a rock in the scorching sun. In*

the background a celebratory fairground noise, like a Bank Holiday Monday.)

JONAH. It should happen to a dog, what happens to me. Here after all this the King himself takes my personal word that in forty days it is the end of the world; and what happens? The forty-first day is proclaimed a national holiday. Government stock rises, and I am the biggest bloody fool in the Middle East. I am a laughingstock, that's all, a laughingstock. I don't move. I'm going to sit here until I get a sunstroke. You can do what you like with Nineveh, Miniver, Shminever. I'm finished. "Yet forty days and Nineveh shall be overthrown." *(Laughter off and voices singing: "Jonah, Jonah— He pulled a boner.")* Listen to 'em. Laugh your heads off! Three-four hours I won't hear you anymore. And I won't hear that damned bird either no more. I hate birds. *(A shadow is thrown over* **JONAH.***)* What's this? By my life. A tree! *(A palm tree has sprung up from nowhere. He reaches down a coconut.)* What do you know? Coconuts as well with a patent zipper. You just pull it open and drink the milk. Ice cold. Delicious. And what's this. The *Tarshish Gazette.* Well, this is certainly a novelty. *(Reads)* Aha. I see that Mrs. Zinkin has been presented with her third daughter. That's bad. Young Fyvel is opening a café espresso bar on the High Street. That's a good position. He should do well. It's just like a summer holiday here now, and believe me, I earned a vacation. This is certainly a wonderful place you made here, Lord. I got to hand it to you. For land development you're the tops.

(Standing beside him is the **MAN** *dressed as an angel.* **JONAH** *sees him and looks away, back to his paper.)*

ANGEL. A beautiful day.

JONAH. Yes, it's certainly marvelous weather we're having.

ANGEL. That's a remarkable palm tree. *(He reaches out for a coconut.)* This I never saw before.

JONAH. It's got a zipper.

ANGEL. What will He think of next, eh?

(He offers the coconut to the irritable **JONAH.***)*

JONAH *(throwing down the newspaper).* All right. Cut out the performance. You are an angel, right?

ANGEL. I must give you credit, Jonah. You're certainly quick off the mark.

JONAH. But an angel?

ANGEL. Archangel.

JONAH. Oh—so now what do I have to do? Go back to Nineveh? Tell the King the Lord has changed his mind again? He is going to give him ten more days and then bring the world to an end? He made a laughingstock of me.

ANGEL. What can you do?

JONAH. Admitted. But at the same time this is a terrible way to treat someone who goes through all the trouble I go through. For what—only He knows. And He won't tell. *(Turns, bangs into tree.)* Feh! Fancy trees yet!

ANGEL *(wheedling).* That's certainly a *wonderful* tree. Help yourself.

JONAH. Perhaps just another coconut. These coconuts are delicious. *(As he turns the tree withers, collapsing into dust; that is, the coatstand is removed.)* What a terrible thing to happen. Such a wonderful tree. With such trees mankind could live in plenty for ever. A quick death from some palm tree disease, I suppose?

ANGEL. It's a small worm crawls through the arterial system of the tree, cuts off the life from the heart. And boom.

JONAH. A quick death to that worm.

ANGEL. Ah. You notice something. How annoyed you are with this worm which after all only killed a tree, which after all didn't cause you an hour's work. After all, you don't hear God complain; He made the tree to come up in a night. He can make it go down the night after.

JONAH. It cranks me such a beautiful tree should die like that, apart from now I am in the sun again and can catch a sunstroke any minute. Pity about the tree. Hey-hey. This is some kind of parable, ain't it? You are trying to teach me something, isn't it?

cranks: upsets.

ANGEL. That's my boy. By this little experiment He is saying, if you feel sorry for the tree, which after all didn't cost you anything, why shouldn't He feel sorry for Nineveh, that great city, in which there are one hundred and twenty thousand human beings on whom after all He has taken a great deal of trouble even if they still don't know what time it is, or their left hand from the right hand. Also much cattle.

JONAH. You got a point there, there was never any harm in those cattle. But if you don't mind a question——

ANGEL. Any help I can give you.

JONAH. If God knew right from the start exactly what He is going to do about everything—right?

ANGEL. That's right.

JONAH. Then He knows He isn't going to destroy Nineveh. Right?

ANGEL. Right!

JONAH. Then what does He want of my life? What's the point of all this expensive business with whales and palm trees and so on?

ANGEL. You mankind, you can't see no further than your nose.

JONAH. So what's the answer?

ANGEL. You see—*(long pause)* frankly, I don't know.

JONAH. It should happen to a dog.

ANGEL. Me too. After all, it's no joke following you or any other prophet I happen to get assigned to around the whole time. You think it's such a wonderful thing to be an angel and do a few conjuring tricks? It *should* happen to a dog.

JONAH. On the other hand, come to think of it, whose dogs are we?

ANGEL. We are the dogs of God.

JONAH. So——

ANGEL. Nu?

JONAH. Whatever happens to a dog——

ANGEL. —must happen to us, eh? *(He chuckles with admiration.)*

JONAH. Can you give me a lift back home?

ANGEL. It's a pleasure. (**JONAH** *jumps on* **ANGEL***'s back.)*

JONAH. On the way we could call in at Tarshish. I got a lot of friends there.

ANGEL. That's a good idea. So have I. *(As they go out)* Did you hear that young Fyvel opened a café espresso bar on the High Street?

JONAH. I read it in the paper. He's a clever boy.

(Curtain)

For close reading

1 What happens to the sacrifice which Jonah throws overboard during the storm?
2 List at least three details or incidents in the play which are not in the Bible story of Jonah.
3 In this play, why is Jonah angry when Nineveh is spared?

For thought and discussion

4 In this account, Jonah is a salesman as well as a prophet. What might these two roles have in common?
5 Suppose this play was staged as "realistically" as possible—with detailed scenery and special effects—instead of with a coatstand and a rope. How do you think the play would be affected?
6 Why do you think the author adds the detail about the king's dream? Why do you suppose he used an angel, rather than God's voice, in Scene VI?
7 The Bible story ends with God's question. What important question does Jonah ask in the final scene of the play? How is this question answered?
8 In his introduction the author says his play is "faithful to the original." Do you agree? Why or why not? He also calls the play a "serio-comic strip." Which moments of the play seem most comic to you? Most serious?

7

varieties
of
biblical
poetry

The Lord is my shepherd, I shall not want;
he makes me lie down in green pastures.
He leads me beside still waters;
he restores my soul.
He leads me in paths of righteousness
for his name's sake.

restores: renews.
righteousness: virtue, goodness.

Even though I walk through the valley of the shadow
of death,
I fear no evil;
for thou art with me;
thy rod and thy staff,
they comfort me.
Thou preparest a table before me
in the presence of my enemies;
thou anointest my head with oil,
my cup overflows.

anointest . . . oil: a sign of God's blessing.

Surely goodness and mercy shall follow me
all the days of my life;
and I shall dwell in the house of the Lord
for ever.

Psalm 23

For thought and discussion

1 What images suggest safety, comfort, and trust?
Which image do you think is most effective?
2 How can a rod and staff "comfort"?
3 Sum up each of the three stanzas in a sentence.
What different emphasis does each stanza have?

LEFT: Terra cotta plaque of seated harpist from Ischali, Iraq. Old Babylonian Period. Courtesy of the Oriental Institute, University of Chicago.

A SONG OF ZION

[*Zion is the hill in Jerusalem on which the temple was built; it is often used poetically to refer to all Jerusalem, "the city of God."*]

refuge: i.e., protector.

Ｇod is our refuge and strength,
　a very present help in trouble.
Therefore we will not fear though the earth should change,
　though the mountains shake in the heart of the sea;
though its waters roar and foam,
　though the mountains tremble with its tumult.

There is a river whose streams make glad the city of God,
　the holy habitation of the Most High.
God is in the midst of her, she shall not be moved;
　God will help her right early.
totter: shake, as if about to fall.
The nations rage, the kingdoms totter;
　he utters his voice, the earth melts.
The Lord of hosts is with us;
　the God of Jacob is our refuge.

Come, behold the works of the Lord,
  how he has wrought desolations in the earth.
He makes wars cease to the end of the earth;
  he breaks the bow, and shatters the spear,
  he burns the chariots with fire!
"Be still, and know that I am God.
  I am exalted among the nations,
  I am exalted in the earth!"
The Lord of hosts is with us;
  the God of Jacob is our refuge.

Psalm 46

wrought desolation: made deserts or ruined places.

exalted: glorified, honored.

For thought and discussion

1 In the second stanza, who or what does "her" refer to?

2 "The nations rage, the kingdoms totter;/he utters his voice, the earth melts." What makes this passage particularly vivid?

3 Both Psalm 23 and Psalm 46 describe God. What other similarities can you find between the two? What differences? Read the two psalms aloud. What other similarities and differences do you notice?

4 Often in Hebrew poetry, one line will be followed by another that is very similar in rhythm and meaning. For example: "The Lord of hosts is with us;/the God of Jacob is our refuge." What other examples can you find in Psalms 23 and 46? What are some of the effects of this technique?

I
THANK
YOU
GOD

E. E. Cummings

i thank You God for most this amazing
day:for the leaping greenly spirits of trees
and a blue true dream of sky;and for everything
which is natural which is infinite which is yes

5 (i who have died am alive again today,
and this is the sun's birthday;this is the birth
day of life and of love and wings:and of the gay

illimitably: infinitely.

great happening illimitably earth)

how should tasting touching hearing seeing
10 breathing any—lifted from the no
of all nothing—human merely being
doubt unimaginable You?

(now the ears of my ears awake and
now the eyes of my eyes are opened)

For thought and discussion

1 Why is the speaker grateful to God? What do you
think is meant by "i who have died"?
2 What special meanings does the speaker give to
the words "yes" and "no"?
3 Cummings is known for the unusual punctuation
and phrasing of his poems. How does the style of "i
thank You God" help express the speaker's emotions?

SONGS
OF
LAMENT

[These poems refer to a time of exile. Jerusalem has been conquered by the Babylonians and many people of Judah have been taken away as captives. This period of exile will be explored further in Chapter 9.]

How lonely sits the city
   that was full of people!
How like a widow has she become,
   she that was great among the nations!
She that was a princess among the cities
   has become a vassal.

vassal: servant.

She weeps bitterly in the night,
   tears on her cheeks;
among all her lovers
   she has none to comfort her;
all her friends have dealt treacherously with her,
   they have become her enemies.

treacherously: disloyally.

Judah has gone into exile because of affliction
   and hard servitude;
she dwells now among the nations,
   but finds no resting place;
her pursuers have all overtaken her
   in the midst of her distress.

affliction . . . servitude: misery and slavery.

The roads to Zion mourn,
   for none come to the appointed feasts;
all her gates are desolate,
   her priests groan;
her maidens have been dragged away,
   and she herself suffers bitterly. . . .

Lamentations 1:1–4

Ｈow the Lord in his anger
　　has set the daughter of Zion under a cloud!
He has cast down from heaven to earth
　　the splendor of Israel;
he has not remembered his footstool
　　in the day of his anger.

footstool: a metaphor for Jerusalem as the earthly extension of God's throne.

The Lord has destroyed without mercy
　　all the habitations of Jacob;
in his wrath he has broken down
　　the strongholds of the daughter of Judah;
he has brought down to the ground in dishonor
　　the kingdom and its rulers.

He has cut down in fierce anger
　　all the might of Israel;
he has withdrawn from them his right hand
　　in the face of the enemy;
he has burned like a flaming fire in Jacob,
　　consuming all around.
He has bent his bow like an enemy,
　　with his right hand set like a foe;
and he has slain all the pride of our eyes
　　in the tent of the daughter of Zion;
he has poured out his fury like fire. . . .

Lamentations 2:1–4

Ｂut thou, O Lord, dost reign for ever;
　　thy throne endures to all generations.
Why dost thou forget us for ever,
　　why dost thou so long forsake us?
Restore us to thyself, O Lord, that we may be
　　　restored!
　　Renew our days as of old!
Or hast thou utterly rejected us?
　　Art thou exceedingly angry with us?

Lamentations 5:19–22

By the waters of Babylon, there we sat down and
    wept,
  when we remembered Zion.
On the willows there
  we hung up our lyres.
For there our captors
  required of us songs,
and our tormentors, mirth, saying,
  "Sing us one of the songs of Zion!"
How shall we sing the Lord's song
  in a foreign land?

If I forget you, O Jerusalem,
  let my right hand wither!
Let my tongue cleave to the roof of my mouth,
  if I do not remember you,
if I do not set Jerusalem
  above my highest joy! . . .

Psalm 137:1–6

lyres: harplike musical
instruments.

cleave: stick.

For thought and discussion

1 These songs use many words that have sad meanings or connotations. For example, the first song has
"lonely" and "widow" in the opening three lines.
What other words and phrases have a similar effect?
2 How is God portrayed in Lam. 2:1-4? How is this
description different from the descriptions of God
given in Psalms 23 and 46?
3 What feelings are expressed about Zion/Jerusalem
in these poems?
4 Which of these poems do you think is most
effective? Why?

A
SONG
OF
COMFORT

Comfort, comfort my people,
   says your God.
Speak tenderly to Jerusalem,
   and cry to her
that her warfare is ended,

   that her iniquity is pardoned,
that she has received from the Lord's hand
   double for all her sins.

A voice cries:
"In the wilderness prepare the way of the Lord,
   make straight in the desert a highway for our
     God.
Every valley shall be lifted up,
   and every mountain and hill be made low;
the uneven ground shall become level,
   and the rough places a plain.
And the glory of the Lord shall be revealed,
   and all flesh shall see it together,
   for the mouth of the Lord has spoken."

A voice says, "Cry!"
   And I said, "What shall I cry?"
All flesh is grass,
   and all its beauty is like the flower of the field.
The grass withers, the flower fades,
   when the breath of the Lord blows upon it;
   surely the people is grass.
The grass withers, the flower fades;
   but the word of our God will stand for ever.

Get you up to a high mountain,
   O Zion, herald of good tidings;
lift up your voice with strength,

   O Jerusalem, herald of good tidings,
   lift it up, fear not;
say to the cities of Judah,

"Behold your God!"
Behold, the Lord God comes with might,
    and his arm rules for him;
behold, his reward is with him,
    and his recompense before him.
He will feed his flock like a shepherd,
    he will gather the lambs in his arms,
he will carry them in his bosom,
    and gently lead those that are with young. . . .

Why do you say, O Jacob,
    and speak, O Israel,
"My way is hid from the Lord,
    and my right is disregarded by my God"?
Have you not known? Have you not heard?
The Lord is the everlasting God,
    the Creator of the ends of the earth.
He does not faint or grow weary,
    his understanding is unsearchable.
He gives power to the faint,
    and to him who has no might he increases
        strength.
Even youths shall faint and be weary,
    and young men shall fall exhausted;
but they who wait for the Lord shall renew their
        strength,
    they shall mount up with wings like eagles,
they shall run and not be weary,
    they shall walk and not faint.

Isaiah 40:1–11, 27–31

recompense: i.e.,
justice, fairness.

unsearchable: cannot
be discovered;
mysterious.

For thought and discussion

1 What are the "good tidings" of this song?
2 As in Psalm 23, God is described in this passage as

a "shepherd." Why do you suppose this image is used?

3 Explain the meaning of "All flesh is grass."

4 One technique of Hebrew poetry is to use similar language and meaning in two or more lines; another technique is to *contrast* two or more lines. For example: "The grass withers, the flower fades;/but the word of our God will stand for ever." What other examples of this use of contrast can you find in this poem and other biblical poetry you have read? What are some of the effects of this pattern?

Activities

1 Create your own title for each of the biblical poems.

2 Make a poster or a banner (using scraps of cloth) which illustrates a phrase from one of these poems.

3 Psalms and other Hebrew poetry are the source of many later religious songs and hymns—and some popular music as well. You may wish to listen to recordings of religious music based on biblical poetry (for example, the "Song of Comfort," Isaiah 40, is part of the text of Handel's oratorio *The Messiah*). You might also obtain one or more hymnals to see how many hymns are based on biblical poetry.

4 Set one or more of these poems to music (adapting a tune or composing your own) and perform it for the class.

PROVERBS

1

Three things are too wonderful for me;
four I do not understand:
the way of an eagle in the sky,
the way of a serpent on a rock,
the way of a ship on the high seas,
and the way of a man with a maiden.

2

The words of a whisperer are like delicious
  morsels;
they go down into the inner parts of the body.

morsels: small bits of food.

3

He who sings songs to a heavy heart
is like one who takes off a garment on a cold day,
and like vinegar on a wound.

4

Better is a neighbor who is near
than a brother who is far away.

Proverbs (1) 30:18–19; (2) 18:8; (3) 25:20; (4) 27:10; (5) 27:7; (6) 6:6–11; (7) 11:16; (8) 23:4–5; (9) 22:2; (10) 30:33; (11) 26:27; (12) 10:9; (13) 21:13; (14) 23:29–35; (15) 14:13; (16) 14:10; (17) 27:19; (18) 21:2 (RSV).

5

sated: fully satisfied.

He who is sated loathes honey,
but to one who is hungry everything bitter is sweet.

6

sluggard: lazy person.

Go to the ant, O sluggard;
consider her ways, and be wise.
Without having any chief,
officer or ruler,
she prepares her food in summer,

sustenance: food,
provisions.

and gathers her sustenance in harvest.
How long will you lie there, O sluggard?
When will you arise from your sleep?
A little sleep, a little slumber,
a little folding of the hands to rest,

vagabond: tramp.

and poverty will come upon you like a vagabond,
and want like an armed man.

7

A gracious woman gets honor,
and violent men get riches.

8

Do not toil to acquire wealth;
be wise enough to desist.
When your eyes light upon it, it is gone;
for suddenly it takes to itself wings,
flying like an eagle toward heaven.

9

The rich and the poor meet together;
the Lord is the maker of them all.

10

For pressing milk produces curds,
pressing the nose produces blood,
and pressing anger produces strife.

curds: thickened part of sour milk, used to form cheese.

11

He who digs a pit will fall into it,
and a stone will come back upon him who starts it
   rolling.

12

He who walks in integrity walks securely,
but he who perverts his ways will be found out.

integrity: honesty, uprightness.
perverts: corrupts.

13

He who closes his ear to the cry of the poor
will himself cry out and not be heard.

14

Who has woe? Who has sorrow?
Who has strife? Who has complaining?
Who has wounds without cause?
Who has redness of eyes?
Those who tarry long over wine,
those who go to try mixed wine.
Do not look at wine when it is red,
when it sparkles in the cup
and goes down smoothly.
At the last it bites like a serpent,
and stings like an adder.
Your eyes will see strange things,
and your mind utter perverse things.

tarry: stay, remain.

adder: a poisonous snake.

You will be like one who lies down in the midst of
    the sea,
like one who lies on the top of a mast.
"They struck me," you will say, but I was not hurt;
they beat me, but I did not feel it.
When shall I awake?
I will seek another drink."

15

Even in laughter the heart is sad,
and the end of joy is grief.

16

The heart knows its own bitterness,
and no stranger shares its joy.

17

As in water face answers to face,
so the mind of man reflects the man.

18

Every way of a man is right in his own eyes,
but the Lord weighs the heart.

For thought and discussion

1 What seem to be the main topics or concerns of these proverbs? How would you describe the kind of "wisdom" they express?
2 Some of these proverbs are based on the similarities of two or more things (see 3). Others are based on the differences between two things (see 5). Find at least one more example of each type.
3 Which of these proverbs seem most closely related to your own experiences of life? Which proverb appealed to you most? Why?

Activities

1 Give a short talk on one of these proverbs, explaining why it interests you. Use at least one illustration from your own experience or reading.
2 Think of as many non-biblical proverbs and sayings as you can (for example: "A penny saved is a penny earned"; "A rolling stone gathers no moss"). What similarities and what differences do you find between these and the Bible proverbs? Report your findings to the class.

A
SONG
OF
LOVE

I am a rose of Sharon,
  a lily of the valleys.

As a lily among brambles,
  so is my love among maidens.

As an apple tree among the trees of the wood,
  so is my beloved among young men.
With great delight I sat in his shadow,
  and his fruit was sweet to my taste.
He brought me to the banqueting house,
  and his banner over me was love.
Sustain me with raisins,
  refresh me with apples;
  for I am sick with love.
O that his left hand were under my head,
  and that his right hand embraced me!
I adjure you, O daughters of Jerusalem,
  by the gazelles or the hinds of the field,
that you stir not up nor awaken love
  until it please.

The voice of my beloved!
  Behold, he comes,
leaping upon the mountains,
  bounding over the hills.
My beloved is like a gazelle,
  or a young stag.
Behold, there he stands
  behind our wall,
gazing in at the windows,
  looking through the lattice.

My beloved speaks and says to me:
"Arise, my love, my fair one,
   and come away;
for lo, the winter is past,
   the rain is over and gone.
The flowers appear on the earth,
   the time of singing has come,
and the voice of the turtledove
   is heard in our land.
The fig tree puts forth its figs,
   and the vines are in blossom;
   they give forth fragrance.
Arise, my love, my fair one,
   and come away.
O my dove, in the clefts of the rock,
   in the covert of the cliff,   covert: hiding place.
let me see your face,
   let me hear your voice,
for your voice is sweet,
   and your face is comely.
Catch us the foxes,
   the little foxes,
that spoil the vineyards,
   for our vineyards are in blossom."

My beloved is mine and I am his,
   he pastures his flock among the lilies.
Until the day breathes
   and the shadows flee,
turn, my beloved, be like a gazelle,
   or a young stag upon rugged mountains.

Song of Solomon 2:1–17

For thought and discussion

1 Who seems to be speaking in this poem? Who is being spoken to? In some versions, this poem is printed as a dialogue. What details suggest that two people are speaking back and forth?

2 In line 8 the speaker mentions "taste." What other physical senses are mentioned or implied in this poem? Why do you think this is done?

3 What impression or association do you receive from words like "dove" and "gazelle"? How do the references to the creatures and fruits of nature help express the emotions of the two lovers?

SHALL I COMPARE THEE TO A SUMMER'S DAY?

William Shakespeare

Shall I compare thee to a summer's day?
Thou art more lovely and more temperate:
Rough winds do shake the darling buds of May,
And summer's lease hath all too short a date:
5 Sometime too hot the eye of heaven shines,
And often is his gold complexion dimm'd;
And every fair from fair sometime declines,
By chance or nature's changing course untrimm'd;
But thy eternal summer shall not fade
10 Nor lose possession of that fair thou ow'st;
Nor shall Death brag thou wand'rest in his shade,
When in eternal lines to time thou grow'st:
   So long as men can breathe or eyes can see,
   So long lives this and this gives life to thee.

Sonnet XVIII

fair . . . declines: i.e., every beautiful thing will lose beauty.

ow'st: own.

For thought and discussion

1 In line 14, what is "this"?
2 Why does the speaker feel that the loved one's beauty will last forever?
3 Compare this poem with the biblical love song on page 248. What differences do you find in each poem's use of nature? What different feelings about the loved one are expressed?

8

why
do the
righteous
suffer?

THE STORY OF JOB

Job

There was a man in the land of Uz, whose name was Job; and that man was blameless and upright, one who feared God, and turned away from evil. There were born to him seven sons and three daughters. He had seven thousand sheep, three thousand camels, five hundred yoke of oxen, and five hundred she-asses, and very many servants; so that this man was the greatest of all the people of the east. His sons used to go and hold a feast in the house of each on his day; and they would send and invite their three sisters to eat and drink with them. And when the days of the feast had run their course, Job would send and sanctify them, and he would rise early in the morning and offer burnt offerings according to the number of them all; for Job said, "It may be that my sons have sinned, and cursed God in their hearts." Thus Job did continually.

Now there was a day when the sons of God came to present themselves before the Lord, and Satan also came among them. The Lord said to Satan, "Whence have you come?" Satan answered the Lord, "From going to and fro on the earth, and from walking up and down on it." And the Lord said to Satan, "Have you considered my servant Job, that

sanctify: bless, make holy.

sons of God: members of God's heavenly court.

Job 1:1–3:4, 20–23; 4:1–2, 4–9; 5:17–18; 6:1, 14, 21, 24 1; 7:9–12, 16–18, 20–21; 8:1–3, 8–10, 20–21; 9:1–2, 19–24, 30–33; 11:1–8; 12:1–3; 13:4–9, 12; 14:1–2, 14–22; 19:23–27; 27:1–6; 29:2, 7–10, 15–16; 31:5–6, 9, 13, 16–17, 19–20, 29, 33, 35–37; 38:1–7, 34–38; 39:19–22, 25–28; 40:2–8, 10, 12–14; 41:1–5, 31–34; 42:1–17 (RSV).
LEFT: *Oppressed Man*, sculpture of pine painted white by Leonard Baskin, 1960. Whitney Museum of American Art, New York.

there is none like him on the earth, a blameless and upright man, who fears God and turns away from evil?" Then Satan answered the Lord, "Does Job fear God for nought? Hast thou not put a hedge about him and his house and all that he has, on every side? Thou hast blessed the work of his hands, and his possessions have increased in the land. But put forth thy hand now, and touch all that he has, and he will curse thee to thy face." And the Lord said to Satan, "Behold, all that he has is in your power; only upon himself do not put forth your hand." So Satan went forth from the presence of the Lord.

Now there was a day when his sons and daughters were eating and drinking wine in their eldest brother's house; and there came a messenger to Job, and said, "The oxen were plowing and the asses feeding beside them; and the Sabeans fell upon them and took them, and slew the servants with the edge of the sword; and I alone have escaped to tell you." While he was yet speaking, there came another, and said, "The fire of God fell from heaven and burned up the sheep and the servants, and consumed them; and I alone have escaped to tell you." While he was yet speaking, there came another, and said, "The Chaldeans formed three companies, and made a raid upon the camels and took them, and slew the servants with the edge of the sword; and I alone have escaped to tell you." While he was yet speaking, there came another, and said, "Your sons and daughters were eating and drinking wine in their eldest brother's house; and behold, a great wind came across the wilderness, and struck the four corners of the house, and it fell upon the young people, and they are dead; and I alone have escaped to tell you."

Then Job arose, and rent his robe, and shaved his head, and fell upon the ground, and worshiped. And he said, "Naked I came from my mother's womb, and naked shall I return; the Lord gave, and the Lord has taken away; blessed be the name of the Lord."

In all this Job did not sin or charge God with wrong.

Again there was a day when the sons of God came to present themselves before the Lord, and Satan also came among them to present himself before the Lord. And the Lord said to Satan, "Whence have you come?" Satan answered the Lord, "From going to and fro on the earth, and from walking up and down on it." And the Lord said to Satan, "Have you considered my servant Job, that there is none like him on the earth, a blameless and upright man, who fears God and turns away from evil? He still holds fast his integrity, although you moved me against him, to destroy him without cause." Then Satan answered the Lord, "Skin for skin! All that a man has he will give for his life. But put forth thy hand now, and touch his bone and his flesh, and he will curse thee to thy face." And the Lord said to Satan, "Behold, he is in your power; only spare his life."

So Satan went forth from the presence of the Lord, and afflicted Job with loathsome sores from the sole of his foot to the crown of his head. And he took a potsherd with which to scrape himself, and sat among the ashes.

loathsome: disgusting.

potsherd: broken piece of pottery.

Then his wife said to him, "Do you still hold fast your integrity? Curse God, and die." But he said to her, "You speak as one of the foolish women would speak. Shall we receive good at the hand of God, and shall we not receive evil?" In all this Job did not sin with his lips.

Now when Job's three friends heard of all this evil that had come upon him, they came each from his own place, Eliphaz the Temanite, Bildad the Shuhite, and Zophar the Naamathite. They made an appointment together to come to condole with him and comfort him. And when they saw him from afar, they did not recognize him; and they raised their voices and wept; and they rent their robes and sprinkled dust upon their heads toward heaven. And they sat with him on the ground seven days and seven nights, and no one spoke a word to him, for they saw that his suffering was very great.

condole: sympathize.

After this Job opened his mouth and cursed the day of his birth. And Job said:

"Let the day perish wherein I was born,
    and the night which said, 'A man-child is
    conceived.'
Let that day be darkness!
    May God above not seek it, nor light shine
    upon it. . . .
Why is light given to him that is in misery,

and life to the bitter in soul,
who long for death, but it comes not,
  and dig for it more than for hid treasures;
who rejoice exceedingly,
  and are glad, when they find the grave?
Why is light given to a man whose way is hid,
  whom God has hedged in? . . . "

Then Eliphaz the Temanite answered:

"If one ventures a word with you, will you be
  offended?
Yet who can keep from speaking? . . .
Your words have upheld him who was stumbling,
  and you have made firm the feeble knees.
But now it has come to you, and you are
  impatient;
  it touches you, and you are dismayed.
Is not your fear of God your confidence,
  and the integrity of your ways your hope?
Think now, who that was innocent ever perished?
  Or where were the upright cut off?

plow iniquity: commit sins.

As I have seen, those who plow iniquity
  and sow trouble reap the same.
By the breath of God they perish,
  and by the blast of his anger they are
  consumed. . . .
Behold, happy is the man whom God re-
  proves;

chastening (chā′sən ing): disciplining.

  therefore despise not the chastening of the
  Almighty.
For he wounds, but he binds up;
  he smites, but his hands heal. . . . "

Then Job answered: . . .

"He who withholds kindness from a friend
  forsakes the fear of the Almighty. . . .
Such you have now become to me;
  you see my calamity, and are afraid. . . .
Teach me, and I will be silent;
  make me understand how I have erred.
As the cloud fades and vanishes,

Sheol: place of the dead; the underworld.

  so he who goes down to Sheol does not
  come up;

he returns no more to his house,
   nor does his place know him anymore.
Therefore I will not restrain my mouth;
   I will speak in the anguish of my spirit;
   I will complain in the bitterness of my soul.
Am I the sea, or a sea monster,
   that thou settest a guard over me?
I loathe my life; I would not live forever.
   Let me alone, for my days are a breath.
What is man, that thou dost make so much of
   him,
   and that thou dost set thy mind upon him,
dost visit him every morning,
   and test him every moment? . . .
If I sin, what do I do to thee, thou watcher of
   men?
   Why hast thou made me thy mark?   **mark:** target.
   Why have I become a burden to thee?
Why dost thou not pardon my transgression
   and take away my iniquity?
For now I shall lie in the earth;
   thou wilt seek me, but I shall not be."

Then Bildad the Shuhite answered:

   "How long will you say these things,
      and the words of your mouth be a great
         wind?
Does God pervert justice?
   Or does the Almighty pervert the right? . . .
For inquire, I pray you, of bygone ages,
   and consider what the fathers have found;
for we are but of yesterday, and know nothing,
   for our days on earth are a shadow.
Will they not teach you, and tell you,
   and utter words out of their understand-
      ing? . . .
Behold, God will not reject a blameless man,
   nor take the hand of evildoers.
He will yet fill your mouth with laughter,
   and your lips with shouting. . . . "

Then Job answered:

   "Truly I know that it is so:
   But how can a man be just before God? . . .
   If it is a contest of strength, behold him!

If it is a matter of justice, who can summon
   him?
Though I am innocent, my own mouth would
   condemn me;
  though I am blameless, he would prove me
    perverse.
I am blameless; I regard not myself;
  I loathe my life.
It is all one; therefore I say,
  he destroys both the blameless and the
   wicked.
When disaster brings sudden death,
  he mocks at the calamity of the innocent.
The earth is given into the hand of the wicked;

covers . . . judges:
makes judges blind to
justice.

  he covers the faces of its judges——
   if it is not he, who then is it? . . .
If I wash myself with snow,
  and cleanse my hands with lye,
yet thou wilt plunge me into a pit,
  and my own clothes will abhor me.
For he is not a man, as I am, that I might
   answer him,
  that we should come to trial together.
There is no umpire between us,
  who might lay his hand upon us both. . . ."

Then Zophar the Naamathite answered:

"Should a multitude of words go unanswered,

vindicated: proved
right.

  and a man full of talk be vindicated?
Should your babble silence men,
  and when you mock, shall no one shame
   you?
For you say, 'My doctrine is pure,
  and I am clean in God's eyes.'
But oh, that God would speak,
  and open his lips to you,
and that he would tell you the secrets of wisdom!

manifold: broad;
having many kinds or
forms.

  For he is manifold in understanding.
Know then that God exacts of you less than
   your guilt deserves.
Can you find out the deep things of God?
  Can you find out the limit of the Almighty?
It is higher than heaven—what can you do?
  Deeper than Sheol—what can you
   know? . . ."

Then Job answered:

"No doubt you are the people,
and wisdom will die with you.
But I have understanding as well as you;
   I am not inferior to you.
   Who does not know such things as
     these? . . .
As for you, you whitewash with lies;
   worthless physicians are you all.
Oh that you would keep silent,
   and it would be your wisdom!
Hear now my reasoning,
   and listen to the pleadings of my lips.
Will you speak falsely for God,
   and speak deceitfully for him?
Will you show partiality toward him,
   will you plead the case for God?
Will it be well with you when he searches you
     out?
   Or can you deceive him, as one deceives a
     man? . . .
Your maxims are proverbs of ashes,
   your defenses are defenses of clay. . . .

Man that is born of a woman is of few days,
     and full of trouble.
He comes forth like a flower, and withers;
   he flees like a shadow, and continues
     not. . . .
If a man die, shall he live again?
   All the days of my service I would wait,
   till my release should come.
Thou wouldest call, and I would answer thee;
   thou wouldest long for the work of thy
     hands.
For then thou wouldest number my steps,
   thou wouldest not keep watch over my sin;
my transgression would be sealed up in a bag,
   and thou wouldest cover over my iniquity.
But the mountain falls and crumbles away,
   and the rock is removed from its place;
the waters wear away the stones;
   the torrents wash away the soil of the earth;
   so thou destroyest the hope of man.
Thou prevailest for ever against him, and he
   passes;

thou prevailest: you
are successful.

countenance: the expression of his face.

thou changest his countenance, and sendest
   him away.
His sons come to honor, and he does not
   know it;
   they are brought low, and he perceives it
   not.
He feels only the pain of his own body,
   and he mourns only for himself." . . .

"Oh that my words were written!
   Oh that they were inscribed in a book!
Oh that with an iron pen and lead
   they were graven in the rock for ever!
For I know that my Redeemer lives,
   and at last he will stand upon the earth,
and after my skin has been thus destroyed,
   then from my flesh I shall see God,
whom I shall see on my side,
   and my eyes shall behold, and not another.
My heart faints within me! . . ."

inscribed: written.

graven: carved.

And Job again took up his discourse, and said:

"As God lives, who has taken away my right,
   and the Almighty, who has made my soul
      bitter;
as long as my breath is in me,
   and the spirit of God is in my nostrils;
my lips will not speak falsehood,
   and my tongue will not utter deceit.
Far be it from me to say that you are right;
   till I die I will not put away my integrity
      from me.
I hold fast my righteousness, and will not let
   it go;
   my heart does not reproach me for any of
      my days. . . .

Oh, that I were as in the months of old,
   as in the days when God watched over
      me; . . .
When I went out to the gate of the city,
   when I prepared my seat in the square,
the young men saw me and withdrew,
   and the aged rose and stood;
the princes refrained from talking,

refrained: held back.

and laid their hand on their mouth;
the voice of the nobles was hushed,
    and their tongue cleaved to the roof of their
        mouth. . . .
I was eyes to the blind,
    and feet to the lame.
I was a father to the poor,
    and I searched out the cause of him whom I
        did not know. . . .
If I have walked with falsehood,
    and my foot has hastened to deceit;
(Let me be weighed in a just balance,
    and let God know my integrity!) . . .
If my heart has been enticed to a woman,
    and I have lain in wait at my neighbor's
        door . . .
If I have rejected the cause of my manservant
    or my maidservant,
    when they brought a complaint against
        me . . .
If I have withheld anything that the poor de-
    sired,
    or have caused the eyes of the widow to
        fail,
or have eaten my morsel alone,
    and the fatherless has not eaten of it . . .
if I have seen any one perish for lack of cloth-
    ing,
    or a poor man without covering;
if his loins have not blessed me,
    and if he was not warmed with the fleece of
        my sheep . . .
If I have rejoiced at the ruin of him that hated
    me,
    or exulted when evil overtook him . . .   **exulted:** greatly
if I have concealed my transgressions from   rejoiced.
    men,
    by hiding my iniquity in my bosom . . .
Oh, that I had one to hear me!
    (Here is my signature! let the Almighty an-
        swer me!)
    Oh, that I had the indictment written by my   **indictment:** list of
        adversary!   accusations.
Surely I would carry it on my shoulder;   **adversary:** opponent,
    I would bind it on me as a crown;   enemy.
I would give him an account of all my steps;
    like a prince I would approach him. . . ."

Then the Lord answered Job out of the whirlwind:

"Who is this that darkens counsel by
    words without knowledge?
Gird up your loins like a man,
    I will question you, and you shall declare to
    me.
Where were you when I laid the foundation of
    the earth?
    Tell me, if you have understanding.
Who determined its measurements—surely
    you know!
    Or who stretched the line upon it?
On what were its bases sunk,
    or who laid its cornerstone,
when the morning stars sang together,
    and all the sons of God shouted for joy? . . .
Can you lift up your voice to the clouds,
    that a flood of waters may cover you?
Can you send forth lightnings, that they may
    go
    and say to you, 'Here we are'?
Who has put wisdom in the clouds,
    or given understanding to the mists?
Who can number the clouds by wisdom?
    Or who can tilt the waterskins of the heav-
    ens,
when the dust runs into a mass
    and the clods cleave fast together? . . .

Do you give the horse his might?
    Do you clothe his neck with strength?
Do you make him leap like the locust?
    His majestic snorting is terrible.
He paws in the valley, and exults in his
    strength;
    he goes out to meet the weapons.
He laughs at fear, and is not dismayed;
    he does not turn back from the sword. . . .
When the trumpet sounds, he says 'Aha!'
    He smells the battle from afar,
    the thunder of the captains, and the shout-
    ing.
Is it by your wisdom that the hawk soars,
    and spreads his wings toward the south?
Is it at your command that the eagle mounts
    up
    and makes his nest on high?

On the rock he dwells and makes his
    home in the fastness of the rocky crag. . . .
Shall a faultfinder contend with the Almighty?
    He who argues with God, let him answer it."

fastness: stronghold; safe place.

Then Job answered the Lord:

"Behold, I am of small account; what shall I
    answer thee?
I lay my hand on my mouth.
I have spoken once, and I will not answer;
    twice, but I will proceed no further."

Then the Lord answered Job out of the whirlwind:

"Gird up your loins like a man;
    I will question you, and you declare to me.
Will you even put me in the wrong?
    Will you condemn me that you may be
        justified? . . .
Deck yourself with majesty and dignity;
    clothe yourself with glory and splendor. . . .
Look on every one that is proud, and bring
        him low;
    and tread down the wicked where they
        stand.
Hide them all in the dust together;
    bind their faces in the world below.
Then will I also acknowledge to you,
    that your own right hand can give you
        victory. . . .
Can you draw out Leviathan with a fishhook,
    or press down his tongue with a cord?
Can you put a rope in his nose,
    or pierce his jaw with a hook?
Will he make many supplications to you?
    Will he speak to you soft words?
Will he make a covenant with you
    to take him for your servant for ever?
Will you play with him as with a bird,
    or will you put him on leash for your
        maidens? . . .
He makes the deep boil like a pot;
    he makes the sea like a pot of ointment.
Behind him he leaves a shining wake;
    one would think the deep to be hoary.
Upon earth there is not his like,

Leviathan (lə vī′ə thən): a sea monster representing disorder and evil.

supplications: pleading requests.

covenant: agreement.

the deep: the ocean.

hoary: white.

a creature without fear.
He beholds everything that is high;
    he is king over all the sons of pride."

Then Job answered the Lord:

"I know that thou canst do all things,
    and that no purpose of thine can be
    thwarted.
'Who is this that hides counsel without knowl-
    edge?'
Therefore I have uttered what I did not under-
    stand,
    things too wonderful for me, which I did
    not know.
'Hear, and I will speak;
    I will question you, and you declare to me.'
I had heard of thee by the hearing of the ear,
    but now my eye sees thee;
therefore I despise myself,
    and repent in dust and ashes."

After the Lord had spoken these words to Job, the
Lord said to Eliphaz the Temanite: "My wrath is
kindled against you and against your two friends; for
you have not spoken of me what is right, as my
servant Job has. Now therefore take seven bulls and
seven rams, and go to my servant Job, and offer up
for yourselves a burnt offering; and my servant Job
shall pray for you, for I will accept his prayer not to
deal with you according to your folly; for you have
not spoken of me what is right, as my servant Job
has." So Eliphaz the Temanite and Bildad the
Shuhite and Zophar the Naamathite went and did
what the Lord had told them; and the Lord accepted
Job's prayer.

And the Lord restored the fortunes of Job, when
he had prayed for his friends; and the Lord gave Job
twice as much as he had before. Then came to him
all his brothers and sisters and all who had known
him before, and ate bread with him in his house;
and they showed him sympathy and comforted him
for all the evil that the Lord had brought upon him;
and each of them gave him a piece of money and a
ring of gold. And the Lord blessed the latter days of
Job more than his beginning; and he had fourteen
thousand sheep, six thousand camels, a thousand

yoke of oxen, and a thousand she-asses. He had also seven sons and three daughters. And he called the name of the first Jemimah; and the name of the second Keziah; and the name of the third Keren-happuch. And in all the land there were no women so fair as Job's daughters; and their father gave them inheritance among their brothers. And after this Job lived a hundred and forty years, and saw his sons, and his sons' sons, four generations. And Job died, an old man, and full of days.

For close reading

1 What limits does God place upon Satan before each of the times Job is tested?
2 How do Eliphaz, Bildad, and Zophar respond when they first meet Job? Does their attitude change during their talks with him? If so, how?
3 Give three points or arguments made by Job's comforters.
4 How does Job's wealth at the end compare with his possessions at the beginning of the story?
5 Explain what you think Job means when he says "my days are a breath" and "I was eyes to the blind."

For thought and discussion

6 What impression do you get of Satan from his discussions with God? Who do you consider responsible for Job's suffering, Satan or God? Explain.
7 In the early sections, what effect is gained by the repetition of the phrase "While he was yet speaking"?
8 Even after his last, "loathsome" affliction, Job

refuses to curse God and seems to accept his fate: "Shall we receive good at the hand of God, and shall we not receive evil?" How do you account for the seeming change in attitude expressed in Job's very next speech?

9 In what ways does "dialogue" help explore a complex issue? In what ways does it get in the way? What would be gained or lost if Job had had only one comforter? No comforters?

10 What is your opinion of the comforters as friends? As advisers? Why do you think God criticizes these men at the end of the story?

11 What would you say is Job's tone of voice when he tells his comforters "No doubt you are the people/and wisdom will die with you"?

12 On pages 260–261 Job defends his righteousness. Do you find any flaw or flaws in this self-portrait? Explain. Why do you suppose God finally accepts Job's challenge after this speech?

13 What do you think is the purpose of God's questions to Job? In what tone of voice do you think God asks these questions?

14 Do you think Job repents: *(a)* because he has been overwhelmed by a full understanding of God's power; *(b)* because his questions have been answered; *(c)* because he has had a first-hand experience of God; *(d)* because he is convinced, after all, that he deserved the suffering he received? Can you suggest any other possible reasons for Job's repentance?

15 Select a passage from the story of Job that you find particularly powerful or moving. What features of language—rhythm, imagery, etc.—make the passage effective? Do you respond more to the content and meaning or to the style of language? Explain.

Activities

1 Write a conversation between Job and his wife about his troubles. If possible, act out this scene before the class.

2 Without using a dictionary, arrange these words in the order of the intensity of feeling in them: suffering, affliction, torment, misery, grief, distress, anxiety, agony, anguish.

3 Suppose that a close friend of yours is going through a period of suffering. Write a letter of comfort to this friend, referring as much as possible to the story of Job.

4 Give a dramatic reading before the class of God's speech from the whirlwind, or some other excerpt of your choice.

5 Collect and record passages of music that express the mood or feeling of various parts of the story of Job. For example, what kind of music would you use to suggest the peace and prosperity that Job enjoys at the beginning? What music would you use to suggest the catastrophes? The dialogues with the comforters? God's speeches? Job's recovery? If possible, tape record your sequence of music to make a "tone poem" of the story of Job.

from
A MASQUE OF REASON

Robert Frost

*[In this passage from a dramatic
poem, God is speaking to Job.]*

Yes, by and by. But first a larger matter.
I've had you on my mind a thousand years
To thank you someday for the way you helped me
Establish once for all the principle
5 There's no connection man can reason out
Between his just deserts and what he gets.
Virtue may fail and wickedness succeed.
'Twas a great demonstration we put on.
I should have spoken sooner had I found
10 The word I wanted. You would have supposed
One who in the beginning *was* the Word
Would be in a position to command it.
I have to wait for words like anyone.
Too long I've owed you this apology
15 For the apparently unmeaning sorrow
You were afflicted with in those old days.
But it was of the essence of the trial
You shouldn't understand it at the time.
It had to seem unmeaning to have meaning.
20 And it came out all right. I have no doubt
You realize by now the part you played
To stultify the Deuteronomist
And change the tenor of religious thought.
My thanks are to you for releasing me
25 From moral bondage to the human race.
The only free will there at first was man's,

just deserts (di
zėrts′): deserved
reward or punishment.

**stultify . . . Deuteron-
omist:** i.e., frustrate
the lawmaker.
Deuteronomy is a book
of the Bible which
stresses that breaking
the law will bring God's
judgment, while
obedience will bring
blessing.

Who could do good or evil as he chose.
I had no choice but I must follow him
With forfeits and rewards he understood—
30 Unless I liked to suffer loss of worship.
I had to prosper good and punish evil.
You changed all that. You set me free to reign.
You are the Emancipator of your God,
And as such I promote you to a saint.

Emancipator: one who frees.

For thought and discussion

1 What impression do you get of God from this speech? Choose three words to describe him.
2 According to this speech, what "principle" was established by Job's ordeal (lines 4-7)?
3 How do you suppose Job responded to this explanation of his suffering?
4 If the system of reward and punishment is as unfair as this speech suggests, what reasons still exist for being good and virtuous?

THE PROLOGUE IN HEAVEN

H. G. Wells

[In this passage from the novel
The Undying Fire, *God and Satan continue
their discussion about Job.]*

Now, as in the ancient story, it is a reception of the sons of God.

The Master of the gathering, to whom one might reasonably attribute a sublime boredom, seeing that everything that can possibly happen is necessarily known to him, displays on the contrary as lively an interest in his interlocutor as ever. This interlocutor is of course Satan, the Unexpected. . . .

interlocutor (in′tər lok′yə tər): participant in a conversation.

"There was a certain man in the land of Uz whose name was Job."

"We remember him."

"We had a wager of sorts," said Satan. "It was some time ago."

"The wager was never very distinct—and now that you remind me of it, there is no record of your paying."

"Did I lose or win? The issue was obscured by discussion. How those men did talk! You intervened. There was no decision."

"You lost, Satan," said a great Being of Light who bore a book. "The wager was whether Job would lose faith in God and curse him. He was afflicted in every way, and particularly by the conversation of his friends. But there remains an undying fire in man."

Satan rested his dark face on his hand, and looked down between his knees through the pellucid floor

pellucid: transparent.

to that little eddying in the ether which makes our world. "Job," he said, "lives still."

Then after an interval: "The whole earth is now— Job."

Satan delights equally in statistics and in quoting scripture. He leant back in his seat with an expression of quiet satisfaction. "Job," he said, in easy narrative tones, "lived to a great age. After his disagreeable experiences he lived one hundred and forty years. He had again seven sons and three daughters, and he saw his offspring for four generations. So much is classical. These ten children brought him seventy grandchildren, who again prospered generally and had large families. (It was a prolific strain.) And now if we allow three generations to a century, and the reality is rather more than that, and if we take the survival rate as roughly three to a family, and if we agree with your excellent Bishop Ussher that Job lived about thirty-five centuries ago, that gives us—— How many? Three to the hundred and fifth power? . . . It is at any rate a sum vastly in excess of the present population of the earth. . . . You have globes and rolls and swords and stars here; has anyone a slide rule?"

But the computation was brushed aside.

"A thousand years in my sight are but as yesterday when it is past. I will grant what you seek to prove; that Job has become mankind."

The dark regard of Satan smote down through the quivering universe and left the toiling light waves behind. "See there," he said pointing. "My old friend on his little planet—Adam—Job—Man—like a roast on a spit. It is time we had another wager."

God condescended to look with Satan at mankind, circling between day and night. "Whether he will curse or bless?"

"Whether he will even remember God."

"I have given my promise that I will at last restore Adam."

The downcast face smiled faintly.

"These questions change from age to age," said Satan.

"The Whole remains the same."

"The story grows longer in either direction," said Satan, speaking as one who thinks aloud; "past and future unfold together. . . . When the first atoms

eddying in the ether: i.e., a small whirling current in space.

prolific strain: productive race or breed.

Bishop Ussher: a 17th century churchman and scholar known for his now-disputed dating of biblical events.

regard: gaze.

jarred I was there, and so conflict was there—and progress. The days of the old story have each expanded to hundreds of millions of years now, and still I am in them all. The sharks and crawling monsters of the early seas, the first things that crept out of the water into the jungle of fronds and stems, the early reptiles, the leaping and flying dragons of the great age of life, the mighty beasts of hoof and horn that came later; they all feared and suffered and were perplexed. At last came this Man of yours, out of the woods, hairy, beetle-browed and blood-stained, peering not too hopefully for that Eden-bower of the ancient story. It wasn't there. There never had been a garden. He had fallen before he arose, and the weeds and thorns are as ancient as the flowers. The Fall goes back in time now beyond man, beyond the world, beyond imagination. The very stars were born in sin. . . .

"If we can still call it sin," mused Satan.

"On a little planet this Thing arises, this red earth, this Adam, this Edomite, this Job. He builds cities, he tills the earth, he catches the lightning and makes a slave of it, he changes the breed of beast and grain. Clever things to do, but still petty things. You say that in some manner he is to come up at last to *this*. . . . He is too foolish and too weak. His achievements only illuminate his limitations. Look at his little brain boxed up from growth in a skull of bone! Look at his bag of a body full of rags and rudiments, a haggis of diseases! His life is decay. . . . *Does* he grow? I do not see it. Has he made any perceptible step forward in quality in the last ten thousand years? He quarrels endlessly and aimlessly with himself. . . . In a little while his planet will cool and freeze."

haggis: a kind of stew or meat pudding.

"In the end he will rule over the stars," said the voice that was above Satan. "My spirit is in him."

Satan shaded his face with his hand from the effulgence about him. He said no more for a time, but sat watching mankind as a boy might sit on the bank of a stream and watch the fry of minnows in the clear water of a shallow.

effulgence (i ful′jəns): brilliant light, radiance.

"Nay," he said at last, "but it is incredible. It is impossible. I have disturbed and afflicted him long enough. I have driven him as far as he can be driven. But now I am moved to pity. Let us end this dispute. It has been interesting, but now—— Is it not enough? It grows cruel. He has reached his limit. Let us give him a little peace now, Lord, a little season of sunshine and plenty, and then some painless universal pestilence and so let him die."

"He is immortal and he does but begin."

"He is mortal and near his end. At times no doubt he has a certain air that seems to promise understanding and mastery in his world; it is but an air; give me the power to afflict and subdue him but a little, and after a few squeaks of faith and hope he will whine and collapse like any other beast. He will behave like any kindred creature with a smaller brain and a larger jaw; he too is doomed to suffer to no purpose, to struggle by instinct merely to live, to endure for a season and then to pass. . . . Give me but the power and you shall see his courage snap like a rotten string."

"You may do all that you will to him, only you must not slay him. For my spirit is in him."

"That he will cast out of his own accord—when I have ruined his hopes, mocked his sacrifices, blackened his skies and filled his veins with torture. . . . But it is too easy to do. Let me just slay him now and end his story. Then let us begin another, a different one, and something more amusing. Let us, for example, put brains—and this Soul of yours—into the ants or the bees or the beavers! Or take up the octopus, already a very tactful and intelligent creature!"

"No; but do as you have said, Satan. For you also are my instrument. Try Man to the uttermost. See if he is indeed no more than a little stir amidst the slime, a fuss in the mud that signifies nothing. . . ."

The Satan, his face hidden in shadow, seemed not to hear this, but remained still and intent upon the world of men.

For close reading

1 Describe Satan's and God's views of human nature in one sentence each.

2 According to Satan, what should God do with the human race? Why?

For thought and discussion

3 How is Satan portrayed in this passage? How does this Satan compare with the biblical Satan?

4 Why do you suppose Satan claims "there was no decision" in the "wager" about Job? Do you think he has a point? Explain.

5 What do you think God means by "Job has become mankind"?

6 This passage expresses both optimistic and pessimistic feelings about humanity. Which do you tend to agree with? Why?

Archibald MacLeish

[*J. B. is a modern Job, a millionaire who has lost his children and his fortune through war, accident, and murder. In this scene J. B. and his wife Sarah struggle to find some meaning to their tragedy.*

The setting of the entire play is a huge circus tent, where a sort of sideshow has been set up, including a six-foot-high platform, a wooden ladder, a table, and several chairs. At the beginning of the play two old actors come onstage to put on masks and play the roles of God and Satan; they observe J. B.'s experiences from the "heavenly" platform. Satan is played by Nickles; throughout this scene he speaks to God, who remains silent and unseen on the platform. The other characters in this scene are Mrs. Adams, her young daughter Jolly, Mrs. Murphy, Mrs. Lesure, and Mrs. Botticelli.]

Scene 8

(There is no light but the glow on the canvas sky, which holds the looming, leaning shadows. They fade as a match is struck. It flares in **SARAH'S** *hand, showing her face, and glimmers out against the wick of a dirty lantern. As the light of the lantern rises,* **J. B.** *is seen lying on the broken propped-up table, naked but for a few rags of clothing.* **SARAH** *looks at him in the new light,*

---

shudders, lets her head drop into her hands. There is a long silence and then a movement in the darkness of the open door where four **WOMEN** *and a young* **GIRL** *stand, their arms filled with blankets and newspapers. They come forward slowly into the light.)*

NICKLES *(unseen, his cracked, cackling voice drifting down from the darkness of the platform overhead).*
Never fails! Never fails!
Count on you to make a mess of it!
Every blessed blundering time
You hit at one man you blast thousands.

5 Think of that Flood of yours—a massacre!
Now you've fumbled it again:
Tumbled a whole city down
To blister one man's skin with agony.

*(***NICKLES'S*** white coat appears at the foot of the ladder. The* **WOMEN,** *in the circle of the lantern, are walking slowly around* **J. B.** *and* **SARAH,** *staring at them as though they were figures in a show window.)*

NICKLES. Look at your works! Those shivering women

10 Sheltering under any crumbling
Heap to keep the sky out! Weeping!

MRS. ADAMS. That's him.

JOLLY ADAMS.   Who's him?

MRS. ADAMS.   Grammar, Jolly.

15 **MRS. LESURE.** Who did she say it was?

MRS. MURPHY.   Him she said it was.
Poor soul!

MRS. LESURE. Look at them sores on him!

MRS. ADAMS. Don't look, child. You'll remember them.

20 **JOLLY ADAMS** *(proudly).* Every sore I seen I remember.

MRS. BOTTICELLI. Who did she say she said it was?

MRS. MURPHY.   Him.

MRS. ADAMS. That's his wife.

MRS. LESURE.   She's pretty.

25 **MRS. BOTTICELLI.**   Ain't she.
Looks like somebody we've seen.

MRS. ADAMS *(snooting her).* I don't believe you
would have seen her:
Pictured possibly—her picture
Posted in the penthouse.

puce (pyüs): a purplish brown.

30 **MRS. BOTICELLI.**   Puce with pants?
MRS. ADAMS. No, the negligee.
MRS. BOTICELLI.   The net?
MRS. ADAMS. The simple silk.
                        Oh la! With sequins?
35 **MRS. MURPHY.** Here's a place to park your poo-
       dle—
    Nice cool floor.
MRS. LESURE.   Shove over, dearie.
*(The **WOMEN** settle themselves on their newspa-
pers off at the edge of the circle of light. **NICKLES**
has perched himself on a chair at the side. Si-
lence.)*
J. B. *(a whisper).* God let me die!
(NICKLES *leers up into the dark toward the unseen
platform.)*
SARAH. *(her voice dead).* You think He'd help you
Even to that?
*(Silence. **Sarah** looks up, turning her face away from
J. B.
She speaks without passion, almost mechanical-
ly.)*
SARAH.   God is our enemy.
J. B. No. . . . No. . . . No. . . . Don't
Say that Sarah!
(SARAH's *head turns toward him slowly as though
dragged against her will. She stares and cannot
look away.)*
                    God had something
45   Hidden from our hearts to show.
NICKLES. She knows! She's looking at it!
J. B.   Try to
       sleep.
SARAH *(bitterly).* He should have kept it hidden.
J. B. Sleep now.
50 **SARAH.**   You don't have to see it:
    I do.
J. B.   Yes, I know.
NICKLES *(a cackle).* He knows!
    He's back behind it and he knows!
55   If he could see what she can see
    There's something else he might be knowing.
J. B. Once I knew a charm for sleeping—
    Not as forgetfulness but gift,
    Not as sleep but second sight,
60   Come and from my eyelids lift
    The dead of night.

SARAH.   The dead . . .
                                    of night . . .
(She drops her head to her knees, whispering.)
        Come and from my eyelids lift
65   The dead of night.
(Silence.)
J. B.   Out of sleep
        Something of our own comes back to us:
        A drowned man's garment from the sea.
*(**SARAH** turns the lantern down. Silence. Then the
        voices of the **WOMEN,** low.)*
MRS. BOTTICELLI. Poor thing!
70   **MRS. MURPHY:**   Poor thing!
        Not a chick not a child between them.
MRS. ADAMS. First their daughters. Then their
        sons.
MRS. MURPHY. First son first. Blew him to pieces.

mischance: bad luck.   More mischance it was than war.
75   Asleep on their feet in the frost they walked
                into it.

two . . . viaduct: two   **MRS. ADAMS.** Two at the viaduct. That makes
of J. B.'s and Sarah's   three.
children were killed in   **JOLLY ADAMS** *(a child's chant).* Jolly saw the pic-
an auto accident.   ture! The picture!
                          MRS. ADAMS. Jolly Adams, you keep quiet.
                          JOLLY ADAMS. Wanna know? The whole of the
                                viaduct. . . .
80   **MRS. ADAMS.** Never again will you look at them!
                Never!
                          MRS. LESURE. Them magazines! They're awful!
                Which?
the little one: J. B.'s   **MRS. MURPHY.** And after that the little one.
youngest daughter had   **MRS. BOTTICELLI.**   Who in the
been murdered.   World are they talking about, the little one?
85   What are they talking?
                          MRS. LESURE.   I don't know.
                Somebody dogged by death it must be.
                          MRS. BOTTICELLI. Him it must be.
                          MRS. LESURE.   Who's him?
90   **MRS. ADAMS.** You know who.
                          MRS. MURPHY.   You remember. . . .
                          MRS. ADAMS. Hush! The child!
                          MRS. MURPHY.   Back of the lumberyard.
                          MRS. LESURE. Oh! Him!
95   **MRS. MURPHY.**   Who did you think it was—
                Penthouse and negligees, daughters and dying?

MRS. BOTTICELLI. Him? That's him? The millionaire?

MRS. LESURE. Millionaires he buys like cabbages.

MRS. MURPHY. He couldn't buy cabbages now by
the look of him:

100   The rags he's got on.

MRS. BOTTICELLI.   Look at them sores!

MRS. MURPHY. All that's left him now is her.

MRS. BOTTICELLI. Still that's something—a good
woman.

MRS. MURPHY. What good is a woman to him
with that hide on him?—

105   Or he to her if you think of it.

MRS. ADAMS.   Don't!

MRS. LESURE. Can you blame her?

MRS. MURPHY.   I don't blame her.
All I say is she's no comfort.

110   She won't cuddle.

MRS. ADAMS.   Really, Mrs. . . .

MRS. MURPHY. Murphy call me. What's got into
you? . . .

                .   .   .

MRS. ADAMS. None of that! We have a child here!
(Silence.)

                .   .   .

115 **MRS. MURPHY.** Roll a little nearer, dearie,
Me backside's froze.

MRS. LESURE.   You smell of roses.

MRS. MURPHY. Neither do you but you're warm.

MRS. BOTTICELLI.   Well,

120   Good night, ladies. Good night, ladies. . . .
*(Silence. Out of the silence, felt rather than heard at
first, a sound of sobbing, a muffled, monotonous
sound like the heavy beat of a heart.)*

J. B. If you could only sleep a little
Now they're quiet, now they're still.

SARAH *(her voice broken).* I try. But oh I close my
eyes and . . .
Eyes are open there to meet me!
(Silence. Then **SARAH'S** *voice in an agony of bitterness.)*

125   My poor babies! Oh, my babies!
*(***J. B.*** pulls himself up, sits huddled on his table in
the feeble light of the lamp, his rags about him.)*

J. B. *(gently).* Go to sleep.

SARAH.   Go! Go where?

If there were darkness I'd go there.
If there were night I'd lay me down in it.
130 God has shut the night against me.
God has set the dark alight
With horror blazing blind as day
When I go toward it . . .

close my eyes.

135 **J. B.** I know. I know those waking eyes.
His will is everywhere against us—
Even in our sleep, our dreams. . . .
NICKLES *(a snort of laughter up toward the dark of
the platform). Your* will, *his* peace!
Doesn't seem to grasp that, does he?
140 Give him another needling twinge

Between the withers and the works—
He'll understand you better.
J. B. If I
Knew. . . . If I knew why!
145 **NICKLES.** If he knew
Why he wouldn't be there. He'd be
Strangling, drowning, suffocating,
Diving for a sidewalk somewhere. . . .
J. B. What I *can't* bear is the blindness—
150 Meaninglessness—the numb blow
Fallen in the stumbling night.
SARAH *(starting violently to her feet).* Has death
no meaning? Pain no meaning?
(She points at his body.)

Even these suppurating sores—
Have they no meaning for you?
155 **NICKLES.** Ah!
J. B. *(from his heart's pain).* God will not punish
without cause.
*(***NICKLES** *doubles up in spasms of soundless laugh-
ter.)*
J. B. God is just.
SARAH *(hysterically).* God is just!
If God is just our slaughtered children
160 Stank with sin, were rotten with it!
*(She controls herself with difficulty, turns toward
him, reaches her arms out, lets them fall.)*
Oh, my dear! my dear! my dear!
Does God demand deception of us?—
Purchase His innocence by ours?
Must we be guilty for Him?—bear

165 The burden of the world's malevolence
For Him who made the world?

J. B.   *He*
Knows the guilt is mine. He must know:
Has He not punished it? He knows its
170   Name, its time, its face, its circumstance,
The figure of its day, the door,
The opening of the door, the room, the mo-
        ment. . . .
SARAH *(fiercely).* And you? Do you? You do not
        know it.
Your punishment is all you know.
(She moves toward the door, stops, turns.)
175   I will not stay here if you lie—   **connive:** cooperate
Connive in your destruction, cringe to it: secretly.
Not if you betray my children . . .

I will not stay to listen. . . .

180   They are
Dead and they were innocent: I will not
Let you sacrifice their deaths
To make injustice justice and God good!
J. B. *(covering his face with his hands).* My heart
        beats. I cannot answer it.
185   **SARAH.** If you buy quiet with their innocence—
Theirs or yours . . .
(Softly.)
                                    I will not love you.
J.B. I have no choice but to be guilty.
SARAH *(her voice rising).* We have the choice to
        live or die,
190   All of us . . .
                        curse God and die. . . .
(Silence.)
J. B. God is God or we are nothing—
Mayflies that leave their husks behind—
Our tiny lives ridiculous—a suffering
195   Not even sad that Someone Somewhere
Laughs at as we laugh at apes.
We have no choice but to be guilty.
God is unthinkable if we are innocent.
*(**SARAH** turns, runs soundlessly out of the circle of
light, out of the door. The **WOMEN** stir. **MRS.
MURPHY** comes up on her elbow.)*
MRS. MURPHY. What did I say? I said she'd walk
        out on him.
200   **MRS. LESURE.** She did.
MRS. BOTTICELLI.   Did she?

MRS. MURPHY. His hide was too much for her.

MRS. BOTTICELLI. His hide or his heart.

MRS. MURPHY. The hide comes between.

205 **MRS. BOTTICELLI.** The heart is the stranger.

MRS. MURPHY. Oh, stranger!
It's always strange, the heart is: only
It's the skin we ever know.

J. B. *(raising his head).* Sarah, why do you not speak to me? Sarah!

(Silence.)

210 **MRS. ADAMS.** Now he knows.

MRS. MURPHY. And he's alone now.

*(**J. B.**'s head falls forward onto his knees. Silence.
Out of the silence his voice in an agony of prayer.)*

J. B. Show me my guilt, O God!

NICKLES. His
Guilt! His! You heard that didn't you?
215 He wants to feel the feel of guilt—
That putrid poultice of the soul
That draws the poison in, not out—
Inverted catheter! You going to show him?

*(Silence. **NICKLES** rises, moves toward the ladder.)*
Well? You going to show him . . . Jahveh?

(Silence. He crosses to the ladder's foot.)
220 Where are those cold comforters of yours
Who justify the ways of God to
Job by making Job responsible?—
Those three upholders of the world—
Defenders of the universe—where are they?

*(Silence. He starts up the ladder. Stops. The jeering
tone is gone. His voice is bitter.)*
225 Must be almost time for comfort! . . .

*(**NICKLES** vanishes into the darkness above. The
light fades.)*

poultice: a soft mass or pack applied to an injury to reduce swelling and pain.
catheter (kath′ə tər): a slender tube inserted into any cavity of the body to drain fluids.
Jahveh (yä′vä): a name of God; also *Yahweh* or *Jehovah.*

For close reading

1 Even before the first speech a grim, depressing mood is created in this scene. How is this done?
2 How many directions for silence do you find in this scene?
3 What information about J. B. and Sarah is given in the women's conversation in lines 69-120?

For thought and discussion

4 Why do you think this scene includes so many silences?
5 How would you describe the conversations of the women in lines 69-120? How are you affected by the contrast of these conversations and the dialogue of J. B. and Sarah?
6 What feelings about J. B. and Sarah are expressed by Nickles? By the women? What would be gained or lost if Nickles and the women were omitted from the scene?
7 Job's wife is only mentioned once in the Bible story. Do you think the playwright's portrayal of Sarah seems reasonable? Which character do you feel closer to, J. B. or Sarah? Why? In your opinion, who seems to be suffering more?
8 Why does J. B. insist that he must be guilty? Why does Sarah disagree so strongly?

NEW HAMPSHIRE, FEBRUARY

Richard Eberhart

Nature had made them hide in crevices,
Two wasps so cold they looked like bark.
Why I do not know, but I took them
And I put them
5 In a metal pan, both day and dark.

Like God touching his finger to Adam
I felt, and thought of Michaelangelo,
For whenever I breathed on them,
The slightest breath,
10 They leaped, and preened as if to go.

My breath controlled them always quite.
More sensitive than electric sparks
They came into life
Or they withdrew to ice,
15 While I watched, suspending remarks.

Then one in a blind career got out,
And fell to the kitchen floor. I
Crushed him with my cold ski boot,
By accident. The other
20 Had not the wit to try or die.

And so the other is still my pet.
The moral of this is plain.
But I will shirk it.
You will not like it. And
25 God does not live to explain.

Like God . . .
Michaelangelo: a
reference to a
well-known scene by
the artist Michaelangelo
on the ceiling of the
Sistine Chapel in Rome.
preened: i.e., seemed
to groom themselves.

career: rush; rapid
movement.

shirk: avoid.

For thought and discussion

1 Controlling the wasps makes the speaker feel "like God." Have you ever had such "godlike" feelings? What were the circumstances?
2 Although this poem makes no mention of Job, what connections do you find between the story of Job and this poem?
3 What do you think is the "moral" of this poem? The speaker claims "You will not like it." Is he right? Why or why not?

9

in
the midst
of the
enemy

THE
VICTORY
OF
JUDITH

Judith

[*Nebuchadnezzar* (neb/ə kəd nez/ər), *here described as king of Assyria, has sent his commander-in-chief Holofernes* (hol/ə fér/nēz) *with a huge army to attack the countries west of his kingdom. To protect Jerusalem and the temple, the Israelites decide to resist. The citizens of Bethulia, under the leadership of Uzziah, try to block Holofernes's army in the hill-country passes, but the situation seems hopeless until Judith comes forward with a plan.*

Catholic Bibles include the Book of Judith in the Old Testament; Protestant and Jewish Bibles do not. In some versions of the Bible, Judith appears in a section called "The Apocrypha."]

The next day Holofernes ordered his whole army, and all the allies who had joined him, to break camp and move against Bethulia, and to seize the passes up into the hill country and make war on the Israelites. So all their warriors moved their camp that day; their force of men of war was one hundred and seventy thousand infantry and twelve thousand cavalry, together with the baggage and the foot soldiers handling it, a very great multitude. . . .

The people of Israel cried out to the Lord their God, for their courage failed, because all their enemies had surrounded them and there was no

Judith 7:1–2, 19–20, 23–24, 26–27; 8:1a, 2–3a, 4–11, 32b–34; 10:1–6a, 9–17, 21–23; 12:10–12, 15–20; 13:1–17; 14:11–18; 15:1–3, 12–13 (RSV).
LEFT: *Daniel in the Den of Lions,* detail from an illustration by Gustave Doré, 1866.

way of escape from them. The whole Assyrian army, their infantry, chariots, and cavalry, surrounded them for thirty-four days, until all the vessels of water belonging to every inhabitant of Bethulia were empty. . . .

Then all the people, the young men, the women, and the children, gathered about Uzziah and the rulers of the city and cried out with a loud voice, and said before all the elders, "God be judge between you and us! For you have done us a great injury in not making peace with the Assyrians. . . . Now call them in and surrender the whole city to the army of Holofernes and to all his forces, to be plundered. For it would be better for us to be captured by them; for we will be slaves, but our lives will be spared, and we shall not witness the death of our babies before our eyes, or see our wives and children draw their last breath. . . ."

At that time Judith heard about these things . . . . Her husband Manasseh, who belonged to her tribe and family, had died during the barley harvest. For as he stood overseeing the men who were binding sheaves in the field, he was overcome by the burning heat, and took to his bed and died in Bethulia his city. . . . Judith had lived at home as a widow for three years and four months. She set up a tent for herself on the roof of her house, and girded sackcloth about her loins and wore the garments of her widowhood. She fasted all the days of her widowhood, except the day before the sabbath and the sabbath itself, the day before the new moon and the day of the new moon, and the feasts and days of rejoicing of the house of Israel. She was beautiful in appearance, and had a very lovely face; and her husband Manasseh had left her gold and silver, and men and women slaves, and cattle, and fields; and she maintained this estate. No one spoke ill of her, for she feared God with great devotion.

When Judith heard the wicked words spoken by the people against the ruler, because they were faint for lack of water, and when she heard all that Uzziah said to them, and how he promised them under oath to surrender the city to the Assyrians after five days, she sent her maid, who was in charge of all she possessed, to summon Chabris and Charmis, the elders of her city. They came to her, and she said to them,

binding sheaves: tying up bundles of grain.

girded . . . loins: dressed herself in rough cloth as a sign of mourning.

"Listen to me, rulers of the people of Bethulia! What you have said to the people today is not right; you have even sworn and pronounced this oath between God and you, promising to surrender the city to our enemies unless the Lord turns and helps us within so many days. . . .

"I am about to do a thing which will go down through all generations of our descendants. Stand at the city gate tonight, and I will go out with my maid; and within the days after which you have promised to surrender the city to our enemies, the Lord will deliver Israel by my hand. Only, do not try to find out what I plan; for I will not tell you until I have finished what I am about to do." . . .

When Judith had ceased crying out to the God of Israel and had ended all these words, she rose from where she lay prostrate and called her maid and went down into the house where she lived on sabbaths and on her feast days; and she removed the sackcloth which she had been wearing, and took off her widow's garments, and bathed her body with water, and anointed herself with precious ointment, and combed her hair and put on a tiara, and arrayed herself in her gayest apparel, which she used to wear while her husband Manasseh was living. And she put sandals on her feet, and put on her anklets and bracelets and rings, and her earrings and all her ornaments, and made herself very beautiful, to entice the eyes of all men who might see her. And she gave her maid a bottle of wine and a flask of oil, and filled a bag with parched grain and a cake of dried fruit and fine bread; and she wrapped up all her vessels and gave them to her to carry.

Then they went out to the city gate of Bethulia. . . .

Then she said to them, "Order the gate of the city to be opened for me, and I will go out and accomplish the things about which you spoke with me." So they ordered the young men to open the gate for her, as she had said. When they had done this, Judith went out, she and her maid with her; and the men of the city watched her until she had gone down the mountain and passed through the valley and they could no longer see her.

The women went straight on through the valley; and an Assyrian patrol met her and took her into

prostrate: face downward.

tiara: band of jewelry worn on the head.

entice: tempt.

custody, and asked her, "To what people do you belong, and where are you coming from, and where are you going?" She replied, "I am a daughter of the Hebrews, but I am fleeing from them, for they are about to be handed over to you to be devoured. I am on my way to the presence of Holofernes the commander of your army, to give him a true report; and I will show him a way by which he can go and capture all the hill country without losing one of his men, captured or slain."

When the men heard her words, and observed her face—she was in their eyes marvelously beautiful—they said to her, "You have saved your life by hurrying down to the presence of our lord. Go at once to his tent; some of us will escort you and hand you over to him. And when you stand before him, do not be afraid in your heart, but tell him just what you have said, and he will treat you well."

They chose from their number a hundred men to accompany her and her maid, and they brought them to the tent of Holofernes. . . . Holofernes was resting on his bed, under a canopy which was woven with purple and gold and emeralds and precious stones. When they told him of her he came forward to the front of the tent, with silver lamps carried before him. And when Judith came into the presence of Holofernes and his servants, they all marveled at the beauty of her face; and she prostrated herself and made obeisance to him, and his slaves raised her up. . . .

On the fourth day Holofernes held a banquet for his slaves only, and did not invite any of his officers. And he said to Bagoas, the eunuch who had charge of all his personal affairs, "Go now and persuade the Hebrew woman who is in your care to join us and eat and drink with us. For it will be a disgrace if we let such a woman go without enjoying her company, for if we do not embrace her she will laugh at us." . . . So she got up and arrayed herself in all her woman's finery, and her maid went and spread on the ground for her before Holofernes the soft fleeces which she had received from Bagoas for her daily use, so that she might recline on them when she ate.

Then Judith came in and lay down, and Holofernes's heart was ravished with her and he was moved with great desire to possess her; for he had been

devoured: i.e., completely conquered.

made obeisance (ō bā′sns): bowed low.

waiting for an opportunity to deceive her, ever since the day he first saw her. So Holofernes said to her, "Drink now, and be merry with us!" Judith said, "I will drink now, my lord, because my life means more to me today than in all the days since I was born." Then she took and ate and drank before him what her maid had prepared. And Holofernes was greatly pleased with her, and drank a great quantity of wine, much more than he had ever drunk in any one day since he was born.

When evening came, his slaves quickly withdrew, and Bagoas closed the tent from outside and shut out the attendants from his master's presence; and they went to bed, for they all were weary because the banquet had lasted long. So Judith was left alone in the tent, with Holofernes stretched out on his bed, for he was overcome with wine.

Now Judith had told her maid to stand outside the bedchamber and to wait for her to come out, as she did every day; for she said she would be going out for her prayers. And she had said the same thing to Bagoas. So every one went out, and no one, either small or great, was left in the bedchamber. Then Judith, standing beside his bed, said in her heart, "O Lord God of all might, look in this hour upon the work of my hands for the exaltation of Jerusalem. For now is the time to help thy inheritance, and to carry out my undertaking for the destruction of the enemies who have risen up against us."

exaltation: increased power and glory.

She went up to the post at the end of the bed, above Holofernes's head, and took down his sword that hung there. She came close to his bed and took hold of the hair of his head, and said, "Give me strength this day, O Lord God of Israel!" And she struck his neck twice with all her might, and severed his head from his body. Then she tumbled his body off the bed and pulled down the canopy from the posts; after a moment she went out, and gave Holofernes's head to her maid, who placed it in her food bag.

Then the two of them went out together, as they were accustomed to go for prayer; and they passed through the camp and circled around the valley and went up the mountain to Bethulia and came to its gates. Judith called out from afar to the watchmen at the gates, "Open, open the gate! God, our God, is still with us, to show his power in Israel, and his strength against our enemies, even as he has done this day!"

When the men of her city heard her voice, they hurried down to the city gate and called together the elders of the city. They all ran together, both small and great, for it was unbelievable that she had returned; they opened the gate and admitted them, and they kindled a fire for light, and gathered around them. Then she said to them with a loud voice, "Praise God, O praise him! Praise God, who has not withdrawn his mercy from the house of Israel, but has destroyed our enemies by my hand this very night!"

Then she took the head out of the bag and showed it to them, and said, "See, here is the head of Holofernes, the commander of the Assyrian army, and here is the canopy beneath which he lay in his drunken **stupor**. The Lord has struck him down by the hand of a woman. As the Lord lives, who has protected me in the way I went, it was my face that tricked him to his destruction, and yet he committed no act of sin with me, to **defile** and shame me."

All the people were greatly astonished, and bowed down and worshiped God, and said with one accord, "Blessed art thou, our God, who hast brought into contempt this day the enemies of thy people." . . .

As soon as it was dawn they hung the head of Holofernes on the wall, and every man took his weapons, and they went out in companies to the passes in the mountains. And when the Assyrians saw them they sent word to their commanders, and they went to the generals and the captains and to all their officers. So they came to Holofernes's tent and said to the **steward** in charge of all his personal affairs, "Wake up our lord, for the slaves have been so bold as to come down against us to give battle, in order to be destroyed completely."

So Bagoas went in and knocked at the door of the tent, for he supposed that he was sleeping with Judith. But when no one answered, he opened it and went into the bedchamber and found him thrown down on the platform dead, with his head cut off and missing. And he cried out with a loud voice and wept and groaned and shouted, and rent his garments. Then he went to the tent where Judith

stupor: dazed or numb condition.

defile: dishonor.

with one accord: in complete agreement.

steward: servant.

had stayed, and when he did not find her he rushed out to the people and shouted, "The slaves have tricked us! One Hebrew woman has brought disgrace upon the house of King Nebuchadnezzar! For look, here is Holofernes lying on the ground, and his head is not on him!" . . .

When the men in the tents heard it, they were amazed at what had happened. Fear and trembling came over them, so that they did not wait for one another, but with one impulse all rushed out and fled by every path across the plain and through the hill country. Those who had camped in the hills around Bethulia also took to flight. Then the men of Israel, every one that was a soldier, rushed out upon them. . . .

Then all the women of Israel gathered to see her, and blessed her, and some of them performed a dance for her; and she took branches in her hands and gave them to the women who were with her; and they crowned themselves with olive wreaths, she and those who were with her; and she went before all the people in the dance, leading all the women, while all the men of Israel followed, bearing their arms and wearing garlands and with songs on their lips.

garlands: strings of flowers.

For close reading

1 What details of the story emphasize the power of the Assyrians? What details emphasize the troubles of the Israelites?
2 What do you learn about Judith from the description on page 288? Choose three words to describe her.
3 How does Judith meet the enemy commander? After she kills Holofernes, how is she able to escape?
4 At what points in the story are people surprised or amazed?

For thought and discussion

5 Why do you suppose Judith does not reveal her plans before she leaves Bethulia? How is the story affected by this withholding of information?
6 "My life means more to me today than in all the days since I was born." What does Judith mean? How do you suppose Holofernes interprets her statement?
7 Why do you think Judith brings Holofernes's head and canopy back to Bethulia?
8 What methods does the story use to create suspense and increase the tension at key moments?
9 Some people would say that Judith was able to succeed only because of her great beauty. What other qualities of Judith might be equally important or more important? Explain.

Activities

1 You are one of the men of Bethulia watching Judith as she leaves the city on a mission that she has declined to tell you about. What are your thoughts?
2 Using whatever method you wish, create a portrait of Judith in all her finery.
3 Write a "moral" to go at the end of the Judith story.

Susanna

[*King Nebuchadnezzar defeated Judah and brought many Jewish captives back to Babylonia, home of the Chaldeans. The king chose certain promising young men from the Jews to serve at the royal court, where they were educated and given new names. One of these young men was Daniel, who was renamed Belteshazzar.*

Susanna, like the story of Judith (page 287) appears as an "apocryphal" book in some versions of the Bible. Catholic Bibles include Susanna in the Book of Daniel. It does not appear in Jewish Bibles.]

There was a man living in Babylon whose name was Joakim. And he took a wife named Susanna, the daughter of Hilkiah, a very beautiful woman and one who feared the Lord. Her parents were righteous, and had taught their daughter according to the law of Moses. Joakim was very rich, and had a spacious garden adjoining his house; and the Jews used to come to him because he was the most honored of them all.

In that year two elders from the people were appointed as judges. . . . These men were frequently at Joakim's house, and all who had suits at law came to them.

elders: older men, leaders in the Jewish community.

When the people departed at noon, Susanna would go into her husband's garden to walk. The two elders used to see her every day, going in and walking about, and they began to desire her. And they perverted their minds and turned away their eyes from looking to heaven or remembering right-

perverted: twisted; corrupted.

Susanna 1:1–5a, 6–56, 58–64 (RSV).

eous judgments. Both were overwhelmed with passion for her, but they did not tell each other of their distress, for they were ashamed to disclose their lustful desire to possess her. And they watched eagerly, day after day, to see her.

They said to each other, "Let us go home, for it is mealtime." And when they went out, they parted from each other. But turning back, they met again; and when each pressed the other for the reason, they confessed their lust. And then together they arranged for a time when they could find her alone.

opportune: favorable.

Once, while they were watching for an opportune day, she went in as before with only two maids, and wished to bathe in the garden, for it was very hot. And no one was there except the two elders, who had hid themselves and were watching her. She said to her maids, "Bring me oil and ointments, and shut the garden doors so that I may bathe." They did as she said, shut the garden doors, and went out by the side doors to bring what they had been commanded; and they did not see the elders, because they were hidden.

Note that there are both main doors to the garden from the house and side doors that could be entered from outside.

When the maids had gone out, the two elders rose and ran to her, and said: "Look, the garden doors are shut, no one sees us, and we are in love with you; so give your consent, and lie with us. If you refuse, we will testify against you that a young man was with you, and this was why you sent your maids away."

hemmed in: trapped.
death: i.e., the penalty for adultery in Jewish law.

Susanna sighed deeply, and said, "I am hemmed in on every side. For if I do this thing, it is death for me; and if I do not, I shall not escape your hands. I choose not to do it and to fall into your hands, rather than to sin in the sight of the Lord."

Then Susanna cried out with a loud voice, and the two elders shouted against her. And one of them ran and opened the garden doors. When the household servants heard the shouting in the garden, they rushed in at the side door to see what had happened to her. And when the elders told their tale, the servants were greatly ashamed, for nothing like this had ever been said about Susanna.

Susanna at the Bath, oil on wood by Albrecht Altdorfer, 1526. The Alte Pinakothek, Munich. Photograph, Joachim Blauel.

The Three Hebrews in the Fiery Furnace, painting in the Chamber of Velatio, Cemetery of Priscilla, Rome, mid-third century. Courtesy Benedittine Di Priscilla, Rome.

OVERLEAF: *Belshazzar Sees the Writing on the Wall,*
oil painting by Rembrandt Van Rijn. Reproduced by courtesy of
the Trustees, The National Gallery, London.
Daniel, detail from a stained-glass window,
twelfth century, Augsburg. Courtesy The Cathedral
of Augsburg, Germany.

The next day, when the people gathered at the house of her husband Joakim, the two elders came, full of their wicked plot to have Susanna put to death. They said before the people, "Send for Susanna, the daughter of Hilkiah, who is the wife of Joakim." So they sent for her. And she came, with her parents, her children, and all her kindred.

Now Susanna was a woman of great refinement, and beautiful in appearance. As she was veiled, the wicked men ordered her to be unveiled, that they might feast upon her beauty. But her family and friends and all who saw her wept.

Then the two elders stood up in the midst of the people, and laid their hands upon her head. And she, weeping, looked up toward heaven, for her heart trusted in the Lord. The elders said, "As we were walking in the garden alone, this woman came in with two maids, shut the garden doors, and dismissed the maids. Then a young man, who had been hidden, came to her and lay with her. We were in a corner of the garden, and when we saw this wickedness we ran to them. We saw them embracing, but we could not hold the man, for he was too strong for us, and he opened the doors and dashed out. So we seized this woman and asked her who the young man was, but she would not tell us. These things we testify."

The assembly believed them, because they were elders of the people and judges; and they condemned her to death.

Then Susanna cried out with a loud voice, and said, "O eternal God, who dost discern what is secret, who art aware of all things before they come to be, thou knowest that these men have borne false witness against me. And now I am to die! Yet I have done none of the things that they have wickedly invented against me!"

The Lord heard her cry. And as she was being led away to be put to death, God aroused the holy spirit of a young lad named Daniel; and he cried with a loud voice, "I am innocent of the blood of this woman."

All the people turned to him, and said, "What is this that you have said?" Taking his stand in the midst of them, he said, "Are you such fools, you sons of Israel? Have you condemned a daughter of Israel without examination and without learning the

THE RESCUE OF SUSANNA   **301**

facts? Return to the place of judgment. For these men have borne false witness against her."

Then all the people returned in haste. And the elders said to him, "Come, sit among us and inform us, for God has given you that right." And Daniel said to them, "Separate them far from each other, and I will examine them."

elders: other men, not the two accusers.

When they were separated from each other, he summoned one of them and said to him, "You old relic of wicked days, your sins have now come home, which you have committed in the past, pronouncing unjust judgments, condemning the innocent and letting the guilty go free, though the Lord said, 'Do not put to death an innocent and righteous person.' Now then, if you really saw her, tell me this: Under what tree did you see them being intimate with each other?" He answered, "Under a mastic tree." And Daniel said, "Very well! You have lied against your own head, for the angel of God has received the sentence from God and will immediately cut you in two."

relic of wicked days: i.e., hardened old sinner.

Then he put him aside, and commanded them to bring the other. And he said to him, "You offspring of Canaan and not of Judah, beauty has deceived you and lust has perverted your heart. . . . Now then, tell me: Under what tree did you catch them being intimate with each other?" He answered, "Under an evergreen oak." And Daniel said to him, "Very well! You also have lied against your own head, for the angel of God is waiting with his sword to saw you in two, that he may destroy you both."

offspring of Canaan: i.e., pagan, heathen.

Then all the assembly shouted loudly and blessed God, who saves those who hope in him. And they rose against the two elders, for out of their own mouths Daniel had convicted them of bearing false witness; and they did to them as they had wickedly planned to do to their neighbor; acting in accordance with the law of Moses, they put them to death. Thus innocent blood was saved that day.

And Hilkiah and his wife praised God for their daughter Susanna, and so did Joakim her husband and all her kindred, because nothing shameful was found in her. And from that day onward Daniel had a great reputation among the people.

For close reading

1 Why are Daniel and the other Jews living in Babylon?

2 What is the reaction of the servants when they first hear the charge against Susanna?

3 Reread the description of the actions and testimony of the two elders at the beginning of the trial. What details should have made the people suspicious of their story?

4 What method does Daniel use to reveal the lies of the two elders?

For thought and discussion

5 What kind of person is Susanna? What evidence can you find in the story—from her own actions and words and those of other people—to support your opinion?

6 Susanna comes to the trial modestly veiled, as was the custom for a married woman. The two elders have the power to make her remove the veil in public. How does this small detail affect the story?

7 Why do you suppose the people accepted the word of the two elders without question? Why do you suppose the other elders immediately agreed to listen to Daniel? Can you think of modern examples of such behavior?

8 Whose story is being told in this passage— Susanna's or Daniel's? Explain.

Activities

1 Draw a map or picture of Susanna's garden showing the various gates and other things that appear in the story.

2 You are Susanna's lawyer. Aside from Daniel's method, how would you prove that she is innocent?

3 You are a reporter at the trial. Write a newspaper story, complete with headline and lead paragraph.

THE SHEPHERDESS

Mihailo Lalić
Translated by Zora Depolo

[*In Yugoslavia in World War II, two groups formed to resist the Nazi occupation: the Četniks* (chet′niks), *who supported the exiled monarchy, and the Partisans, who were Communist. The two resistance groups could not agree to cooperate and fighting broke out between them, a "war within a war." "The Shepherdess" is the story of a young Partisan who is captured by the Četniks.*]

Kolašin (kô′lä shin):
city in Yugoslavia.
Brujić (brü′yěch).
decrepit: weak, feeble.

Minić (mi′něch).
Selić (se′lěch).
Zečević (ze che′věch).
Lakičević (la kē che′věch).

On a late spring Monday in 1942, on the eve of a large-scale operation, they were captured by Četnik sentinels right at the entrance to Kolašin. First came Veko Brujić, a decrepit old man, the father of an executed Partisan. Either he was recognized or else someone had given him away—but the fact was that they took him by surprise so that he did not even have time to pull his revolver out of his vest pocket. After they disarmed him, the old man no longer concealed his purpose—that he had come to kill Commander Minić and thus avenge his son's death. In the afternoon he was shot along with Selić, Zečević, and Lakičević. Bent over and exhausted, at the last moment of his life, scornfully he straightened himself, saying: "I am glad to die with such company, with such good honest people and with heroes representing two great Montenegrin tribes." Shot in an upright position, he was buried deep in the earth, and because of the fame of those who had fallen with him, his own reputation was forgotten so that practically nothing was either mentioned or known about him later.

Another person was more interesting from the very start: a girl of medium stature, a healthy peasant whose beauty was hidden under her rough clothes, sunburned and with a sturdy look in her silvery-gray eyes and black eyebrows. Her name was Djurdja Vlahović, a shepherdess from the small village of Trebaljevo. On that day she was leading about twenty lambs to be exchanged with those of her relatives. At other times this might have been nothing unusual, because at the end of spring, lambs are separated from their mothers and given to other sheep so that they can forget about milk and learn how to live exclusively on grass. But that spring, when everything had changed and there was continuous fighting in different parts of the Tara valley, both shepherds and lambs, as well as anything alive and mobile, seemed suspicious to the Četniks.

The girl walked along calmly, knitting stockings and concentrating on her work as she passed the sentinels, pretending not to see them. Her composure was an insult to the sentinels and it did not increase their suspicion so much as it heightened their eagerness to see her face and to arouse her fears, as they were accustomed to doing. The commander of the guard, an ex-policeman whose beard sometimes covered the soiled collar of his buttoned-up jacket, cleared his throat and asked maliciously: "Well, where are you coming from, my pretty one?"

She stopped and turned around as if she had not noticed them before. She shook her head slightly, but her look became all the more resolute, cold, and angry. She replied without haste: "I? I'm from right there, from the mountain."

"Which mountain? There's more than one mountain around here."

"Well, I'm from that one over there, Mount Biograd," the girl said, looking at her stocking as she knitted. She wanted to proceed, but one of the men dashed in front of her.

Montenegrin tribes: Slavic ethnic groups in Yugoslavia.

Djurdja Vlahović (jür′jä vlä′hô vēch).

Trebaljevo (tre bäl′ye vô).

"Wait, wait a minute: why don't you say you're coming from the zone controlled by the Partisans? Give me your pass!"

She had no pass and even pretended that she did not know what the pass was or why it was important. They took her to an inn to see whether the innkeeper could recognize her and to search her belongings. Milena Tutova, a fat widow who had helped the Četnik movement in many ways, was the innkeeper. She could not recognize the girl; she did not know the peasant-folk, especially the women. The shepherdess said that she belonged to the Vlahović family of Trebaljevo, but that did not mean very much because Vlahovićs, like all the other families, were separated as they fought each other in deadly combat, some favoring the Četniks and others the Partisans. The girl tried to prevent them from searching her on the excuse that she had to catch up with the lambs, but the sentinels were not at all interested in her lambs. They kept her at the inn by force, and with a sly look the innkeeper unbuttoned the girl's blouse and discovered a package of leaflets concealed beneath it. The leaflets contained an appeal, calling upon the people to join in the struggle against the invader and his mercenaries. As soon as they heard the paper rattling, the sentinels knew what the matter was even without looking at the text of the leaflets. They began to beat the shepherdess. Her face began to bleed; her eye was injured, her hair was disheveled, and three times her white kerchief was pulled off her head. She was totally silent but grabbed her kerchief again and again to cover her head because, according to the strict custom of her village, women's hair was not supposed to be exposed to men's eyes.

mercenaries: soldiers fighting only for pay.

Then the sentinels took her to security headquarters. They could not beat her in the street in front of the people, but they could scream and curse, thus giving vent to their hatred and showing their devotion to duty and authority, as well as attracting people's attention to their big catch and success. Suddenly it seemed to them as if they had grown bigger, that they were a foot taller than the other passers-by—the startled and frightened townspeople who with uneasy curiosity frequently stopped, turned, and attached themselves to the enraged, screaming group. And thus the quiet procession grew ever longer and in it each individual silently wondered what had driven that unknown shepherdess of Trebaljevo to choose a martyr's path, what had brought her to the Četnik's Kolašin, and who had given her away to the murderers. What was going to happen to her? No one asked the question because everybody knew the answer. All heads were bent because of the weight of that heavy thought. No one paid any attention to the abandoned lambs, which now lagged behind, sniffing and grazing the dusty grass along the fences in the street in that sordid place where they knew only the shepherdess; and then they rushed to catch up with her. But she had obviously forgotten about her lambs as she was pushed along at the head of the procession.

In front of headquarters the group came to a stop. The girl was taken inside and the crowd stayed for a while staring at the dark black square gap leading to the corridor. In silence they stared at one another questioningly, but no one either asked or said anything. They dispersed to tell what had happened, and by using this as an example to frighten their families, they tried to put a check on daring—that evil, unfortunate quality of young and able people who are punished in this manner or even more drastically simply because of it.

The area in front of the headquarters building was soon deserted. For a little while only the lambs lingered, involved in their innocent play, but then, attracted by the green grass, they, too, ran away to the meadow below the dam. The guard, who did not know whose lambs they were and how they had gotten there, mentally selected the fattest one for himself, imagining a barbecue and fire and licking his lips in anticipation.

He watched them sadly as they went away and soon forgot about them as they disappeared out of sight.

Puzzled by their sudden freedom, the lambs stopped a while to think, and called their mothers and the shepherdess by their feeble bleating, and then again forgot everything in their play. They advanced, passing through slanting fences and uncultivated gardens and fields, across the hard and dusty road that did not appeal to them, and then across the barren fallow land where many Partisans were buried without tombstones. And so they

fallow: plowed but unseeded for a time.

reached the sandy woods near the Tara and gazed with their frightened little eyes at the skinny, molting, and ugly coachman's horse grazing there. The big animal, with his calmness, made them feel confident. Hesitating to approach him very closely, the lambs remained in his vicinity all day, grazing and skipping over the natural green carpet and playing like butterflies. In the evening the coachman came and took the horse away. The abandoned lambs, although frightened and startled, hopefully ran after him at a distance. They stopped in front of the stable and spent the night there, alone, frightened, and huddled together in a warm little group.

In the meantime the shepherdess was interrogated at police headquarters.

She was questioned by Božanić, the illegitimate son of a laundress, who had previously served at police headquarters. The laundress had not lived long enough to see the authority and fame of her illegitimate offspring. Before the war Božanić had been a small police agent in Belgrade, a homeless spy who had long forgotten and completely dismissed Kolašin. In the second year of the war, he returned to his "native town" with the identity papers of Nedić's intelligence officer. He alleged that he had escaped from Nedić, who maintained close ties with the Germans, to serve Draža, because he trusted the English more than the Germans. He boasted how he had machine-gunned handcuffed Communists at Banjica and how he had skillfully captured them in various Serbian villages. The people there believed the former statement, but they doubted the latter. Četnik officers, mostly conceited higher-class people, did not, in spite of everything, accept him as one of their own kind; remembering his low origin and obscure birth, they believed that he had escaped from Serbia because he had been caught as a thief. On the other hand, other more cautious people tried to guess whether Božanić was a Nedić or a Gestapo spy, sent to Kolašin to control Draža's headquarters; therefore they were very careful not to offend him.

Božanić interrogated the girl "in the Belgrade fashion": that is, he would tie the victim's hands and legs and bind them both together behind the victim's back, thus tightly arching the body; he would then hang that living bundle on a horizontal stick

molting: shedding hair.

Božanić (bô′zhä nēch).

Nedić (ne′dēch).
Draža (drä′zhä).

Banjica (bän′yē tsä).

whose ends rested on two especially arranged little tables. The stick was called the bridge and the victim was called the bell clapper. When the assistants hung the victim to oscillate under the bridge, Božanić would grab a whip and skillfully begin a bastinado.

That day he had difficulty. He had to hang the obstinate girl three times, and three times he had to let the fainted girl go. At intervals, when his assistants sprinkled water on her to make her come to her senses, he scratched his small ugly head furiously as locks of his colorless hair stuck to his sweaty fingers. Everything was in vain. In the beginning it seemed as if the girl had accepted the torture as something necessary and compulsory. The torturers did their best to explain to her that the length of the torture depended on her own confessions, and that she could put a stop to it as soon as she made up her mind to talk. But she was very stubborn and persistent and refused to accept the explanations. She remained as mute as a fish and thus she did not even try either to confirm or deny her original statement. That first statement was: that she had found the leaflets tucked in a haystack and had taken them to give them to her mother and brother as cigarette paper. This explanation was given prior to the bastinado and was obviously false, and Božanić even refused to put it down. Tired and angry, his face twisted because of a severe toothache, he ordered that the girl be put into prison and he himself dashed out of his gloomy office, rushing headlong down the stairs across the dam to the nearest cafe.

The girl was brought before the court the next day.

The Četnik court of Kolašin was formed for purely formal reasons—to amuse the public and to create an impression that capital punishment was meted out there on the basis of evidence. In fact, that punishment was decided prior to the court trial itself and outside the courtroom at Četnik headquarters, where no evidence was taken very seriously. Marko Milović-Čoro, a drunkard and quarreler, was the pillar of the court; his face was pale and bloated because of drinking. Before the war he had been a lawyer and an admirer of the notorious Fascist Ljotić; he himself liked to tell how, as a candidate for parliamentary office on Ljotić's list, he had not

oscillate: swing to and fro.

bastinado (bas tə nä′dō): beating.

Milović-Čoro (mē lô′věch chô′rô).

Ljotić (lyô těch).

received a single vote, and so from that time on he had begun to hate the human race. He would wink with his left eye for a long time and when asked to explain this action he said: "This way I can see fewer loathsome people in this world."

Vule Vlahović (vü′le vlä′hô vēch).

Vuksanović (vük sän′ô vēch).

Milović's assistant, Vule Vlahović, was seated to the right; Vlahović was a very tall man with hazy eyes, suffering from tuberculosis, who, on principle, asked capital punishment for every accused Communist. Vuksanović, the third judge, crouched on the left-hand side of Milović. Vuksanović was scared to death day and night, he could neither eat, drink, nor smoke, and, as Milović put it, "fear constituted his only food and sustenance." However, despite that fear, or perhaps because of it, Vuksanović sometimes was courageous enough to disapprove a death penalty, but that, of course, was not even taken into consideration.

When they brought the girl in, they could see that she was limping and this incited Milović's first remark, which was meant to puzzle the defendant and to amuse the public.

"Bent-backed one," he addressed her, "what kind of change is this? Yesterday you did not limp, while today you do."

She stopped, as if wondering whether she had heard him correctly. Although her face was covered with black and blue marks, still the insult brought a blush to her face. Lifting her head, she frowned and stared: "You, too, have changed," she said. "Last year you were a Montenegrin, whereas this year you are an Italian. You'd become a Turk and change nine creeds to avoid suffering only half the tortures I have gone through." . . .

Milović, pale and with bulging eyes, rose to his feet, banging on the desk: "Do you know where you are?" he screamed in a hoarse voice.

"I do: in front of executioners!" the girl replied almost simultaneously.

Judge Vuksanović's pencil slipped out of his hand and rolled down on the floor. He bent down to pick it up and in the terrible silence one could hear the squeaking of his chair and the rattling of the pencil in his trembling hand. Milović said, "Hm," his head dropping over a pile of documents. He closed his eyes, meaning that he had surrendered his position in the court to Judge Vule Vlahović. The people in the courtroom, a major part of whom came mostly to have a good time listening to Milović cursing the defendants, were instantly disappointed and lost interest in the trial. Vlahović's interrogation was dull, he spoke with a gravelike voice, had a literary accent, and did not conceal the fact that what was taking place was a mere comedy and not a court trial; the decisive sentence had been irrevocably passed in advance.

He calmly took the usual data of names and dates, and then grimly asked: "This means . . . you've brought the lambs . . . Well, but where are they now?"

The girl said she could not tell exactly where they were, but that they had most probably been prepared as food for the Četniks.

"All right, all right," the judge waved his hand, and asked another question: "To whom should you have delivered those leaflets?"

The girl frowned again, as if trying to find the right answer. Looking him straight in the eyes, she said: "You'll die before you know."

"I see," the tubercular tall man admitted bitterly as he smiled spitefully. "That's . . . that means, how long have you been a Party member?"

"That, too, you are never going to know!" the girl replied scornfully, staring at Milović's bristling beard.

Obviously tired, Vlahović looked at Judge Vuksanović observing the girl's composed face covered with blue marks, her resolute eyebrows on which all her spite seemed to have accumulated. He waved his hand; he had no more questions to ask.

They took her back to prison and during the last two hours of life the girl washed her face, combed her hair, and straightened her clothes. At lunch she could not eat at all but, to mislead and encourage the others to eat, she plucked and chewed a single bite for a long time and crumbled a small ball of corn bread with her fingers.

In the afternoon they called her name out and informed her that she was sentenced to death by hanging and that the sentence was to be carried out immediately. She was asked to get ready. Listening to all this, she did not even blink: it was as if she had known her fate long ago and did nothing else than to make ready for it. And really, she was prepared for it—she knew that in Četnik's Kolašin, women, being unworthy of a death by shooting, were as a rule sentenced to death by hanging. Ruža Rip, a "Partisan doctor," had also ended her life hanging from a snare, while Djurdja Vlahović did not doubt for a moment that she could get anything better from the Četniks. People talked about how Ruza had faced her death quietly and how she gathered her long, thick hair and pushed it through the snare with her small, almost childlike hands. That story showed the girl that even such a humiliating death chosen for a woman and a Jew had some traits of beauty and sadness and was also human.

Before she shook hands with her comrades in the women's prison, Djurdja crossed the yard to the men's prison and went from one cell to another taking leave of the comrades she had not even had time to get to know. Resolute and composed, she deceived many prisoners by her cheerfulness, so they thought she was going home and only later regretted that she was no longer among them and that they had not seen more of her while she was there. As she walked along the pebbled path across the yard on her way back to the women's prison, drumbeating resounded in the street in front of the prison gate, and then the shrill voice of the town crier was heard inviting the townspeople of Kolašin not to miss the opportunity to attend the execution of the Communist organizer, Djurdja Vlahović. The girl stopped in front of the open gate of the women's prison and, looking pale and smiling, said bitterly: "He's calling together my wedding guests, have you heard him? Mother, my poor mother, can you imagine what my wedding will be like. . . ."

Frowning and terrified as a result of the tension, the guards, with their faces hidden in their woolly beards, escorted the girl beyond the locked gate. Out on the street she started to run and the guards ran after her. By the time she reached the dam overlooking the meadow, the girl noticed the assembled crowd and became aware of the hundreds of people staring at her. This was the moment she dreaded most: isolation and loneliness before such a glare of eyes. Her head drooped and her legs began to tremble under their burden. But the next moment she straightened herself up and began to walk resolutely through the huge crowd, which made room for her to advance, and soon she reached the wooden poles of the gallows, surrounded by armed men and hordes of people whispering in admiration.

This admiration redoubled her strength and spite. In a wink she jumped to the stool beneath the gallows. Looking down from that height, it seemed to her as if the crowd was silenced by her appearance. She looked around for the face of an acquaintance, but among the first she saw was the bloodless face with its goat beard of Commander Minić, slyly smiling. She addressed him with her hoarse, biting voice that rang as cold and sharp as metal itself: "Are you pleased, Ljubo Minić, commander of the macaroni? Laugh, you sly fox, but remember: your fate will not be a lucky one either!"

Taken by surprise, Minić did not hear her first words and knew in advance that he would not be able to give her the right answer. He only muttered: "Well, you magpie, Mehmed will now baptize you, since the first baptism did not help you!"

Besides the blacksmith Jogaz, Mehmed was the only Moslem who could have survived under the Četnik rule in Kolašin. This insane and timid street-cleaner and domestic servant would perform any humiliating task out of fear; he had also consented to hang the condemned Partisan women since no one else wanted to do so. Short, ugly, and stumpy in his filthy, ragged clothes, he stood on the stool waiting for a sign, gazing stupidly, listening with pricked ears to what the girl was saying but unable to trust his own ears.

"Pull it, what are you gaping at?" screamed Minić to Mehmed.

"Hey, fool! You're listening to a speech, ah, Turkish rogue!" Minić's commander of the guards added, ready to assume the executioner's role.

Mehmed was puzzled. He tried to catch the swaying snare but the girl pushed him abruptly and vigorously with her elbow. Surprised, he clutched his chest and fell from the shaken stool.

"Ah," the people sighed with admiration, approval, and congratulations along with a dozen forbidden, dangerous, and suppressed feelings and desires.

The girl stood firm and pulled the snare around her thin white neck.

She pulled off her white kerchief and uncovered her hair, which was divided into two fair braids. She threw the braids across the snare and let them fall on her bosom, reaching as far as her waist. Framed by her pale forehead, her shining hair and eyes made her face more beautiful. For a few seconds in these last moments her great beauty radiated forth.

"I know how to hang myself unaided," she said in the dead silence, and with an almost invisible gesture pushed and turned the stool under her feet.

She jerked and hung down, stretched out straight and stiff, hung by the snare.

Women began to scream and cover their eyes so as not to see what they had come to watch. The citizens realized that they had fulfilled their despicable duties and rushed to the dam. Mehmed was the last to leave. He felt dizzy, his legs trembled, something urged him to turn around, but he lacked the courage to do so.

despicable: to be despised; contemptible.

The hanged girl remained alone. The first to approach her were her lambs. Fewer in number, huddled together, gone wild by the chase, they had descended along the river and followed the trampled grass on the meadow. Below the gallows they came to a stop and one after the other lifted their heads. They stared at the shepherdess, astonished and sad—as if imploring her to come down and protect them. A mild wind blowing from the summits of Mount Ključ swayed the hanged girl's body, and her shadow moved over the grass as if she were alive, frightening the lambs. Huddled together, alone and abandoned, they rushed in terror in the direction of the Tara and its muddy waters, which have never recorded a worse spring than that one.

For close reading

1 Why is the shepherdess arrested?

2 How are the Četniks described in this story? List some of the specific words and phrases used.

3 What details in the story show the helplessness of the shepherdess in the hands of the enemy? What details show her courage?

For thought and discussion

4 How do the references to lambs affect this story? How would the story be changed if the girl had been herding other animals instead (for instance, geese or pigs)?

5 The narrator is obviously sympathetic to the Partisans and opposed to the Četniks. In your opinion, would the story be more effective if the narrator were "neutral"? Explain.

6 The shepherdess must stand alone before the enemy and face a test of her courage and ideals— just as the heroes and heroines must do in the Bible stories in this chapter. What similarities can you find between Djurdja's experiences and those of Judith and Susanna? In what ways is "The Shepherdess" different from the Bible stories?

THE
FIERY
FURNACE

Daniel

[*Another story from the period of the Babylonian Captivity concerns three young Jews who, like Daniel, were brought to the royal court to be educated. Their names Hananiah, Mishael, and Azariah were changed to Shadrach, Meshach, and Abednego.*]

image: statue.
cubit: about eighteen inches.

satraps: regional governors.
prefects: administrative officials.
magistrates: local judges.

and languages: of every language.
lyre, trigon (lir, tri'gon): stringed musical instruments.

King Nebuchadnezzar made an image of gold, whose height was sixty cubits and its breadth six cubits. He set it up on the plain of Dura, in the province of Babylon. Then King Nebuchadnezzar sent to assemble the satraps, the prefects, and the governors, the counselors, the treasurers, the justices, the magistrates, and all the officials of the provinces to come to the dedication of the image which King Nebuchadnezzar had set up. Then the satraps, the prefects, and the governors, the counselors, the treasurers, the justices, the magistrates, and all the officials of the provinces, were assembled for the dedication of the image that King Nebuchadnezzar had set up; and they stood before the image that Nebuchadnezzar had set up. And the herald proclaimed aloud, "You are commanded, O peoples, nations, and languages, that when you hear the sound of the horn, pipe, lyre, trigon, harp, bagpipe, and every kind of music, you are to fall down and worship the golden image that King Nebuchadnezzar has set up; and whoever does not fall down and

Daniel 3:1–8, 12–14, 15b–30 (RSV).

worship shall immediately be cast into a burning fiery furnace." Therefore, as soon as all the peoples heard the sound of the horn, pipe, lyre, trigon, harp, bagpipe, and every kind of music, all the peoples, nations, and languages fell down and worshiped the golden image which King Nebuchadnezzar had set up.

Therefore at that time certain Chaldeans came forward and maliciously accused the Jews. . . . "There are certain Jews whom you have appointed over the affairs of the province of Babylon: Shadrach, Meshach, and Abednego. These men, O king, pay no heed to you; they do not serve your gods or worship the golden image which you have set up."

Then Nebuchadnezzar in furious rage commanded that Shadrach, Meshach, and Abednego be brought. Then they brought these men before the king. Nebuchadnezzar said to them, "Is it true, O Shadrach, Meshach, and Abednego, that you do not serve my gods or worship the golden image which I have set up? . . . if you do not worship, you shall immediately be cast into a burning fiery furnace; and who is the god that will deliver you out of my hands?"

Shadrach, Meshach, and Abednego answered the king, "O Nebuchadnezzar, we have no need to answer you in this matter. If it be so, our God whom we serve is able to deliver us from the burning fiery furnace; and he will deliver us out of your hand, O king. But if not, be it known to you, O king, that we will not serve your gods or worship the golden image which you have set up."

Then Nebuchadnezzar was full of fury, and the expression of his face was changed against Shadrach, Meshach, and Abednego. He ordered the furnace heated seven times more than it was wont to be heated. And he ordered certain mighty men of his army to bind Shadrach, Meshach, and Abednego, and to cast them into the burning fiery furnace. Then these men were bound in their mantles, their tunics, their hats, and their other garments, and they were cast into the burning fiery furnace. Because the king's order was strict and the furnace very hot, the flame of the fire slew those men who took up Shadrach, Meshach, and Abednego. And these three men, Shadrach, Meshach, and Abednego, fell bound into the burning fiery furnace.

wont to be: usually.

mantles: coats, cloaks.
tunics: suits.

a son of the gods: an
angel or other heavenly
being.

Then King Nebuchadnezzar was astonished and rose up in haste. He said to his counselors, "Did we not cast three men bound into the fire?" They answered the king, "True, O king." He answered, "But I see four men loose, walking in the midst of the fire, and they are not hurt; and the appearance of the fourth is like a son of the gods."

Then Nebuchadnezzar came near to the door of the burning fiery furnace and said, "Shadrach, Meshach, and Abednego, servants of the Most High God, come forth, and come here!" Then Shadrach, Meshach, and Abednego came out from the fire. And the satraps, the governors, and the king's counselors gathered together and saw that the fire had not had any power over the bodies of those men; the hair of their heads was not singed, their mantles were not harmed, and no smell of fire had come upon them. Nebuchadnezzar said, "Blessed be the God of Shadrach, Meshach, and Abednego, who has sent his angel and delivered his servants, who trusted in him, and set at nought the king's command, and yielded up their bodies rather than serve and worship any god except their own God. Therefore I make a decree: Any people, nation, or language that speaks anything against the God of Shadrach, Meshach, and Abednego shall be torn limb from limb, and their houses laid in ruins; for there is no other god who is able to deliver in this way." Then the king promoted Shadrach, Meshach, and Abednego in the province of Babylon.

nought: nothing.

For close reading

1 How do Shadrach, Meshach, and Abednego answer when questioned by King Nebuchadnezzar?
2 What details in the story emphasize the king's power? What details emphasize the king's anger at the young Jews?
3 What does the king see when he looks in the furnace?

For thought and discussion

4 Why do you think the power and fury of the king are described in such detail?

5 What is the effect of the repetition of certain phrases in this story?

6 How does the story increase the dramatic impact of the Jews' survival in the furnace?

7 Reread the king's last words. To what extent has he changed? Is he completely won over to the God of Israel? Explain.

Activities

1 You are one of the accusers of the three Jews. Write your diary entries for the week, beginning before you go to the king and ending after the three men have been promoted.

2 Make a clay model of the furnace, or portray in painting, collage, needlework, or some other medium, the three Jews in the furnace.

3 With musical accompaniment and in your own words, retell the story of Shadrach, Meshach, and Abednego to an audience.

BELSHAZZAR'S FEAST

Daniel

Belshazzar (bel shaz′ər).

King Belshazzar made a great feast for a thousand of his lords, and drank wine in front of the thousand.

Belshazzar, when he tasted the wine, commanded that the vessels of gold and of silver which Nebuchadnezzar his father had taken out of the temple in Jerusalem be brought, that the king and his lords, his wives, and his concubines might drink from them. . . . They drank wine, and praised the gods of gold and silver, bronze, iron, wood, and stone.

concubines: lower-ranking wives.

Immediately the fingers of a man's hand appeared and wrote on the plaster of the wall of the king's palace, opposite the lampstand; and the king saw the hand as it wrote. Then the king's color changed, and his thoughts alarmed him; his limbs gave way, and his knees knocked together. The king cried aloud to bring in the enchanters, the Chaldeans, and the astrologers. The king said to the wise men of Babylon, "Whoever reads this writing, and shows me its interpretation, shall be clothed with purple, and have a chain of gold about his neck, and shall be the third ruler in the kingdom." Then all the king's wise men came in, but they could not read the writing or make known to the king the interpretation. Then King Belshazzar was greatly alarmed, and his color changed; and his lords were perplexed. . . .

enchanters: people who could cast spells.

purple: the royal color.

third ruler: i.e., third highest.

Daniel 5:1–2, 4–9, 13–14, 16b–18, 20, 22–30 (RSV).

Then Daniel was brought in before the king. The king said to Daniel, "You are that Daniel, one of the exiles of Judah, whom the king my father brought from Judah. I have heard of you that the spirit of the holy gods is in you, and that light and understanding and excellent wisdom are found in you. . . . Now if you can read the writing and make known to me its interpretation, you shall be clothed with purple, and have a chain of gold about your neck, and shall be the third ruler in the kingdom."

Then Daniel answered before the king, "Let your gifts be for yourself, and give your rewards to another; nevertheless I will read the writing to the king and make known to him the interpretation. O king, the Most High God gave Nebuchadnezzar your father kingship and greatness and glory and majesty . . . . But when his heart was lifted up and his spirit was hardened so that he dealt proudly, he was deposed from his kingly throne, and his glory was taken from him . . . . And you his son, Belshazzar, have not humbled your heart, though you knew all this, but you have lifted up yourself against the Lord of heaven; and the vessels of his house have been brought in before you, and you and your lords, your wives, and your concubines have drunk wine from them; and you have praised the gods of silver and gold, of bronze, iron, wood, and stone, which do not see or hear or know, but the God in whose hand is your breath, and whose are all your ways, you have not honored.

"Then from his presence the hand was sent, and this writing was inscribed. And this is the writing that was inscribed: MENE, MENE, TEKEL, and PARSIN. This is the interpretation of the matter: MENE, God has numbered the days of your kingdom and brought it to an end; TEKEL, you have been weighed in the balances and found wanting; PERES, your kingdom is divided and given to the Medes and Persians."

Then Belshazzar commanded, and Daniel was clothed with purple, a chain of gold was put about his neck, and proclamation was made concerning him, that he should be the third ruler in the kingdom.

That very night Belshazzar the Chaldean king was slain. And Darius the Mede received the kingdom . . . .

deposed: removed.

Mene (mē′nē) **Mene, Tekel, and Parsin:** count, count, weigh, divide; Aramaic words. *Parsin (Peres)* is the same as "Persian."

wanting: lacking.

Darius (də rī′əs): king of Persia.

For close reading

1 The fingers of a man's hand appear "immediately" as if in response to something. What in the preceding lines might have caused this abrupt appearance?
2 What is Daniel's response when told of the reward he will receive for interpreting the writing?
3 What are the three charges that Daniel brings against Belshazzar?

For thought and discussion

4 What hints in the story prepare us for the news of Belshazzar's downfall? How does the story keep that outcome in suspense?
5 Belshazzar honors Daniel even though Daniel predicts that Belshazzar will lose his kingdom. Why do you suppose he does so? What would you have done?
6 You have probably read other stories which have a theme of "pride goes before a fall." Choose one and compare it with the story of Belshazzar. What other Bible stories have this theme?

Activities

1 Illustrate—in painting, sculpture, collage, needlework, film, or recorded music—the scene in which Belshazzar sees the hand as it writes on the wall.
2 The words which appear on the wall have various explanations. Look them up in a reference book and report to the class.

IN A
DEN
OF
LIONS

Daniel

It pleased Darius to set over the kingdom a hundred and twenty satraps, to be throughout the whole kingdom; and over them three presidents, of whom Daniel was one, to whom these satraps should give account, so that the king might suffer no loss. Then this Daniel became distinguished above all the other presidents and satraps, because an excellent spirit was in him; and the king planned to set him over the whole kingdom. Then the presidents and the satraps sought to find a ground for complaint against Daniel with regard to the kingdom; but they could find no ground for complaint or any fault, because he was faithful, and no error or fault was found in him. Then these men said, "We shall not find any ground for complaint against this Daniel unless we find it in connection with the law of his God."

Then these presidents and satraps came by agreement to the king and said to him, "O King Darius, live for ever! All the presidents of the kingdom, the prefects and the satraps, the counselors and the governors are agreed that the king should establish an ordinance and enforce an interdict, that whoever makes petition to any god or man for thirty days, except to you, O king, shall be cast into the den of lions. Now, O king, establish the interdict and sign the document, so that it cannot be changed, according to the law of the Medes and the Persians, which

satraps: regional governors.

sought: tried.

interdict: order forbidding something.
makes petition: i.e., prays.

Daniel 6:1–28 (RSV).

revoked: canceled.

supplication: humble prayer.

labored . . . rescue him: i.e., tried all day to think of some way around the law.

signet: stamp, seal.

diversions: entertainment.

anguish: suffering.

cannot be revoked." Therefore King Darius signed the document and interdict.

When Daniel knew that the document had been signed, he went to his house where he had windows in his upper chamber open toward Jerusalem; and he got down upon his knees three times a day and prayed and gave thanks before his God, as he had done previously. Then these men came by agreement and found Daniel making petition and supplication before his God. Then they came near and said before the king, concerning the interdict, "O king! Did you not sign an interdict, that any man who makes petition to any god or man within thirty days except to you, O king, shall be cast into the den of lions?" The king answered, "The thing stands fast, according to the law of the Medes and Persians, which cannot be revoked." Then they answered before the king, "That Daniel, who is one of the exiles from Judah, pays no heed to you, O king, or the interdict you have signed, but makes his petition three times a day."

Then the king, when he heard these words, was much distressed, and set his mind to deliver Daniel; and he labored till the sun went down to rescue him. Then these men came by agreement to the king, and said to the king, "Know, O king, that it is a law of the Medes and Persians that no interdict or ordinance which the king establishes can be changed."

Then the king commanded, and Daniel was brought and cast into the den of lions. The king said to Daniel, "May your God, whom you serve continually, deliver you!" And a stone was brought and laid upon the mouth of the den, and the king sealed it with his own signet and with the signet of his lords, that nothing might be changed concerning Daniel. Then the king went to his palace, and spent the night fasting; no diversions were brought to him, and sleep fled from him.

Then, at break of day, the king arose and went in haste to the den of lions. When he came near to the den where Daniel was, he cried out in a tone of anguish and said to Daniel, "O Daniel, servant of the living God, has your God, whom you serve continually, been able to deliver you from the lions?" Then Daniel said to the king, "O king, live for ever! My God sent his angel and shut the lions' mouths, and they have not hurt me, because I was found blameless before him; and also before you, O king, I have done no wrong." Then the king was exceedingly glad, and commanded that Daniel be taken up out of the den. So Daniel was taken up out of the den, and no kind of hurt was found upon him, because he had trusted in his God. And the king commanded, and those men who had accused Daniel were brought and cast into the den of lions—they, their children, and their wives; and before they reached the bottom of the den the lions overpowered them and broke all their bones in pieces.

exceedingly: very.

Then King Darius wrote to all the peoples, nations, and languages that dwell in all the earth: "Peace be multiplied to you. I make a decree, that in all my royal dominion men tremble and fear before the God of Daniel,

dominion: empire.

> for he is the living God,
> enduring for ever;
> his kingdom shall never be destroyed,
> and his dominion shall be to the end.
> He delivers and rescues,
> he works signs and wonders
> in heaven and on earth,
> he who has saved Daniel
> from the power of the lions."

So this Daniel prospered during the reign of Darius and the reign of Cyrus the Persian.

For close reading

1 How many times does the story mention that the law of Darius cannot be changed and that the punishment must be carried out?

2 What details of the story show the king's concern for Daniel?

3 What happens to the people who accused Daniel?

For thought and discussion

4 After Daniel is thrown into the lions' den, the story focuses completely on Darius. Why do you think the story does so?

5 What is Darius's attitude toward Daniel's God at the end? Is his attitude different from the attitudes of Nebuchadnezzar and Belshazzar when they acknowledged the power of the God of the Jews?

6 According to Daniel's jealous enemies, the only way they could attack him was through his religion. Where else, in the Bible and in history, have Jews been in trouble because of their religion? What other religious groups have suffered for similar reasons? Why do you think this is so?

7 Daniel plays a part in three stories in this chapter. What do you learn about Daniel's character and abilities in these stories? Describe Daniel in two sentences.

8 What similarities do you find among the stories from the Babylonian Captivity (Susanna, the fiery furnace, the writing on the wall, the lions' den)? For example, in several of the stories, Jews are put to a test of their faith in the God of Israel; often they must face a foreign king. What other similarities do you find? Try to make a general outline, or pattern for these stories.

9 Though the stories in this chapter have grim settings of exile and danger, they often have moments of humor. What incidents struck you as humorous?

Activities

1 Using whatever medium you wish, depict Daniel in the lions' den.

2 You are one of the lions in the den. What is your reaction to the episode with Daniel?

3 Make up a comic book or picture book that would help you teach very young children about the various stories of Daniel and other Jews in Babylon.

ESTHER

Esther

[*This story describes the experiences of Jews living in Persia during the reign of King Ahasuerus* (ə haz′yü ėr′əs).]

In the days of Ahasuerus, the Ahasuerus who reigned from India to Ethiopia over one hundred and twenty-seven provinces, . . . the king gave for all the people present in Susa the capital, both great and small, a banquet lasting for seven days, in the court of the garden of the king's palace. . . . Queen Vashti also gave a banquet for the women in the palace which belonged to King Ahasuerus.

On the seventh day, when the heart of the king was merry with wine, he commanded Mehuman, Biztha, Harbona, Bigtha and Abagtha, Zethar and Carkas, the seven eunuchs who served King Ahasuerus as chamberlains, to bring Queen Vashti before the king with her royal crown, in order to show the peoples and the princes her beauty; for she was fair to behold. But Queen Vashti refused to come at the king's command conveyed by the eunuchs. At this the king was enraged, and his anger burned within him.

chamberlains: high officials.

Then the king said to the wise men who knew the times . . . "According to the law, what is to be done to Queen Vashti, because she has not performed the command of King Ahasuerus conveyed by the eunuchs?" Then Memucan said in presence of the

Esther 1:1, 3b, 9–10a, 10c–13, 15–17a, 19a, 19c–21; 2:2, 4–5a, 7–8c, 10–11, 16a, 17, 21–23a; 3:1a, 2, 5–6, 8–9, 11; 4:1, 4–7a, 8b–14; 5:1–4, 9–14; 6:1–7:10; 8:15–17 (RSV).

king and the princes, "Not only to the king has Queen Vashti done wrong, but also to all the princes and all the peoples who are in all the provinces of King Ahasuerus. For this deed of the queen will be made known to all women, causing them to look with contempt upon their husbands. . . . If it please the king, let a royal order go forth from him . . . that Vashti is to come no more before King Ahasuerus; and let the king give her royal position to another who is better than she. So when the decree made by the king is proclaimed throughout all his kingdom, vast as it is, all women will give honor to their husbands, high and low." This advice pleased the king and the princes, and the king did as Memucan proposed . . . .

. . . Then the king's servants who attended him said, "Let beautiful young virgins be sought out for the king. . . . And let the maiden who pleases the king be queen instead of Vashti." This pleased the king, and he did so.

Now there was a Jew in Susa the capital whose name was Mordecai . . . . He had brought up Hadassah, that is Esther, the daughter of his uncle, for she had neither father nor mother; the maiden was beautiful and lovely, and when her father and her mother died, Mordecai adopted her as his own daughter. So when the king's order and his edict were proclaimed, and when many maidens were gathered in Susa the capital in custody of Hegai, Esther also was taken into the king's palace . . . Esther had not made known her people or kindred, for Mordecai had charged her not to make it known. And every day Mordecai walked in front of the court of the harem, to learn how Esther was and how she fared.

. . . And when Esther was taken to King Ahasuerus . . . the king loved Esther more than all the women, and she found grace and favor in his sight more than all the virgins, so that he set the royal crown on her head and made her queen instead of Vashti.

. . . And in those days, as Mordecai was sitting at the king's gate, Bigthan and Teresh, two of the king's eunuchs, who guarded the threshold, became angry and sought to lay hands on King Ahasuerus. And this came to the knowledge of Mordecai, and he told it to Queen Esther, and Esther told the

Mordecai (môr′də ki).

harem: the section of the palace where the king's women lived.

king in the name of Mordecai. When the affair was investigated and found to be so, the men were both hanged on the gallows. . . .

After these things King Ahasuerus promoted Haman the Agagite . . . . And all the king's servants who were at the king's gate bowed down and did obeisance to Haman; for the king had so commanded concerning him. But Mordecai did not bow down or do obeisance. . . . And when Haman saw that Mordecai did not bow down or do obeisance to him, Haman was filled with fury. But he disdained to lay hands on Mordecai alone. So, as they had made known to him the people of Mordecai, Haman sought to destroy all the Jews, the people of Mordecai, throughout the whole kingdom of Ahasuerus.

disdained: i.e., felt it was not worthwhile.

. . . Then Haman said to King Ahasuerus, "There is a certain people scattered abroad and dispersed among the peoples in all the provinces of your kingdom; their laws are different from those of every other people, and they do not keep the king's laws, so that it is not for the king's profit to tolerate them. If it please the king, let it be decreed that they be destroyed . . . ." And the king said to Haman, "The money is given to you, the people also, to do with them as it seems good to you." . . .

When Mordecai learned all that had been done, Mordecai rent his clothes and put on sackcloth and ashes, and went out into the midst of the city, wailing with a loud and bitter cry . . . .

When Esther's maids and her eunuchs came and told her, the queen was deeply distressed; she sent garments to clothe Mordecai, so that he might take off his sackcloth, but he would not accept them. Then Esther called for Hathach, one of the king's eunuchs, who had been appointed to attend her, and ordered him to go to Mordecai to learn what this was and why it was. Hathach went out to Mordecai in the open square of the city in front of the king's gate, and Mordecai told him all that had happened to him . . . that he might show it to Esther and explain it to her and charge her to go to the king to make supplication to him and entreat him for her people. And Hathach went and told Esther what Mordecai had said. Then Esther spoke to Hathach and gave him a message for Mordecai, saying, "All the king's servants and the people of the king's provinces know that if any man or woman goes to

supplication: humble request.

scepter: rod or staff
symbolizing the king's
power.

the king inside the inner court without being called,
there is but one law; all alike are to be put to death,
except the one to whom the king holds out the
golden scepter that he may live. And I have not been
called to come in to the king these thirty days." And
they told Mordecai what Esther had said. Then
Mordecai told them to return answer to Esther,
"Think not that in the king's palace you will escape
any more than all the other Jews. For if you keep
silence at such a time as this, relief and deliverance
will rise for the Jews from another quarter, but you
and your father's house will perish. And who knows
whether you have not come to the kingdom for such
a time as this?" . . .

relief . . . quarter: i.e.,
the Jews will be saved
in some other way.

On the third day Esther put on her royal robes and
stood in the inner court of the king's palace, opposite the king's hall. The king was sitting on his royal
throne inside the palace opposite the entrance to
the palace; and when the king saw Queen Esther
standing in the court, she found favor in his sight
and he held out to Esther the golden scepter that
was in his hand. Then Esther approached and
touched the top of the scepter. And the king said to
her, "What is it, Queen Esther? What is your request? It shall be given you, even to the half of my
kingdom." And Esther said, "If it please the king, let
the king and Haman come this day to a dinner that I
have prepared for the king." . . .

And Haman went out that day joyful and glad of
heart. But when Haman saw Mordecai in the king's
gate, that he neither rose nor trembled before him,
he was filled with wrath against Mordecai. Nevertheless Haman restrained himself, and went home; and
he sent and fetched his friends and his wife Zeresh.

And Haman recounted to them the splendor of his
riches, the number of his sons, all the promotions
with which the king had honored him, and how he
had advanced him above the princes and the servants of the king. And Haman added, "Even Queen
Esther let no one come with the king to the banquet
she prepared but myself. And tomorrow also I am
invited by her together with the king. Yet all this
does me no good, so long as I see Mordecai the Jew
sitting at the king's gate." Then his wife Zeresh and
all his friends said to him, "Let a gallows fifty cubits
high be made, and in the morning tell the king to
have Mordecai hanged upon it; then go merrily with

the king to the dinner." This counsel pleased Haman, and he had the gallows made.

On that night the king could not sleep; and he gave orders to bring the book of memorable deeds, the chronicles, and they were read before the king. And it was found written how Mordecai had told about Bigthana and Teresh, two of the king's eunuchs, who guarded the threshold, and who had sought to lay hands upon King Ahasuerus. And the king said, "What honor or dignity has been bestowed on Mordecai for this?" The king's servants who attended him said, "Nothing has been done for him." And the king said, "Who is in the court?" Now Haman had just entered the outer court of the king's palace to speak to the king about having Mordecai hanged on the gallows that he had prepared for him. So the king's servants told him, "Haman is there, standing in the court." And the king said, "Let him come in." So Haman came in, and the king said to him, "What shall be done to the man whom the king delights to honor?" And Haman said to himself, "Whom would the king delight to honor more than me?" And Haman said to the king, "For the man whom the king delights to honor, let royal robes be brought, which the king has worn, and the horse which the king has ridden, and on whose head a royal crown is set; and let the robes and the horse be handed over to one of the king's most noble princes; let him array the man whom the king delights to honor, and let him conduct the man on horseback through the open square of the city, proclaiming before him: 'Thus shall it be done to the man whom the king delights to honor.' " Then the king said to Haman, "Make haste, take the robes and the horse, as you have said, and do so to Mordecai the Jew who sits at the king's gate. Leave out nothing that you have mentioned." So Haman took the robes and the horse, and he arrayed Mordecai and made him ride through the open square of the city, proclaiming, "Thus shall it be done to the man whom the king delights to honor."

Then Mordecai returned to the king's gate. But Haman hurried to his house, mourning and with his head covered. And Haman told his wife Zeresh and all his friends everything that had befallen him. Then his wise men and his wife Zeresh said to him, "If Mordecai, before whom you have begun to fall, is of

counsel: advice.

chronicles: written records.

array: richly dress.

the Jewish people, you will not prevail against him but will surely fall before him.''

While they were yet talking with him, the king's eunuchs arrived and brought Haman in haste to the banquet that Esther had prepared.

So the king and Haman went in to feast with Queen Esther. And on the second day, as they were drinking wine, the king again said to Esther, "What is your petition, Queen Esther? It shall be granted you. And what is your request? Even to the half of my kingdom, it shall be fulfilled." Then Queen Esther answered, "If I have found favor in your sight, O king, and if it please the king, let my life be given me at my petition, and my people at my request. For we are sold, I and my people, to be destroyed, to be slain, and to be annihilated. If we had been sold merely as slaves, men and women, I would have held my peace; for our affliction is not to be compared with the loss to the king." Then King Ahasuerus said to Queen Esther, "Who is he, and where is he, that would presume to do this?" And Esther said, "A foe and enemy! This wicked Haman!" Then Haman was in terror before the king and the queen. And the king rose from the feast in wrath and went into the palace garden; but Haman stayed to beg his life from Queen Esther, for he saw that evil was determined against him by the king. And the king returned from the palace garden to the place where they were drinking wine, as Haman was falling on the couch where Esther was; and the king said, "Will he even assault the queen in my presence, in my own house?" As the words left the mouth of the king, they covered Haman's face. Then said Harbona, one of the eunuchs in attendance on the king, "Moreover, the gallows which Haman has prepared for Mordecai, whose word saved the king, is standing in Haman's house, fifty cubits high." And the king said, "Hang him on that." So they hanged Haman on the gallows which he had prepared for Mordecai. Then the anger of the king abated. . . .

Then Mordecai went out from the presence of the king in royal robes of blue and white, with a great golden crown and a mantle of fine linen and purple, while the city of Susa shouted and rejoiced. The Jews had light and gladness and joy and honor. And in every province and in every city, wherever the king's command and his edict came, there was gladness and joy among the Jews, a feast and a holiday. And many from the peoples of the country declared themselves Jews, for the fear of the Jews had fallen upon them. . . .

For close reading

1 How many times in the story is Ahasuerus given advice? How many times does he act on this advice?
2 What is Esther's first answer when Mordecai asks for help? What arguments does Mordecai use to convince her to help the Jews?
3 How many examples of disobedience or disrespect can you find in this story?

For thought and discussion

4 What is your opinion of Ahasuerus as a king? As a husband? Support your views with details from the story.
5 What effect does the first scene (involving Queen Vashti) have on the rest of the story?
6 In what ways does Esther change or develop during the story? What would you say is the turning point in her life?
7 An ironic situation exists in a story when the opposite of what is intended or expected happens. For example, Haman thinks the honors he suggests to the king are for himself—but actually the honors are for his enemy, Mordecai. Find at least one other ironic situation in the story.
8 What details in the story prepare us for Haman's final downfall and Mordecai's final triumph?
9 Which of the four main characters do you find most interesting? Why?
10 Why do you suppose the story includes so many examples of disobedience and disrespect for authority?
11 The triumph of the underdog is one appealing feature of the story of Esther. What other things in the story make it popular and appealing to many people?

10

jesus:
birth
and early
ministry

WHERE IS HE WHO HAS BEEN BORN KING?

Luke, Matthew

The angel Gabriel was sent from God to a city of Galilee named Nazareth, to a virgin betrothed to a man whose name was Joseph, of the house of David; and the virgin's name was Mary. And he came to her and said, "Hail, O favored one, the Lord is with you!" But she was greatly troubled at the saying, and considered in her mind what sort of greeting this might be. And the angel said to her, "Do not be afraid, Mary, for you have found favor with God. And behold, you will conceive in your womb and bear a son, and you shall call his name Jesus.

Luke 1:26.
betrothed: engaged to be married.

> He will be great, and will be called the Son of
>   the Most High;
> and the Lord God will give to him the throne of
>   his father David,
> and he will reign over the house of Jacob for
>   ever;
> and of his kingdom there will be no end."

And Mary said to the angel, "How can this be, since I have no husband?" And the angel said to her,

> "The Holy Spirit will come upon you,

Luke 1:26–38; 2:1–21. Matthew 2:1–16, 19–23 (RSV).

LEFT: Detail of a bronze crosier (ecclesiastical staff) decorated with a depiction of the annunciation. French, thirteenth century. Musée Departmental des Antiquités de la Seine-Maritime, Rouen. Lauros-Giraudon.

and the power of the Most High will over-
   shadow you;
therefore the child to be born will be called
   holy,
the Son of God.

kinswoman: relative.

handmaid: servant.

And behold, your kinswoman Elizabeth in her old age has also conceived a son; and this is the sixth month with her who was called barren. For with God nothing will be impossible." And Mary said, "Behold I am the handmaid of the Lord; let it be to me according to your word." And the angel depart-ed from her. . . .

**Caesar Augustus . . .
enrolled:** the Roman emperor ordered all people in the empire to return to their ancestral home to register for taxation.

In those days a decree went out from Caesar Augustus that all the world should be enrolled. This was the first enrollment, when Quirinius was gover-nor of Syria. And all went to be enrolled, each to his own city. And Joseph also went up from Galilee, from the city of Nazareth, to Judea, to the city of David, which is called Bethlehem, because he was of the house and lineage of David, to be enrolled with Mary, his betrothed, who was with child. And while they were there, the time came for her to be delivered. And she gave birth to her first-born son and wrapped him in swaddling cloths, and laid him in a manger, because there was no place for them in the inn.

swaddling cloths:
long strips of cloth.

manger: place for food for animals.

And in that region there were shepherds out in the field, keeping watch over their flock by night. And an angel of the Lord appeared to them, and the glory of the Lord shone around them, and they were filled with fear. And the angel said to them, "Be not afraid; for behold, I bring you good news of a great joy which will come to all the people; for to you is born this day in the city of David a Savior, who is Christ the Lord. And this will be a sign for you: you will find a babe wrapped in swaddling cloths and lying in a manger." And suddenly there was with the angel a multitude of the heavenly host praising God and saying,

"Glory to God in the highest,
and on earth peace among men with whom he
   is pleased!"

When the angels went away from them into heaven, the shepherds said to one another, "Let us go over to Bethlehem and see this thing that has happened, which the Lord has made known to us." And they went with haste, and found Mary and Joseph, and the babe lying in a manger. And when they saw it they made known the saying which had been told them concerning this child; and all who heard it wondered at what the shepherds told them. But Mary kept all these things, pondering them in her heart. And the shepherds returned, glorifying and praising God for all they had heard and seen, as it had been told them.

And at the end of eight days, when he was circumcised, he was called Jesus, the name given by the angel before he was conceived in the womb. . . .

pondering them: thinking them over carefully.

Now when Jesus was born in Bethlehem of Judea in the days of Herod the king, behold, wise men from the east came to Jerusalem, saying, "Where is he who has been born king of the Jews? For we have seen his star in the east, and have come to worship him." When Herod the king heard this, he was troubled, and all Jerusalem with him; and assembling all the chief priests and scribes of the people, he inquired of them where the Christ was to be born. They told him, "In Bethlehem of Judea; for so it is written by the prophet:

Matt. 2:1.
Herod: ruler of Judea, by authority of the Romans.
wise men: also called "magi" and "astrologers" in other translations.

'And you, O Bethlehem, in the land of Judah, are by no means least among the rulers of Judah; for from you shall come a ruler who will govern my people Israel.' "

Then Herod summoned the wise men secretly and ascertained from them what time the star appeared; and he sent them to Bethlehem, saying, "Go and search diligently for the child, and when you have found him bring me word, that I too may come and worship him." When they had heard the king they went their way; and lo, the star which they had seen in the east went before them, till it came to rest over the place where the child was. When they saw the star, they rejoiced exceedingly with great joy; and going into the house they saw the child with Mary his mother, and they fell down and worshiped him.

frankincense,
myrrh: incense and
perfume (expensive
items in Judea).

Then, opening their treasures, they offered him gifts, gold and frankincense and myrrh. And being warned in a dream not to return to Herod, they departed to their own country by another way.

Now when they had departed, behold, an angel of the Lord appeared to Joseph in a dream and said, "Rise, take the child and his mother, and flee to Egypt, and remain there till I tell you; for Herod is about to search for the child, to destroy him." And he rose and took the child and his mother by night, and departed to Egypt, and remained there until the death of Herod. This was to fulfil what the Lord had spoken by the prophet, "Out of Egypt have I called my son."

Then Herod, when he saw that he had been tricked by the wise men, was in a furious rage, and he sent and killed all the male children in Bethlehem and in all that region who were two years old or under, according to the time which he had ascertained from the wise men. . . .

But when Herod died, behold, an angel of the Lord appeared in a dream to Joseph in Egypt, saying, "Rise, take the child and his mother, and go to the land of Israel, for those who sought the child's life are dead." And he rose and took the child and his mother, and went to the land of Israel. But when he heard that Archelaus reigned over Judea in place of his father Herod, he was afraid to go there, and being warned in a dream he withdrew to the district of Galilee. And he went and dwelt in a city called Nazareth, that what was spoken by the prophets might be fulfilled, "He shall be called a Nazarene."

For close reading

1 Why do Mary and Joseph travel to Bethlehem?
2 What methods does God use to give messages to people in these passages?
3 What two groups of visitors come to see the baby? How are the two groups similar? How are they different?
4 How does King Herod react when he learns of the birth of "the king of the Jews"?

For thought and discussion

5 Suppose there had been room at the inn. Suppose the birth had occurred during the day. What qualities of the story would be changed in each case?
6 The Matthew section of the birth story (beginning on page 337) makes several references to what prophets had written. What do you think is the purpose of these references?
7 Why do you think Herod reacts as he does to the news the wise men bring him?
8 What details of the birth story suggest lowliness, humbleness? What details suggest kingliness, splendor? What details suggest danger, death? From what you know of Jesus' later life, what might these details foreshadow?

Activities

1 The Bible presents four accounts of the life of Jesus: the Gospels of Matthew, Mark, Luke, and John. Only Matthew and Luke give detailed descriptions of Jesus' birth. Read and compare the complete birth stories in a Bible. What differences can you discover? How do these differences affect the impression the story makes on the reader? Why do you think each story emphasizes different aspects of the Nativity? Report to the class.
2 The Matthew account never mentions how many wise men came to Bethlehem—yet tradition tells us there were three, and even provides their names.

What other features have traditionally been added to what is given in the Bible's story of Jesus' birth? Choose one of these Christmas traditions and try to trace its origins.

3 Find out what you can about astrologers in the ancient world, especially in Persia. What was their work? How were they trained? Write a report.

4 You are a shepherd or a wise man who visited the baby Jesus. Write about your experience.

5 The Nativity has been the source of many works of art and music. Find a work of art to illustrate each part of the birth story. Be prepared to discuss whether the artist based his work on the Matthew or Luke account, and what parts of the work are based on other traditions. From carols, spirituals, and other music, select a song that focuses on each part of the Nativity. You and others in the class may wish to put the art and music together into a tape and slide show.

JOURNEY OF THE MAGI

T. S. Eliot

"A cold coming we had of it,
Just the worst time of the year
For a journey, and such a long journey:
The ways deep and the weather sharp,
5   The very dead of winter."
And the camels galled, sore-footed, refractory,
Lying down in the melting snow.
There were times we regretted
The summer palaces on slopes, the terraces,
10   And the silken girls bringing sherbet.
Then the camel men cursing and grumbling
And running away, and wanting their liquor and
      women,
And the night-fires going out, and the lack of
      shelters,
And the cities hostile and the towns unfriendly
15   And the villages dirty and charging high prices:
A hard time we had of it.
At the end we preferred to travel all night,
Sleeping in snatches,
With the voices singing in our ears, saying
20   That this was all folly.

Then at dawn we came down to a temperate valley,
Wet, below the snow line, smelling of vegetation;
With a running stream and a water mill beating the
      darkness,
And three trees on the low sky,
25   And an old white horse galloped away in the
      meadow.

Lines 1-5 are adapted from a 17th-century Nativity sermon by Lancelot Andrews.

galled: i.e., their skin had sores from the rubbing of packs or straps.
refractory: stubborn.

lintel: horizontal beam over a door.

Then we came to a tavern with vine-leaves over
   the lintel,
Six hands at an open door dicing for pieces of
   silver,
And feet kicking the empty wineskins.
But there was no information, and so we
   continued
30 And arrived at evening, not a moment too soon
Finding the place; it was (you may say) satisfactory.

All this was a long time ago, I remember,
And I would do it again, but set down
This set down
35 This: were we led all that way for
Birth or Death? There was a Birth, certainly,
We had evidence and no doubt. I had seen birth
   and death,
But had thought they were different; this Birth was
Hard and bitter agony for us, like Death, our death.
40 We returned to our places, these Kingdoms,

dispensation: i.e., religious system.

But no longer at ease here, in the old dispensation,
With an alien people clutching their gods.
I should be glad of another death.

For thought and discussion

1 What general impressions do you usually have when you think of the magi or wise men? How do these impressions compare with the impressions given by Eliot in this poem?
2 What different emotions does the narrator reveal in each stanza?
3 What references to Jesus' later life can you find in the second stanza? What is the effect of linking these references to the Nativity?
4 Why do you think the narrator is "no longer at ease" (line 41)?
5 Practice reading this poem aloud. (Pay close attention to the punctuation as you read.) Be prepared to explain how you decided on your interpretation.

A
SHEPHERD

Heywood Broun

The host of heaven and the angel of the Lord had filled the sky with radiance. Now, the glory of God was gone, and the shepherds and the sheep stood under dim starlight. The men were shaken by the wonders they had seen and heard and, like the animals, they huddled close.

"Let us now," said the eldest one of the shepherds, "go even unto Bethlehem, and see this thing which has come to pass, which the Lord hath made known unto us."

The City of David lay beyond a far, high hill, upon the crest of which there danced a star. The men made haste to be away, but as they broke out of the circle there was one called Amos who remained. He dug his crook into the turf and clung to it.

crook: a shepherd's staff, curved on the upper end into a hook.

"Come," cried the eldest of the shepherds, but Amos shook his head. They marveled, and called out: "It is true. It was an angel. You heard the tidings. A Saviour is born!"

"I heard," said Amos. "I will abide."

abide: stay.

The eldest walked back from the road to a little knoll on which Amos stood.

"You do not understand," the old man told him. "We have a sign from God. An angel has commanded us. We go to worship the Saviour, who is even now born in Bethlehem. God has made His will manifest."

manifest: clear; plain.

"It is not in my heart," replied Amos.

"A Shepherd" from the *Collected Edition of Heywood Broun*, published by Harcourt, Brace and Company. Reprinted by permission of Patricia Broun.

And now the eldest of the shepherds was angry.

"With your eyes," he cried out, "you have seen the host of heaven in these dark hills. And you heard, for it was like the thunder when 'Glory to God in the Highest' came ringing to us out of the night."

And again Amos said, "It is not in my heart."

Another shepherd then broke in. "Because the hills still stand and the sky has not fallen, it is not enough for Amos. He must have something louder than the voice of God."

Amos held more tightly to his crook and answered, "I have need of a whisper."

They laughed at him and said, "What should this voice say in your ear?"

He was silent and they pressed about him and shouted mockingly, "Tell us now. What says the God of Amos, the little shepherd of a hundred sheep?"

Meekness fell away from him. He took his hands from off the crook and raised them high.

"I, too, am a God," said Amos in a loud, strange voice, "and to my hundred I am a saviour."

And when the din of the angry shepherds about him slackened Amos pointed to his hundred.

"See my flock," he said. "See the fright of them. The fear of the bright angel and of the voices is still upon them. God is busy in Bethlehem. He has no time for a hundred sheep. They are my sheep. I will abide."

This the others did not take so much amiss, for they saw now that there was a terror in all the flocks, and they, too, knew the ways of sheep. And before the shepherds departed on the road to Bethlehem toward the bright star each one talked to Amos and told him what he should do for the care of the several flocks. And yet one or two turned back a moment to taunt Amos, before they reached the dip in the road which led to the City of David. It was said, "We shall see new glories at the throne of God, and you, Amos—you will see sheep."

Amos paid no heed, for he thought to himself, "One shepherd the less will not matter at the throne of God." Nor did he have time to be troubled that he was not to see the Child who was come to save the world. There was much to be done among the flocks, and Amos walked between the sheep and made under his tongue a clucking noise, which was a way he had, and to his hundred and to the others it was a sound finer and more friendly than the voice of the bright angel. Presently the animals ceased to tremble and they began to graze as the sun came up over the hill where the star had been.

"For sheep," said Amos to himself, "the angels shine too much. A shepherd is better."

With the morning the others came up the road from Bethlehem, and they told Amos of the manger and of the wise men who had mingled there with shepherds. And they described to him the gifts—gold, frankincense, and myrrh. And when they were done they said, "And did you see wonders here in the fields with the sheep?"

Amos told them, "Now my hundred are one hundred and one," and he showed them a lamb which had been born just before the dawn.

"Was there for this a great voice out of heaven?" asked the eldest of the shepherds.

Amos shook his head and smiled, and there was in his face that which seemed to the shepherds a wonder even in a night of wonders.

"To my heart," he said, "there came a whisper."

For thought and discussion

1 In what sense is Amos a "saviour"?
2 If Amos is not listening to the voice of God, what do you think he is listening to? Who or what might the "whisperer" be?
3 How is Amos rewarded for his decision to stay with the flocks?
4 Do you think Amos made the right choice? What would you have done in his place?

SOME SAY THAT EVER 'GAINST THAT SEASON COMES

William Shakespeare

'gainst: just before.

Some say that ever 'gainst that season comes
Wherein our Saviour's birth is celebrated,
The bird of dawning singeth all night long:
And then, they say, no spirit dare stir abroad;
5 The nights are wholesome; then no planets strike,
No fairy takes, nor witch hath power to charm,

hallow'd: holy.

So hallow'd and so gracious is the time.

Hamlet, Act 1, Scene 1

CHRISTMAS COMMENTARY

Harry Reasoner

Christmas is such a unique idea that most non-Christians accept it and I think sometimes envy it: if Christmas is the anniversary of the appearance of the Lord of the universe in the form of a helpless baby, it's quite a day. It's a startling idea, and the theologians, who sometimes love logic more than they love God, find it uncomfortable. But, if God did do it, he had a tremendous insight. People are afraid of God and standing in his very bright light. But everyone has seen babies and almost everyone likes them—so if God wanted to be loved as well as feared, he moved correctly here. And if he wanted to know people as well as rule them he moved correctly, because a baby, growing up, learns all there is to know about people. If God wanted to be intimately a part of man, he moved correctly—for the experience of birth and familyhood is our most intimate and precious experience.

So it comes beyond logic. It is what a bishop I used to know called a kind of divine insanity. It is either all falsehood or it is the truest thing in the world. It is the story of the great innocence of God, the baby, God in the power of man, and it is such a dramatic shot toward the heart that if it is not true, for Christians nothing is true. . . .

Abridgement of "Commentary" by Harry Reasoner from *The ABC Evening News with Howard K. Smith and Harry Reasoner,* December 25, 1973. Reprinted by permission of Harry Reasoner.

TO JESUS
ON HIS
BIRTHDAY

Edna St. Vincent Millay

For this your mother sweated in the cold,
For this you bled upon the bitter tree:
A yard of tinsel ribbon bought and sold;
A paper wreath; a day at home for me.
5 The merry bells ring out, the people kneel;
Up goes the man of God before the crowd;
With voice of honey and with eyes of steel
He drones your humble gospel to the proud.
Nobody listens. Less than the wind that blows
10 Are all your words to us you died to save.
O Prince of Peace! O Sharon's dewy Rose!
How mute you lie within your vaulted grave.
The stone the angel rolled away with tears
Is back upon your mouth these thousand years.

Sharon's dewy
Rose: see page 248.

mute: silent.

For thought and discussion

1 The three preceding selections ("Some say . . . ," "Christmas Commentary," and "To Jesus on His Birthday") are all reflections on the meaning of the Christmas season. What different impression do you get from each selection?

2 In the "Commentary" notice these words: *most, I think, sometimes, almost everyone,* and five repetitions of the word *if.* What do these words suggest about Reasoner's way of presenting his thoughts? Why do you think he chooses this way?

3 The title "To Jesus on His Birthday" suggests a gift. What is given to Jesus in the poem?

4 The Millay poem makes several ironic contrasts. For example, the efforts and sufferings of Mary and Jesus are contrasted with such trivial things as "a yard of tinsel ribbon." What other contrasts can you find in this poem?

IS NOT THIS THE CARPENTER?

Mark, John

Mark 1:4.

John: the son of Elizabeth (see page 336).

baptism of repentance: a ceremony using water to symbolize washing away what is impure.

John the baptizer appeared in the wilderness, preaching a baptism of repentance for the forgiveness of sins. And there went out to him all the country of Judea, and all the people of Jerusalem; and they were baptized by him in the river Jordan, confessing their sins. Now John was clothed with camel's hair, and had a leather girdle around his waist, and ate locusts and wild honey. And he preached, saying, "After me comes he who is mightier than I, the thong of whose sandals I am not worthy to stoop down and untie. I have baptized you with water; but he will baptize you with the Holy Spirit."

In those days Jesus came from Nazareth of Galilee and was baptized by John in the Jordan. And when he came up out of the water, immediately he saw the heavens opened and the Spirit descending upon him like a dove; and a voice came from heaven, "Thou art my beloved Son; with thee I am well pleased."

The Spirit immediately drove him out into the wilderness. And he was in the wilderness forty days, tempted by Satan; and he was with the wild beasts; and the angels ministered to him.

Now after John was arrested, Jesus came into Galilee, preaching the gospel of God, and saying,

---

Mark 1:4–15; 4:35–41; 5:1–17, 21–43; 6:1–6, 14–52. John 6:25–40 (RSV).

"The time is fulfilled, and the kingdom of God is at hand; repent, and believe in the gospel." . . .

gospel: message of good news.

[Jesus called certain men to be his personal followers. Accompanied by these disciples (also called apostles) he spoke to a large crowd beside the Sea of Galilee.]

On that day, when evening had come, he said to them, "Let us go across to the other side." And leaving the crowd, they took him with them in the boat, just as he was. And other boats were with him. And a great storm of wind arose, and the waves beat into the boat, so that the boat was already filling. But he was in the stern, asleep on the cushion; and they woke him and said to him, "Teacher, do you not care if we perish?" And he awoke and rebuked the wind, and said to the sea, "Peace! Be still!" And the wind ceased, and there was a great calm. He said to them, "Why are you afraid? Have you no faith?" And they were filled with awe, and said to one another, "Who then is this, that even wind and sea obey him?"

rebuked: scolded.

They came to the other side of the sea, to the country of the Gerasenes. And when he had come out of the boat, there met him out of the tombs a man with an unclean spirit, who lived among the tombs; and no one could bind him any more, even with a chain; for he had often been bound with fetters and chains, but the chains he wrenched apart, and the fetters he broke in pieces; and no one had the strength to subdue him. Night and day among the tombs and on the mountains he was always crying out, and bruising himself with stones. And when he saw Jesus from afar, he ran and worshiped him; and crying out with a loud voice, he said, "What have you to do with me, Jesus, Son of the Most High God? I adjure you by God, do not torment me." For he had said to him, "Come out of the man, you unclean spirit!" And Jesus asked him, "What is your name?" He replied, "My name is Legion; for we are many." And he begged him eagerly not to send them out of the country. Now a great herd of swine was feeding there on the hillside; and they begged him, "Send us to the swine, let us enter them." So he gave them leave. And the unclean spirits came out, and entered the swine;

tombs: usually caves.
with an unclean spirit: possessed by demons; insane.

adjure: beg.

my name is Legion: i.e., there is a legion, an army of us.

and the herd, numbering about two thousand, rushed down the steep bank into the sea, and were drowned in the sea.

The herdsmen fled, and told it in the city and in the country. And people came to see what it was that had happened. And they came to Jesus, and saw the demoniac sitting there, clothed and in his right mind, the man who had had the legion; and they were afraid. And those who had seen it told what had happened to the demoniac and to the swine. And they began to beg Jesus to depart from their neighborhood. . . .

And when Jesus had crossed again in the boat to the other side, a great crowd gathered about him; and he was beside the sea. Then came one of the rulers of the synagogue, Jairus by name; and seeing him, he fell at his feet, and besought him, saying, "My little daughter is at the point of death. Come and lay your hands on her, so that she may be made well, and live." And he went with him.

synagogue: place of worship and religious study.

And a great crowd followed him and thronged about him. And there was a woman who had had a flow of blood for twelve years, and who had suffered much under many physicians, and had spent all that she had, and was no better but rather grew worse. She had heard the reports about Jesus, and came up behind him in the crowd and touched his garment. For she said, "If I touch even his garments, I shall be made well." And immediately the hemorrhage ceased; and she felt in her body that she was healed of her disease. And Jesus, perceiving in himself that power had gone forth from him, immediately turned about in the crowd, and said, "Who touched my garments?" And his disciples said to him, "You see the crowd pressing around you, and yet you say, 'Who touched me?' " And he looked around to see who had done it. But the woman, knowing what had been done to her, came in fear and trembling and fell down before him, and told him the whole truth. And he said to her, "Daughter, your faith has made you well; go in peace, and be healed of your disease."

While he was still speaking, there came from the ruler's house some who said, "Your daughter is dead. Why trouble the Teacher any further?" But ignoring what they said, Jesus said to the ruler of the synagogue, "Do not fear, only believe." And he allowed no one to follow him except Peter and James and John the brother of James. When they came to the house of the ruler of the synagogue, he saw a tumult, and people weeping and wailing loudly. And when he had entered, he said to them, "Why do you make a tumult and weep? The child is not dead but sleeping." And they laughed at him. But he put them all outside, and took the child's father and mother and those who were with him, and went in where the child was. Taking her by the hand he said to her, "Talitha cumi"; which means, "Little girl, I say to you, arise." And immediately the girl got up and walked (she was twelve years of age), and they were immediately overcome with amazement. And he strictly charged them that no one should know this, and told them to give her something to eat.

He went away from there and came to his own country; and his disciples followed him. And on the sabbath he began to teach in the synagogue; and many who heard him were astonished, saying, "Where did this man get all this? What is the wisdom given to him? What mighty works are wrought by his hands! Is not this the carpenter, the son of Mary and brother of James and Joses and Judas and Simon, and are not his sisters here with us?" And they took offense at him. And Jesus said to them, "A prophet is not without honor, except in his own country, and among his own kin, and in his own house." And he could do no mighty work there, except that he laid his hands upon a few sick people and healed them. And he marveled because of their unbelief.

And he went about among the villages teaching. . . .

King Herod heard of it; for Jesus' name had become known. Some said, "John the baptizer has been raised from the dead; that is why these powers are at work in him." But others said, "It is Elijah." And others said, "It is a prophet, like one of the prophets of old." But when Herod heard of it he said, "John, whom I beheaded, has been raised." For Herod had sent and seized John, and bound him in prison for the sake of Herodias, his brother Philip's wife; because he had married her. For John said to Herod, "It is not lawful for you to have your brother's wife." And Herodias had a grudge against

Peter and James and John: Jesus' closest disciples.

tumult: noisy commotion.

Herod: ruler of Galilee; son of Herod the Great (mentioned in the story of Jesus' birth).

him, and wanted to kill him. But she could not, for Herod feared John, knowing that he was a righteous and holy man, and kept him safe. When he heard him, he was much perplexed; and yet he heard him gladly. But an opportunity came when Herod on his birthday gave a banquet for his courtiers and officers and the leading men of Galilee. For when Herodias's daughter came in and danced, she pleased Herod and his guests; and the king said to the girl, "Ask me for whatever you wish, and I will grant it." And he vowed to her, "Whatever you ask me, I will give you, even half of my kingdom." And she went out, and said to her mother, "What shall I ask?" And she said, "The head of John the baptizer." And she came in immediately with haste to the king, and asked, saying, "I want you to give me at once the head of John the Baptist on a platter." And the king was exceedingly sorry; but because of his oaths and his guests he did not want to break his word to her. And immediately the king sent a soldier of the guard and gave orders to bring his head. He went and beheaded him in the prison, and brought his head on a platter, and gave it to the girl; and the girl gave it to her mother. When his disciples heard of it, they came and took his body, and laid it in a tomb.

[Earlier, Jesus had sent out his disciples in pairs, to preach and to heal the sick.]

The apostles returned to Jesus, and told him all that they had done and taught. And he said to them, "Come away by yourselves to a lonely place, and rest a while." For many were coming and going, and they had no leisure even to eat. And they went away in the boat to a lonely place by themselves. Now many saw them going, and knew them, and they ran there on foot from all the towns, and got there ahead of them. As he went ashore he saw a great throng, and he had compassion on them, because they were like sheep without a shepherd; and he began to teach them many things. And when it grew late, his disciples came to him and said, "This is a lonely place, and the hour is now late; send them away, to go into the country and villages round about and buy themselves something to eat." But he answered them, "You give them something to eat." And they said to him, "Shall we go and buy two

courtiers: attendants at Herod's court.

hundred denarii worth of bread, and give it to them to eat?" And he said to them, "How many loaves have you? Go and see." And when they had found out, they said, "Five, and two fish." Then he commanded them all to sit down by companies upon the green grass. So they sat down in groups, by hundreds and by fifties. And taking the five loaves and the two fish he looked up to heaven, and blessed, and broke the loaves, and gave them to the disciples to set before the people; and he divided the two fish among them all. And they all ate and were satisfied. And they took up twelve baskets full of broken pieces and of the fish. And those who ate the loaves were five thousand men.

Immediately he made his disciples get into the boat and go before him to the other side, to Bethsaida, while he dismissed the crowd. And after he had taken leave of them, he went up on the mountain to pray. And when evening came, the boat was out on the sea, and he was alone on the land. And he saw that they were making headway painfully, for the wind was against them. And about the fourth watch of the night he came to them, walking on the sea. He meant to pass by them, but when they saw him walking on the sea they thought it was a ghost, and cried out; for they all saw him, and were terrified. But immediately he spoke to them and said, "Take heart, it is I; have no fear." And he got into the boat with them and the wind ceased. And they were utterly astounded, for they did not understand about the loaves, but their hearts were hardened. . . .

When they found him on the other side of the sea, they said to him, "Rabbi, when did you come here?" Jesus answered them, "Truly, truly, I say to you, you seek me, not because you saw signs, but because you ate your fill of the loaves. Do not labor for the food which perishes, but for the food which endures to eternal life, which the Son of man will give to you; for on him has God the Father set his seal." Then they said to him, "What must we do, to be doing the works of God?" Jesus answered them, "This is the work of God, that you believe in him whom he has sent." So they said to him, "Then what sign do you do, that we may see, and believe you? What work do you perform? Our fathers ate the

denarii (di ner′ē i): Roman silver coins, each equal to a day's wages in Jesus' time.

by companies: in large groups.

fourth watch: a period of the night beginning at 3 A.M.

John 6:25.
they: part of the crowd that had been fed the day before.
rabbi: teacher.

seal: sign (of authority or approval).

manna in the wilderness; as it is written, 'He gave them bread from heaven to eat.' " Jesus then said to them, "Truly, truly, I say to you, it was not Moses who gave you the bread from heaven; my Father gives you the true bread from heaven. For the bread of God is that which comes down from heaven, and gives life to the world." They said to him, "Lord, give us this bread always."

Jesus said to them, "I am the bread of life; he who comes to me shall not hunger, and he who believes in me shall never thirst. But I said to you that you have seen me and yet do not believe. All that the Father gives me will come to me; and him who comes to me I will not cast out. For I have come down from heaven, not to do my own will, but the will of him who sent me; and this is the will of him who sent me, that I should lose nothing of all that he has given me, but raise it up at the last day. For this is the will of my Father, that every one who sees the Son and believes in him should have eternal life; and I will raise him up at the last day." . . .

For close reading

1 Both John the Baptist and Jesus announce what is coming. What is the difference between their messages?

2 What miracles does Jesus perform in this passage?

3 What words and phrases are used to describe how the various people react to Jesus and what he does?

4 This section contains a long passage from Mark (350-355). In that passage, the opening and closing episodes make a "frame" enclosing the central story of the passage. Can you find other examples of Mark's framing technique in the passage?

5 This section ends with a passage from the Gospel of John—a Gospel which emphasizes the meaning of the events of Jesus' life. In this passage, what seems to be the people's attitude toward miracles? How does Jesus explain the meaning of the feeding of the five thousand?

For thought and discussion

6 There are many connections between the life of John and the life of Jesus, beginning with the angelic foretelling of their births (page 336). What other connections can you find? How is the death of John related to the story of Jesus? Why do you suppose Mark withholds the details of John's death until later in the story?

7 This account describes three different ways by which Jesus heals people. Notice the order in which they are presented. Would it be more effective if they were told in a different order? Explain.

8 Why do you think Jesus "could do no mighty work" in his own country?

9 Twice the disciples are caught in a storm at sea. What might these two stories tell about the disciples and their relationship to Jesus?

10 Do you see any pattern to the ways people respond to Jesus in this account? Explain.

Activities

1 Jesus has so long been presented as "perfect" that sometimes his individual characteristics are passed over. Try to read this section as if it were your first information about Jesus. What personal traits does he seem to have? Where are these traits most clearly revealed? Write about your "discoveries."

2 Read all four Gospel accounts of Jesus' baptism and his stay in the wilderness. Or, read a description of the same miracle in two different Gospels. What differences of detail, emphasis, and style do you find? (A good reference is a "parallel Gospel" edition of the New Testament.)

3 You are the man who was possessed by demons. Write your thoughts at the moment of healing.

4 Show in some medium one of the scenes from Jesus' early ministry.

THE
JESUS
INFECTION

Maxine Kumin

Jesus is with me
on the Blue Grass Parkway going eastbound.
He is with me
on the Old Harrodsburg Road coming home.
5   I am listening
to country gospel music
in the borrowed Subaru.
The gas pedal
and the words
10 leap to the music.
Oh throw out the lifeline!
Someone is drifting away.

Flags fly up in my mind
without my knowing
15 where they've been lying furled
and I am happy
living in the sunlight
where Jesus is near.
A man is driving his polled Herefords
20 across the gleanings of a cornfield
while I am bound for the kingdom of the free.
At the little trestle bridge that has no railing
I see that I won't have to cross Jordan alone.

Signposts every mile exhort me
25 to Get Right With God
and I move over.
There's a neon message blazing
at the crossroad
catty-corner to the Burger Queen:
30 Ye Come With Me.
Is it well with my soul, Jesus?
It sounds so easy
to be happy after the sunrise,
to be washed in the crimson flood.

From *House, Bridge, Fountain, Gate* by Maxine Kumin. Copyright © 1973
by Maxine Kumin. Reprinted by permission of The Viking Press, Inc. and
Curtis Brown, Ltd.

35 Now I am tailgating
   and I read the bumper sticker
   on a Ford truck full of Poland Chinas.

Poland China: a breed of hogs.

   It says: Honk If You Know Jesus
   and I do it.
40 My sound blats out for miles
   behind the pigsqueal
   and it's catching in the front end,
   in the axle,
   in the universal joint,
45 this rich contagion.

contagion: the spreading of any influence from one to another.

   We are going down the valley on a hairpin turn,
   the swine and me, we're breakneck in,
   we're leaning on
   the everlasting arms.

For thought and discussion

1 The narrator is listening to gospel music as she drives. How does this influence her choice of images in the poem?

2 In line 13, what might the "flags" be?

3 What seems to be the narrator's mood? Choose one or two words to describe her feelings.

4 Think back to some moment in your own life when you felt a similar mood, and try to write about it using specific objects and scenes the way the poet does.

11

jesus:
teachings,
death, and
resurrection

THE SERMON ON THE MOUNT

Matthew

Seeing the crowds, he went up on the mountain, and when he sat down his disciples came to him. And he opened his mouth and taught them, saying:

"Blessed are the poor in spirit, for theirs is the kingdom of heaven.

"Blessed are those who mourn, for they shall be comforted.

"Blessed are the meek, for they shall inherit the earth.

"Blessed are those who hunger and thirst for righteousness, for they shall be satisfied.

"Blessed are the merciful, for they shall obtain mercy.

"Blessed are the pure in heart, for they shall see God.

"Blessed are the peacemakers, for they shall be called sons of God.

"Blessed are those who are persecuted for right- eousness' sake, for theirs is the kingdom of heaven. . . .

for righteousness' sake: for doing right.

"You have heard that it was said to the men of old, 'You shall not kill; and whoever kills shall be liable to judgment.' But I say to you that every one who is angry with his brother shall be liable to judgment. . . . So if you are offering your gift at the altar, and there remember that your brother has something

liable: subject to.

Matthew 5:1–10, 21–22a, 23–24, 27–29, 38–41, 43–45; 6:1–4, 7–13, 19–21, 24–34; 7:1–3, 24–29 (RSV).
LEFT: *The Crucifixion* (from a book cover?), bronze, eighth century. National Museum of Ireland, Dublin.

against you, leave your gift there before the altar and go; first be reconciled to your brother, and then come and offer your gift. . . .

"You have heard that it was said, 'You shall not commit adultery.' But I say to you that every one who looks at a woman lustfully has already committed adultery with her in his heart. If your right eye causes you to sin, pluck it out and throw it away; it is better that you lose one of your members than that your whole body be thrown into hell. . . .

"You have heard that it was said, 'An eye for an eye and a tooth for a tooth.' But I say to you, Do not resist one who is evil. But if any one strikes you on the right cheek, turn to him the other also; and if any one would sue you and take your coat, let him have your cloak as well; and if any one forces you to go one mile, go with him two miles. . . .

"You have heard that it was said, 'You shall love your neighbor and hate your enemy.' But I say to you, Love your enemies and pray for those who persecute you, so that you may be sons of your Father who is in heaven; for he makes his sun rise on the evil and on the good, and sends rain on the just and on the unjust. . . .

piety: religious feeling.

"Beware of practicing your piety before men in order to be seen by them; for then you will have no reward from your Father who is in heaven.

alms: charity.

hypocrites: persons who only pretend to be good or religious.

"Thus, when you give alms, sound no trumpet before you, as the hypocrites do in the synagogues and in the streets, that they may be praised by men. Truly, I say to you, they have received their reward. But when you give alms, do not let your left hand know what your right hand is doing, so that your alms may be in secret; and your Father who sees in secret will reward you. . . .

"And in praying do not heap up empty phrases as the Gentiles do; for they think that they will be heard for their many words. Do not be like them, for your Father knows what you need before you ask him. Pray then like this:

hallowed: sacred.

> Our Father who art in heaven,
> Hallowed be thy name.
> Thy kingdom come,
> Thy will be done,
>   On earth as it is in heaven.
> Give us this day our daily bread;

And forgive us our debts,
    As we also have forgiven our debtors;
And lead us not into temptation,
    But deliver us from evil. . . .

debts: In other versions, "trespasses"; i.e., sins.

"Do not lay up for yourselves treasures on earth, where moth and rust consume and where thieves break in and steal, but lay up for yourselves treasures in heaven, where neither moth nor rust consumes and where thieves do not break in and steal. For where your treasure is, there will your heart be also. . . .

consume: destroy.

"No one can serve two masters; for either he will hate the one and love the other, or he will be devoted to the one and despise the other. You cannot serve God and mammon.

"Therefore I tell you, do not be anxious about your life, what you shall eat or what you shall drink, nor about your body, what you shall put on. Is not life more than food, and the body more than clothing? Look at the birds of the air: they neither sow nor reap nor gather into barns, and yet your heavenly Father feeds them. Are you not of more value than they? And which of you by being anxious can add one cubit to his span of life? And why are you anxious about clothing? Consider the lilies of the field, how they grow; they neither toil nor spin; yet I tell you, even Solomon in all his glory was not arrayed like one of these. But if God so clothes the grass of the field, which today is alive and tomorrow is thrown into the oven, will he not much more clothe you, O men of little faith? Therefore do not be anxious, saying, 'What shall we eat?' or 'What shall we drink?' or 'What shall we wear?' For the Gentiles seek all these things; and your heavenly Father knows that you need them all. But seek first his kingdom and his righteousness, and all these things shall be yours as well.

mammon: money, riches.

cubit: about eighteen inches.

"Therefore do not be anxious about tomorrow, for tomorrow will be anxious for itself. Let the day's own trouble be sufficient for the day.

sufficient: enough.

"Judge not, that you be not judged. For with the judgment you pronounce you will be judged, and the measure you give will be the measure you get. Why do you see the speck that is in your brother's eye, but do not notice the log that is in your own eye? . . .

measure: quantity.

"Every one then who hears these words of mine and does them will be like a wise man who built his house upon the rock; and the rain fell, and the floods came, and the winds blew and beat upon that house, but it did not fall, because it had been founded on the rock. And every one who hears these words of mine and does not do them will be like a foolish man who built his house upon the sand; and the rain fell, and the floods came, and the winds blew and beat against that house, and it fell; and great was the fall of it."

And when Jesus finished these sayings, the crowds were astonished at his teaching, for he taught them as one who had authority, and not as their scribes.

scribes: professional experts in the Law of Moses.

For close reading

1 To whom is Jesus speaking in this passage? How do they respond to his message?
2 What patterns can you find in Jesus' speaking style?
3 According to this passage, what does Jesus say people's attitude should be toward such things as food and clothing?

For thought and discussion

4 "If your right eye causes you to sin, pluck it out and throw it away." What do you think Jesus means? What other statements in the sermon strike you as unusual or surprising? What would you say they mean?

(Continued on page 373.)

RIGHT: *The Annunciation,* painting by Romare Bearden, 1942. Courtesy of Mrs. Nanette Bearden. *The Adoration of the Magi,* detail from a tempera on wood painting by Gentile da Fabriano, 1423. SCALA/Florence.

The Flight into Egypt, serigraph by Sadao Watanabe, Japan, 1970. Lee Boltin.

The Baptism of Christ, detail from the Baptistry doors (south side), Florence. Bronze gilt relief by Andrea Pisano, c. 1330. SCALA/Florence.

Page 368: *The Miracle of the Loaves and the Fishes,* lithograph by Jean Heiberg, USA, contemporary. Lee Boltin.
Page 369: *The Good Samaritan* (after Delacroix), oil painting by Vincent Van Gogh, 1890. The Rijksmuseum, Kröller-Müller, Otterlo, The Netherlands.

ABOVE: *The Return of the Prodigal Son,* etching by Rembrandt Van Rijn. Rijksprenten-kabinet-Rijksmuseum, Amsterdam.
RIGHT: *Christ with the Crown of Thorns,* wood, Africa, twentieth century. Lee Boltin.
BELOW: *The Last Supper,* mural by Richard West. Courtesy of Richard West.

Black Cross, New Mexico, oil painting by Georgia O'Keeffe. Courtesy of the Art Institute of Chicago.

(Continued from page 364.)

5 The sermon frequently uses *you, your,* and *I.* What is the effect of these pronouns? Suppose Jesus had said "people should not" or "humanity should not." What would be the difference?

6 Jesus presents many examples of how people should act toward each other. List six examples. If the examples presented in this sermon were followed by everyone, how might our society be affected? Do you think a society based on these examples is possible? Explain.

7 Jesus concludes his sermon with a parable, a short story with a moral. What is Jesus saying in this story about houses? How does this teaching relate to what Jesus said about the lilies of the field?

Activities

1 Many phrases from the Sermon on the Mount have become well known sayings. List as many as are familiar to you.

2 Select one of the following topics and give a talk before the class based on your reading and personal experience. "Let the day's own trouble be sufficient for the day." "Do not lay up for yourselves treasures on earth, where moth and rust consume." "He makes his sun rise on the evil and on the good, and sends rain on the just and on the unjust." Instead of that kind of talk, you may wish to create a parable with one of these sayings (or another from the sermon) as the last line.

3 Make a collage illustrating one of the points in Jesus' sermon. Write the quotation on the back of your collage. See whether your classmates can tell which point you illustrate.

4 The "blessed" portions of Jesus' sermon are known as the Beatitudes. Select or compose some music to accompany an oral reading or a singing of the Beatitudes.

IN PLACE OF A CURSE

John Ciardi

At the next vacancy for God, if I am elected,
I shall forgive last the delicately wounded
who, having been slugged no harder than anyone
   else,
never got up again, neither to fight back,
5   nor to finger their jaws in painful admiration.

They who are wholly broken, and they in whom
mercy is understanding, I shall embrace at once
and lead to pillows in heaven. But they who are
the meek by trade, baiting the best of their betters
10   with the extortions of a mock-helplessness

I shall take last to love, and never wholly.
Let them all into Heaven—I abolish Hell—
but let it be read over them as they enter:
"Beware the calculations of the meek, who gam-
   bled nothing,
15   gave nothing, and could never receive enough."

baiting: annoying, tormenting.

For thought and discussion

1 What two types of people does the poet mention? Which type would he "forgive last" and "take last to love"?
2 How is it possible to extort (obtain) something by pretending to be helpless (line 10)? Can you think of an example?
3 Some years ago a song entitled "If I Ruled the World" was popular. What one thing would you do if you ruled the world?

PARABLES

Luke, Matthew

And behold, a lawyer stood up to put him to the test, saying, "Teacher, what shall I do to inherit eternal life?" He said to him, "What is written in the law? How do you read?" And he answered, "You shall love the Lord your God with all your heart, and with all your soul, and with all your strength, and with all your mind; and your neighbor as yourself." And he said to him, "You have answered right; do this, and you will live."

Luke 10:25.

But he, desiring to justify himself, said to Jesus, "And who is my neighbor?" Jesus replied, "A man was going down from Jerusalem to Jericho, and he fell among robbers, who stripped him and beat him, and departed, leaving him half dead. Now by chance a priest was going down that road; and when he saw him he passed by on the other side. So likewise a Levite, when he came to the place and saw him, passed by on the other side. But a Samaritan, as he journeyed, came to where he was; and when he saw him, he had compassion, and went to him and bound up his wounds, pouring on oil and wine; then he set him on his own beast and brought him to an inn, and took care of him. And the next day he took out two denarii and gave them to the innkeeper, saying, 'Take care of him; and whatever more you spend, I will repay you when I come back.' Which of these three, do you think, proved neighbor to the man who fell among the robbers?" He said, "The one who showed mercy on him." And Jesus said to him, "Go and do likewise."

Levite: assistant to a priest.

Samaritan: in Jesus' time, there was ill feeling between Jews and Samaritans, though the two peoples were distantly related to each other.

denarii (di ner′ē i): Roman silver coins each equal to a day's wages in Jesus' time.

Luke 10:25–37. Matthew 18:23–35. Luke 18:9–14. Matthew 13:44–46. Luke 14:16–24, 15:1–32 (RSV).

Matt. 18:25.

reckoning: settling of accounts.
talent: originally a unit of weight, about seventy-five pounds. That weight of silver would be worth a great deal today, as it was then.

besought: begged.

Therefore the kingdom of heaven may be compared to a king who wished to settle accounts with his servants. When he began the reckoning, one was brought to him who owed him ten thousand talents; and as he could not pay, his lord ordered him to be sold, with his wife and children and all that he had, and payment to be made. So the servant fell on his knees, imploring him, 'Lord, have patience with me, and I will pay you everything.' And out of pity for him the lord of that servant released him and forgave him the debt. But that same servant, as he went out, came upon one of his fellow servants who owed him a hundred denarii; and seizing him by the throat he said, 'Pay what you owe.' So his fellow servant fell down and besought him, 'Have patience with me, and I will pay you.' He refused and went and put him in prison till he should pay the debt. When his fellow servants saw what had taken place, they were greatly distressed, and they went and reported to their lord all that had taken place. Then his lord summoned him and said to him, 'You wicked servant! I forgave you all that debt because you besought me; and should not you have had mercy on your fellow servant, as I had mercy on you?' And in anger his lord delivered him to the jailers, till he should pay all his debt. So also my heavenly Father will do to every one of you, if you do not forgive your brother from your heart.''

Luke 18:9.

Pharisee: member of a religious party whose main goal (like that of Jesus) was to make the Law of Moses more relevant to the Jewish community. Pharisees are portrayed unfavorably in the New Testament.

He also told this parable to some who trusted in themselves that they were righteous and despised others: "Two men went up into the temple to pray, one a Pharisee and the other a tax collector. The Pharisee stood and prayed thus with himself, 'God, I thank thee that I am not like other men, extortioners, unjust, adulterers, or even like this tax collector. I fast twice a week, I give tithes of all that I get.' But the tax collector, standing far off, would not even lift up his eyes to heaven, but beat his breast, saying, 'God, be merciful to me a sinner!' I tell you, this man went down to his house justified rather than the other; for every one who exalts himself will be humbled, but he who humbles himself will be exalted.''

The kingdom of heaven is like treasure hidden in a field, which a man found and covered up; then in his joy he goes and sells all that he has and buys that field.

"Again, the kingdom of heaven is like a merchant in search of fine pearls, who, on finding one pearl of great value, went and sold all that he had and bought it."

Matt. 13:44.

A man once gave a great banquet, and invited many; and at the time for the banquet he sent his servant to say to those who had been invited, 'Come; for all is now ready.' But they all alike began to make excuses. The first said to him, 'I have bought a field, and I must go out and see it; I pray you, have me excused.' And another said, 'I have bought five yoke of oxen, and I go to examine them; I pray you, have me excused.' And another said, 'I have married a wife, and therefore I cannot come.' So the servant came and reported this to his master. Then the householder in anger said to his servant, 'Go out quickly to the streets and lanes of the city, and bring in the poor and maimed and blind and lame.' And the servant said, 'Sir, what you commanded has been done, and still there is room.' And the master said to the servant, 'Go out to the highways and hedges, and compel people to come in, that my house may be filled. For I tell you, none of those men who were invited shall taste my banquet.' "

Luke 14:16.

yoke: pair.

maimed: injured, disfigured.

compel: force.

Now the tax collectors and sinners were all drawing near to hear him. And the Pharisees and the scribes murmured, saying, "This man receives sinners and eats with them."

So he told them this parable: "What man of you, having a hundred sheep, if he has lost one of them, does not leave the ninety-nine in the wilderness, and go after the one which is lost, until he finds it? And when he has found it, he lays it on his shoulders, rejoicing. And when he comes home, he calls together his friends and his neighbors, saying to

Luke 15:1.
tax collectors: hated because they paid the Romans for the job and were free to get and keep whatever amount they could from citizens.

them, 'Rejoice with me, for I have found my sheep which was lost.' Just so, I tell you, there will be more joy in heaven over one sinner who repents than over ninety-nine righteous persons who need no repentance.

"Or what woman, having ten silver coins, if she loses one coin, does not light a lamp and sweep the house and seek diligently until she finds it? And when she has found it, she calls together her friends and neighbors, saying, 'Rejoice with me, for I have found the coin which I had lost.' Just so, I tell you, there is joy before the angels of God over one sinner who repents."

diligently: carefully and persistently.

Luke 15:11.

And he said, "There was a man who had two sons; and the younger of them said to his father, 'Father, give me the share of property that falls to me.' And he divided his living between them. Not many days later, the younger son gathered all he had and took his journey into a far country, and there he squandered his property in loose living. And when he had spent everything, a great famine arose in that country, and he began to be in want. So he went and joined himself to one of the citizens of that country, who sent him into his fields to feed swine. And he would gladly have fed on the pods that the swine ate; and no one gave him anything. But when he came to himself he said, 'How many of my father's hired servants have bread enough and to spare, but I perish here with hunger! I will arise and go to my father, and I will say to him, "Father, I have sinned against heaven and before you; I am no longer worthy to be called your son; treat me as one of your hired servants." ' And he arose and came to his father. But while he was yet at a distance, his father saw him and had compassion, and ran and embraced him and kissed him. And the son said to him, 'Father, I have sinned against heaven and before you; I am no longer worthy to be called your son.' But the father said to his servants, 'Bring quickly the best robe, and put it on him; and put a ring on his hand, and shoes on his feet; and bring the fatted calf and kill it, and let us eat and make merry; for this my son was dead, and is alive again; he was lost, and is found.' And they began to make merry.

squandered: wasted.

fatted: fattened for a feast.

"Now his elder son was in the field; and as he came and drew near to the house, he heard music and dancing. And he called one of the servants and asked what this meant. And he said to him, 'Your brother has come, and your father has killed the fatted calf, because he has received him safe and sound.' But he was angry and refused to go in. His father came out and entreated him, but he answered his father, 'Lo, these many years I have served you, and I never disobeyed your command; yet you never gave me a kid, that I might make merry with my friends. But when this son of yours came, who has devoured your living with harlots, you killed for him the fatted calf!' And he said to him, 'Son, you are always with me, and all that is mine is yours. It was fitting to make merry and be glad, for this your brother was dead, and is alive; he was lost, and is found.' "

harlots: prostitutes.

For close reading

1 How does Jesus answer the lawyer's question about eternal life?
2 Which of these parables end with an explanation? Which do not?

For thought and discussion

3 Several of these parables show a lowly or despised person doing the right thing or gaining something, in contrast to the actions of "better" people. Which parables fit that pattern? Why do you suppose Jesus emphasizes this kind of teaching?
4 In the story of the father and two sons, how is the personality of each character revealed? Does the

father love one son more than the other? Whose story is being told: the father's? The older son's? The younger son's? Explain.

5 Which parables seem to illustrate teachings that Jesus presented in his sermon (page 361)? In each case, what does the parable add to the point made in the sermon? In general, which method of teaching—sermon or parables—do you prefer? Why?

6 When "put to the test" by people opposed to his teachings, Jesus usually responded with parables. Why do you think Jesus used this method in these hostile, challenging situations?

Activities

1 Whether you realize it or not, you know a good deal about teaching and teachers. Apply your knowledge to the sermon and parables. What kind of teacher was Jesus? What methods did he use?

2 Express one or more of the parables in art, music, or poetry.

3 Many of these parables are known by popular titles: the Prodigal Son, the Good Samaritan, etc. Create a title of your own for each of the parables, and compare choices with classmates.

4 Imagine that you have been sent to observe Jesus by people who are opposed to his teachings. You overhear several of Jesus' parables, but don't quite understand them. Write a report for your employers.

THE PRODIGAL SON

Edwin Arlington Robinson

You are not merry, brother. Why not laugh,
As I do, and acclaim the fatted calf?
For, unless ways are changing here at home,
You might not have it if I had not come.
5 And were I not a thing for you and me
To execrate in anguish, you would be
As indigent a stranger to surprise,
I fear, as I was once, and as unwise.
Brother, believe, as I do, it is best
10 For you that I'm again in the old nest—
Draggled, I grant you, but your brother still,
Full of good wine, good viands, and good will.
You will thank God, some day, that I returned,
And may be singing for what you have learned,
15 Some other day; and one day you may find
Yourself a little nearer to mankind.
And having hated me till you are tired
You will begin to see, as if inspired,
It was fate's way of educating us.
20 Remembering then when you were venomous,
You will be glad enough that I am gone,
But you will know more of what's going on;
For you will see more of what makes it go,
And in more ways than are for you to know.
25 We are so different when we are dead,
That you, alive, may weep for what you said;
And I, the ghost of one you could not save,
May find you planting lentils on my grave.

execrate: curse.
indigent: poor, needy.

viands: foods.

lentils: plant of the pea family. This is a reference to the Jacob-Esau story (see Gen. 25:34).

For thought and discussion

1 According to this poem, how has the brother who stayed at home benefited from the prodigal's actions?
2 Which brother do you feel closer to? Why?

Reprinted with permission of Macmillan Publishing Co., Inc. from *Collected Poems* by Edwin Arlington Robinson. Copyright 1932 by Edwin Arlington Robinson, renewed 1960 by Ruth Nivison and Barbara R. Holt.

LAST DAYS IN JERUSALEM

Luke, Mark, Matthew

[*Accompanied by his twelve disciples,
Jesus made his way to Jerusalem.*]

Luke 19:29.

those who sold:
merchants who sold
birds and animals for
temple sacrifice.

Whn he drew near to Bethphage and Bethany, at the mount that is called Olivet, he sent two of the disciples, saying, "Go into the village opposite, where on entering you will find a colt tied, on which no one has ever yet sat; untie it and bring it here. If any one asks you, 'Why are you untying it?' you shall say this, 'The Lord has need of it.'" . . . And they brought it to Jesus, and throwing their garments on the colt they set Jesus upon it. And as he rode along, they spread their garments on the road. As he was now drawing near, at the descent of the Mount of Olives, the whole multitude of the disciples began to rejoice and praise God with a loud voice for all the mighty works that they had seen, saying, "Blessed be the King who comes in the name of the Lord! Peace in heaven and glory in the highest!" And some of the Pharisees in the multitude said to him, "Teacher, rebuke your disciples." He answered, "I tell you, if these were silent, the very stones would cry out." . . .

And he entered the temple and began to drive out those who sold, saying to them, "It is written, 'My house shall be a house of prayer'; but you have made it a den of robbers."

Luke 19:29–31, 35–40, 45; 22:1–22. Mark 14:29–31. Luke 22:39–42, 45–48, 54–71; 23:1–23. Matthew 27:24–32. Luke 23:32–45. Matthew 27:46–49. Luke 23:46–57 (RSV).

Now the feast of Unleavened Bread drew near, which is called the Passover. And the chief priests and the scribes were seeking how to put him to death; for they feared the people.

Then Satan entered into Judas called Iscariot, who was of the number of the twelve; he went away and conferred with the chief priests and officers how he might betray him to them. And they were glad, and engaged to give him money. So he agreed, and sought an opportunity to betray him to them in the absence of the multitude.

Then came the day of Unleavened Bread, on which the passover lamb had to be sacrificed. So Jesus sent Peter and John, saying, "Go and prepare the passover for us, that we may eat it." They said to him, "Where will you have us prepare it?" He said to them, "Behold, when you have entered the city, a man carrying a jar of water will meet you; follow him into the house which he enters, and tell the house-holder, 'The Teacher says to you, Where is the guest room, where I am to eat the passover with my disciples?' And he will show you a large upper room furnished; there make ready." And they went, and found it as he had told them; and they prepared the passover.

And when the hour came, he sat at table, and the apostles with him. And he said to them, "I have earnestly desired to eat this passover with you before I suffer; for I tell you I shall not eat it until it is fulfilled in the kingdom of God." And he took a cup, and when he had given thanks he said, "Take this, and divide it among yourselves; for I tell you that from now on I shall not drink of the fruit of the vine until the kingdom of God comes." And he took bread, and when he had given thanks he broke it and gave it to them, saying, "This is my body which is given for you. Do this in remembrance of me." And likewise the cup after supper, saying, "This cup which is poured out for you is the new covenant in my blood. But behold the hand of him who betrays me is with me on the table. For the Son of man goes as it has been determined; but woe to that man by whom he is betrayed!" . . .

. . . Peter said to him, "Even though they all fall away, I will not." And Jesus said to him, "Truly, I say to you, this very night, before the cock crows twice,

Unleavened Bread: bread or cakes baked without yeast; eaten at Passover in celebration of Israel's escape from Egypt (see page 108).

conferred: discussed.

covenant: agreement.

woe to: death and damnation upon.

Mark 14:29.

you will deny me three times." But he said vehemently, "If I must die with you, I will not deny you." And they all said the same. . . .

Luke 22:39.

And he came out, and went, as was his custom, to the Mount of Olives; and the disciples followed him. And when he came to the place he said to them, "Pray that you may not enter into temptation." And he withdrew from them about a stone's throw, and knelt down and prayed, "Father, if thou art willing, remove this cup from me; nevertheless not my will, but thine, be done.". . . And when he rose from prayer, he came to the disciples and found them sleeping for sorrow, and he said to them, "Why do you sleep? Rise and pray that you may not enter into temptation."

While he was still speaking, there came a crowd, and the man called Judas, one of the twelve, was leading them. He drew near to Jesus to kiss him; but Jesus said to him, "Judas, would you betray the Son of man with a kiss?" . . .

Then they seized him and led him away, bringing him into the high priest's house. Peter followed at a distance; and when they had kindled a fire in the middle of the courtyard and sat down together, Peter sat among them. Then a maid, seeing him as he sat in the light and gazing at him, said, "This man also was with him." But he denied it, saying, "Woman, I do not know him." And a little later some one else saw him and said, "You also are one of them." But Peter said, "Man, I am not." And after an interval of about an hour still another insisted, saying, "Certainly this man also was with him; for he is a Galilean." But Peter said, "Man, I do not know what you are saying." And immediately, while he was still speaking, the cock crowed. And the Lord turned and looked at Peter. And Peter remembered the word of the Lord, how he had said to him, "Before the cock crows today, you will deny me three times." And he went out and wept bitterly.

Now the men who were holding Jesus mocked him and beat him; they also blindfolded him and asked him, "Prophesy! Who is it that struck you?" And they spoke many other words against him, reviling him.

reviling: attacking with abusive language.

When day came, the assembly of the elders of the people gathered together, both chief priests and scribes; and they led him away to their council, and they said, "If you are the Christ, tell us." But he said to them, "If I tell you, you will not believe; and if I ask you, you will not answer. But from now on the Son of man shall be seated at the right hand of the power of God." And they all said, "Are you the Son of God, then?" And he said to them, "You say that I am." And they said, "What further testimony do we need? We have heard it ourselves from his own lips."

Then the whole company of them arose, and brought him before Pilate. And they began to accuse him, saying, "We found this man perverting our nation, and forbidding us to give tribute to Caesar, and saying that he himself is Christ a king." And Pilate asked him, "Are you the King of the Jews?" And he answered him, "You have said so." And Pilate said to the chief priests and the multitudes, "I find no crime in this man." But they were urgent, saying, "He stirs up the people, teaching throughout all Judea, from Galilee even to this place."

When Pilate heard this, he asked whether the man was a Galilean. And when he learned that he belonged to Herod's jurisdiction, he sent him over to Herod, who was himself in Jerusalem at that time. When Herod saw Jesus, he was very glad, for he had long desired to see him, because he had heard about him, and he was hoping to see some sign done by him. So he questioned him at some length; but he made no answer. The chief priests and the scribes stood by, vehemently accusing him. And Herod with his soldiers treated him with contempt and mocked him; then, arraying him in gorgeous apparel, he sent him back to Pilate. And Herod and Pilate became friends with each other that very day, for before this they had been at enmity with each other.

Pilate then called together the chief priests and the rulers and the people, and said to them, "You brought me this man as one who was perverting the people; and after examining him before you, behold, I did not find this man guilty of any of your charges against him; neither did Herod, for he sent him back to us. Behold, nothing deserving death has been done by him; I will therefore chastise him and release him."

But they all cried out together, "Away with this

council: also called the Sanhedrin, this assembly had the power to make judgments under Jewish law. Only the Roman government, however, could pronounce and carry out the death penalty.

Pilate: Roman governor in charge of Judea.

Herod: see page 353.

sign: miracle.

vehemently: forcefully, with strong feeling.

gorgeous apparel: clothing fit for a king—mocking Jesus' "royal" status.

chastise: punish physically.

insurrection: revolt.

man, and release to us Barabbas"—a man who had been thrown into prison for an insurrection started in the city, and for murder. Pilate addressed them once more, desiring to release Jesus; but they shouted out, "Crucify, crucify him!" A third time he said to them, "Why, what evil has he done? I have found in him no crime deserving death; I will therefore chastise him and release him." But they were urgent, demanding with loud cries that he should be crucified. And their voices prevailed. . . .

Matt. 27:24.

So when Pilate saw that he was gaining nothing, but rather that a riot was beginning, he took water and washed his hands before the crowd, saying, "I am innocent of this man's blood; see to it your-selves." And all the people answered, "His blood be on us and on our children!" Then he released for them Barabbas, and having scourged Jesus, deliv-ered him to be crucified.

scourged: whipped.

Then the soldiers of the governor took Jesus into the praetorium, and they gathered the whole battal-ion before him. And they stripped him and put a scarlet robe upon him, and plaiting a crown of thorns they put it on his head, and put a reed in his right hand. And kneeling before him they mocked him, saying, "Hail, King of the Jews!" And they spat upon him, and took the reed and struck him on the head. And when they had mocked him, they stripped him of the robe, and put his own clothes on him, and led him away to crucify him.

praetorium (prē tôr′ē əm): local headquarters of the Roman government.

plaiting (plāt′ing): braiding, weaving together.

As they went out, they came upon a man of Cyrene, Simon by name; this man they compelled to carry his cross. . . .

Luke 23:32.

Two others also, who were criminals, were led away to be put to death with him. And when they came to the place which is called The Skull, there they crucified him, and the criminals, one on the right and one on the left. And Jesus said, "Father, forgive them; for they know not what they do." And they cast lots to divide his garments. And the people stood by, watching; but the rulers scoffed at him, saying, "He saved others; let him save himself, if he is the Christ of God, his Chosen One!" The soldiers also mocked him, coming up and offering him vinegar, and saying, "If you are the King of the Jews,

cast lots: method of selecting by chance, probably by using marked stones.

save yourself!" There was also an inscription over him, "This is the King of the Jews."

One of the criminals who were hanged railed at him, saying, "Are you not the Christ? Save yourself and us!" But the other rebuked him, saying, "Do you not fear God, since you are under the same sentence of condemnation? And we indeed justly; for we are receiving the due reward of our deeds; but this man has done nothing wrong." And he said, "Jesus, remember me when you come into your kingdom." And he said to him, "Truly, I say to you, today you will be with me in Paradise."

railed: complained bitterly.

It was now about the sixth hour, and there was darkness over the whole land until the ninth hour, while the sun's light failed; and the curtain of the temple was torn in two. . . .

sixth hour: noon.

curtain: a heavy fabric shield protecting the most holy area of the temple.
Matt. 27:46.

. . . And about the ninth hour Jesus cried with a loud voice, "Eli, Eli, lama sabachthani?" that is, "My God, my God, why hast thou forsaken me?" And some of the bystanders hearing it said, "This man is calling Elijah." And one of them at once ran and took a sponge, filled it with vinegar, and put it on a reed, and gave it to him to drink. But the others said, "Wait, let us see whether Elijah will come to save him." . . .

Elijah: an Old Testament prophet (see page 193). It was thought his return would signal God's reign on earth.

Luke 23:46.

. . . Then Jesus, crying with a loud voice, said, "Father, into thy hands I commit my spirit!" And having said this he breathed his last. Now when the centurion saw what had taken place, he praised God, and said, "Certainly this man was innocent!" And all the multitudes who assembled to see the sight, when they saw what had taken place, returned home beating their breasts. And all his acquaintances and the women who had followed him from Galilee stood at a distance and saw these things.

centurion: Roman officer.

Now there was a man named Joseph from the Jewish town of Arimathea. He was a member of the council, a good and righteous man, who had not consented to their purpose and deed, and he was looking for the kingdom of God. This man went to Pilate and asked for the body of Jesus. Then he took it down and wrapped it in a linen shroud, and laid him in a rock-hewn tomb, where no one had ever yet been laid. It was the day of Preparation, and the

day of Preparation: Friday, before sundown.

sabbath was beginning. The women who had come with him from Galilee followed, and saw the tomb, and how his body was laid; then they returned, and prepared spices and ointments.

On the sabbath they rested according to the commandment.

For close reading

1 Jesus appears before the council, Pilate, and Herod. Compare his responses to each situation. He is asked: "Are you the Son of God?" and "Are you the King of the Jews?" How does he respond to these questions? How do Jesus' accusers interpret his answers?

2 According to his enemies, why should Jesus be put to death?

3 What action does Pilate perform to symbolize his innocence in Jesus' death?

4 What unusual events occur while Jesus is on the cross?

For thought and discussion

5 Jesus is shown in many different situations that reveal many aspects of his character. Write down five words that you feel describe Jesus and support your choices with evidence from these biblical passages.

6 Jesus' last week is filled with many contrasting scenes. For instance, his triumphant entrance into Jerusalem is in sharp contrast to the procession leading to his execution. What other contrasts can you find in these passages?

7 What details in the story emphasize: *(a)* Jesus' isolation and aloneness? *(b)* His humiliation? *(c)* His physical suffering?

8 When Jesus enters Jerusalem, a multitude greets him joyously, and we are told that his enemies "feared the people." Only a few days later a mob is demanding Jesus' death. Can you find any details in these passages that prepare the reader for this turnabout? Explain.

9 Do you see any irony in the fact that a man like Barabbas is released instead of Jesus? Explain.

10 Now that you have read the crucifixion story, reconsider the earlier events of Jesus' life. What similarities, foreshadowings, hints of things to come do you find in these earlier stories in Chapter 10? For example, what similarities do you see between Jesus' birth and his entry into Jerusalem? Where in an earlier story do you find a ruler reluctant to execute an innocent man? What is the effect of these similarities?

Activities

1 Bring a recording of *Jesus Christ, Superstar* to class. How does this musical narrative interpret Jesus' last week?

2 You are Barabbas, or Simon the Cyrene, or Joseph of Arimathea. What were your thoughts and feelings as you became involved in the events of the crucifixion of Jesus? (You may wish to research some of the traditions surrounding each man. Simon the Cyrene, for example, was a black man according to tradition.)

3 Collect and record passages of music that express the mood or feeling at various points of Jesus' last days in Jerusalem—from the joyous entry into the city to the crucifixion and burial. If possible, tape record your sequence of music to make a "tone poem" of the events.

SAINT JUDAS

James Wright

<big>W</big>hen I went out to kill myself, I caught
A pack of hoodlums beating up a man.
Running to spare his suffering, I forgot
My name, my number, how my day began,
5 How soldiers milled around the garden stone
And sang amusing songs; how all that day

javelins: spears.

Their javelins measured crowds; how I alone
Bargained the proper coins, and slipped away.
Banished from heaven, I found this victim beaten,
10 Stripped, kneed, and left to cry. Dropping my rope

rope: in the Gospel of Matthew, Judas hanged himself after Jesus was condemned.

Aside, I ran, ignored the uniforms:
Then I remembered bread my flesh had eaten.
The kiss that ate my flesh. Flayed without hope,
I held the man for nothing in my arms.

flayed: i.e., stripped; laid open.

For thought and discussion

1 Generally, how do people respond to the character of Judas? How does this general attitude compare with the feelings about Judas expressed in this poem?
2 What do "bread my flesh had eaten" and "the kiss that ate my flesh" refer to?
3 What do you think the last line means?

BEN TOBIT

Leonid Andreyev

O n the dread day of that monstrous injustice, when Jesus Christ was crucified among the thieves on Golgotha—on that day, Ben Tobit, a merchant in Jerusalem, had been suffering from an unbearable toothache since the early hours of the morning. It had started the night before; his right jaw had begun to hurt, and one tooth, the one in front of the wisdom tooth, seemed to have risen a little and it hurt when he touched his tongue to it. But after supper the pain disappeared, and Ben Tobit prompt-ly forgot all about it. In fact, he had that very day traded his old donkey advantageously for a young, strong one, and so he was in rather high spirits and totally unconcerned about the ominous symptom.

That night he slept very well and very soundly, but just before dawn something began to bother him, as if someone were calling him on matters of great importance, and when Ben Tobit awakened with annoyance, he found that the toothache had re-turned, a direct and racking one that assailed him with the full force of sharp, stabbing pain. But now he could not tell whether it was the same tooth that had hurt him the night before, or whether other teeth were involved as well; his mouth and his head were filled with excruciating pain, as if he were

excruciating: causing extreme suffering.

being forced to chew a thousand sharp, red-hot nails. He filled his mouth with cool water from an earthen jug, and the fury of the pain subsided for a moment; his mouth began to twitch and throb, and this sensation was almost pleasant compared to the previous one. Ben Tobit lay back on his bed. He thought about his new donkey and he thought of how fortunate he would be if it were not for his teeth.

He tried to fall asleep again, but the water became warm, and in five minutes the pain was back, more savage than before. Ben Tobit sat up in his bed, and soon his body swayed back and forth like a pendulum. His whole face was pulled together and puckered about a big nose, and on that nose, turned white with agony, a drop of cold sweat gathered. Thus it was that, swaying back and forth and moaning in pain, he beheld the first rays of the sun that was destined to see Golgotha with its three crosses and to grow dim with horror and sorrow.

Ben Tobit was a kind and good man who disliked injustice, but when his wife awakened, he had barely opened his mouth before he began to say a great many unpleasant things to her, complaining repeatedly that he was left alone, like a jackal, to howl and to writhe in agony. His wife listened patiently to the undeserved reproaches, for she knew it was not a mean heart that made him say such things, and she brought him many fine remedies: cleansed dung of rats to be applied to the cheek, a strong tincture obtained from a scorpion, and an authentic sliver of the stone tablets that had been smashed to bits by Moses. The rat dung helped a little, but not for long, as did also the tincture and the sliver, but each respite was followed by a violent onslaught of even greater pain. During the brief periods of relief, Ben Tobit comforted himself by thinking of his little donkey and day-dreaming about him; but when he felt worse, he moaned, scolded his wife, and threatened to dash his head against a rock if the pain did not subside. And he kept pacing all the time from one corner of the flat roof of his house to the other, ashamed to get too close to its outer edge because the kerchief he had tied around his head made him look like a woman.

Several times children came running to him to tell him hastily about Jesus of Nazareth. Ben Tobit

tincture (tingk′chər): solution of medicine in alcohol.

would stop for a moment to listen to them; then he would contract his face and, stamping his foot angrily, would send them on their way. He was a kind man and fond of children, but now it irritated him to be pestered with all sorts of silly things.

He was also irritated because many people in the street and on neighboring roofs seemed to have nothing better to do than to stare in curiosity at him with his head wrapped in a kerchief like a woman's. He was just about to go downstairs when his wife called to him:

"Look, there are the thieves! This might interest you!"

"Leave me alone, please. Don't you see how I'm suffering?" Ben Tobit answered angrily.

But his wife's words gave him a slight feeling that his toothache might be lessening. So he reluctantly went to the edge of the roof. With his head tilted to one side, one eye closed, his cheek in the palm of a hand, his face peevish and tearful, he looked down.

peevish: fretful.

A huge, turbulently milling crowd, shrouded in dust, incessantly shouting, was moving up the steep, narrow street. Surrounded by the crowd, the criminals moved along with bodies bent low under the heavy burdens of the crosses, the whips of the Roman soldiers writhing like black snakes above them. One of them—the one who had long, fair hair and who was wearing a torn, blood-stained robe— stumbled on a stone someone had thrown at his feet and fell. The shouting grew louder and the crowd, like a many-colored sea, seemed to close over the fallen man. Ben Tobit suddenly winced with pain, as if someone had stabbed a red-hot needle into his tooth and twisted it there. He moaned, "Oh—oh— oh," and walked away from the edge of the roof, petulantly preoccupied and full of resentment.

petulantly: irritably.

"How they yell!" he said enviously, visualizing wide-open mouths with strong, never-aching teeth and thinking how he himself would be shouting if he were well. This mental image brought on another savage attack of pain. He kept shaking his kerchief-wrapped head, lowing, "M—moo—oo . . ."

"They say he healed the blind," said his wife, who had remained at the edge of the roof and had thrown a small stone at the place where Jesus, brought to his feet by the whips, moved along slowly.

"Yes, of course! Let him heal my toothache!" Ben Tobit retorted mockingly. "What a dust they kick up! Like a herd! They ought to be dispersed with a cane!" he added peevishly, in bitterness. "Help me down, Sarah!"

His wife was right; the spectacle did somewhat divert Ben Tobit, or perhaps it was the rat dung that helped him at last, and he managed to fall asleep. When he awakened, the pain was almost gone; there was only a small swelling on his right jaw, so small it was hardly noticeable. His wife said it was completely unnoticeable, but Ben Tobit smiled knowingly: he knew well what a good wife he had and how much she loved to say pleasant things. His neighbor Samuel, the tanner, came to visit, and Ben Tobit took him to see his little donkey; he listened with pride while Samuel praised him and the animal enthusiastically.

Then, to satisfy Sarah's insistent curiosity, the three of them went to see the men crucified on Golgotha. On the way, Ben Tobit told Samuel the whole story from the beginning, how he had felt an ache in his right jaw the previous evening and how he was wakened by an excruciating pain during the night. For greater effect, he put on the air of a martyr, closed his eyes, shook his head and groaned, while the gray-bearded Samuel nodded sympathetically and said, "Oh, oh, oh—how painful!"

Ben Tobit enjoyed the sympathy and repeated the story, going back to the remote past when he had first had a tooth go bad, down on the left side. So it was, in animated conversation, that they came to Golgotha. The sun that was destined to shine upon the world on this dread day had already set behind the far hills, and in the west a crimson strip like a bloody mark, stretched across the sky. Against this background the crosses stood dark and indistinct, while white-clad figures knelt at the foot of the middle cross.

The crowd had dispersed long before; it was growing cold, and, with a brief glance at the crucified men, Ben Tobit took Samuel's arm and gently turned him homeward. He felt particularly eloquent; he wanted to say more about the toothache. And so they walked away, Ben Tobit resuming the air of a martyr, shaking his head and groaning artfully, while Samuel nodded and exclaimed sympathetically. Black night was rising from the dark, deep gorges and from the distant, burned plains—as though it were trying to hide the enormous misdeed of the earth from the eyes of heaven.

For close reading

1 What details in the story emphasize Ben Tobit's suffering? What details refer to the sufferings of Jesus?
2 How is Ben Tobit affected by watching the procession to Golgotha? By seeing the crucified men?

For thought and discussion

3 "Ben Tobit was a kind and good man who disliked injustice . . . ." How were you affected by this description of Ben Tobit? Choose three words that express your own opinion of Ben Tobit.
4 Suppose Ben Tobit had been dying of cancer, instead of experiencing a toothache. How would that have affected your feelings about the story?
5 "Ben Tobit" presents two kinds of sufferings. Why do you think the author links the two? Why do you think he emphasizes one over the other? What do you think he wants to show?

THE MAKING OF THE CROSS

Brother Antoninus

Rough fir, hauled from the hills. And the tree it
    had been,
Lithe-limbed, wherein the wren had nested,
Whereon the red hawk and the grey
Rested from flight, and the raw-head vulture
5 Shouldered to his feed—that tree went over
Bladed down with a double-bitted axe; was snaked
    with winches;
The wedge split it; hewn with the adze
It lay to season toward its use.

So too with the nails: milleniums under the earth,
10 Pure ore; chunked out with picks; the nail-shape
Struck in the pelt-lunged forge; tonged to a cask
And the wait against that work.

Even the thorn-bush flourished from afar,
As do the flourishing generations of its kind,
15 Filling the shallow soil no one wants;
Wind-sown, it cuts the cattle and the wild horse;
It tears the cloth of man, and hurts his hand.

Just as in life the good things of the earth
Are patiently assembled: some from here, some
    from there;
20 Wine from the hill and wheat from the valley;
Rain that comes blue-bellied out of the sopping
    sea;

adze: an axlike tool for shaping timber.

milleniums: thousands of years.

pelt-lunged: i.e., having leather bellows.

"The Making of the Cross" by Brother Antoninus from *The Crooked Lines of God,* the University of Detroit Press, 1960. Reprinted by permission.

Snow that keeps its drift on the gooseberry ridge,
Will melt with May, go down, take the egg of
   the salmon,
Serve the traffic of otters and fishes,
25 Be ditched to orchards . . .

So too are gathered up the possibles of evil.

And when the Cross was joined, quartered,
As is the earth; spoked, as is the Universal Wheel—
Those radials that led all unregenerate act   **unregenerate:** wicked.
30 Inward to innocence—it met the thorn-wove
   Crown;
It found the Scourges and the Dice;   **scourges:** whips.
The Nail was given and the reed-lifted Sponge;
The Curse caught forward out of the heart corrupt;
The excoriate Foul, stoned with the thunder and   **excoriate:** i.e.,
   the hail—   denouncement.
35 All these made up that miscellaneous wrath
And were assumed.   **assumed:** taken on.

The evil and the wastage and the woe,
As if the earth's old cyst, back down the slough   **cyst** (sist): i.e.,
To Adam's sin-burnt calcinated bones   diseased growth.
40 Rushed out of time and clotted on the Cross.   **calcinated:** burned to
                                            ashes.

Off there the cougar
Coughed in passion when the sun went out;
   the rattler
Filmed his glinty eye, and found his hole.

For thought and discussion

1 The poet begins by describing the beginnings of the wood and the nails used for the cross and by describing how they were made. Then he describes the "good things of the earth." What does he say are the similarities between "the good things" (line 18) and the "possibles of evil" (line 26)?

2 According to the poet, what three things clotted on the cross (line 40)? Why do you think he mentions these three things in connection with the physical or "real" parts of the cross and the crucifixion?

3 Complete the following sentence: "The Making of the Cross" is about . . . . . List as many possibilities as you can think of.

from
BARABBAS

Pär Lagerkvist
Translated by Alan Blair

[*This is the first chapter
of a novel about the man who was
released instead of Jesus.*]

Everyone knows how they hung there on the crosses, and who they were that stood gathered around him: Mary his mother and Mary Magdalene, Veronica, Simon of Cyrene, who carried the cross, and Joseph of Arimathea, who shrouded him. But a little further down the slope, rather to one side, a man was standing with his eyes riveted on the dying man in the middle, watching his death-throes from the first moment to the last. His name was Barabbas. . . .

He was about thirty, powerfully built, with a sallow complexion, a reddish beard and black hair. His eyebrows also were black, his eyes too deep-set, as though they wanted to hide. Under one of them he had a deep scar that was lost to sight in his beard. But a man's appearance is of little consequence.

He had followed the mob through the streets all the way from the governor's palace, but at a distance, somewhat behind the others. When the exhausted rabbi had collapsed beneath his cross, he had stopped and stood still for a while to avoid catching up with the cross, and then they had got hold of that man Simon and forced him to carry it instead. There were not many men in the crowd, except the Roman soldiers of course; they were mostly women following the condemned man and a flock of urchins who were always there when anyone was led out along their street to be crucified—it made a change for them. But they soon tired and

urchins: young children.

went back to their games, pausing a moment to glance at the man with the long scar down his cheek who was walking behind the others.

Now he was standing up here on the gallows-hill looking at the man on the middle cross, unable to tear his eyes away. Actually he had not wanted to come up here at all, for everything was unclean, full of contagion; if a man set foot in this potent and accursed place part of him would surely remain, and he could be forced back there, never to leave it again. Skulls and bones lay scattered about everywhere, together with fallen, half-mouldering crosses, no longer of any use but left to lie there all the same, because no one would touch anything. Why was he standing here? He did not know this man, had nothing to do with him. What was he doing at Golgotha, he who had been released?

The crucified man's head hung down and he was breathing heavily; it would not be long now. There was nothing vigorous about the fellow. His body was lean and spindly, the arms slender as though they had never been put to any use. A queer man. The beard was sparse and the chest quite hairless, like a boy's. He did not like him.

From the first moment Barabbas had seen him in the courtyard of the palace, he had felt there was something odd about him. What it was he could not say; it was just something he felt. He didn't remember ever having seen anyone like him before. Though it must have been because he came straight from the dungeon and his eyes were still unused to the glare. That is why at first glance the man seemed to be surrounded by a dazzling light. Soon afterwards the light vanished, of course, and his sight grew normal again and took in other things besides the figure standing out there alone in the courtyard. But he still thought there was something very strange about him and that he was not like anyone else. It seemed quite incredible that he was a prisoner and had been condemned to death, just as he himself had been. He could not grasp it. Not that it concerned him—but how could they pass a sentence like that? It was obvious he was innocent.

Then the man had been led out to be crucified— and he himself had been unshackled and told he was free. It was none of his doing. It was their business. They were quite at liberty to choose

unclean: according to Jewish law, contact with dead bodies made one impure, requiring a cleansing ritual.

whomever they liked, and it just turned out that way. They had both been sentenced to death, but one of them was to be released. He was amazed himself at their choice. As they were freeing him from his chains, he had seen the other man between the soldiers disappear through the archway, with the cross already on his back.

He had remained standing, looking out through the empty arch. Then the guard had given him a push and bellowed at him:—What are you standing there gaping for, get out of here, you're free! And he had awakened and gone out through the same archway, and when he saw the other dragging his cross down the street he had followed behind him. Why, he did not know. Nor why he had stood here hour after hour watching the crucifixion and the long death agony, though it was nothing whatever to do with him.

Those standing around the cross up there surely need not have been here? Not unless they had wanted to. Nothing was forcing them to come along and defile themselves with uncleanness. But they were no doubt relations and close friends. Odd that they didn't seem to mind being made unclean.

That woman must be his mother. Though she was not like him. But who could be like him? She looked like a peasant woman, stern and morose, and she kept wiping the back of her hand across her mouth and nose, which was running because she was on the brink of tears. But she did not cry. She did not grieve in the same way as the others, nor did she look at him in the same way as they did. So it was evidently his mother. She probably felt far more sorry for him than they did, but even so she seemed to reproach him for hanging there, for having let himself be crucified. He must have done something to let himself in for it, however pure and innocent he was, and she just could not approve of it. She knew he was innocent because she was his mother. Whatever he had done she would have thought so.

He himself had no mother. And no father either, for that matter; he had never even heard one mentioned. And he had no relatives, as far as he knew. So if he had been the one to be crucified there would not have been many tears shed. Not like this. They were beating their breasts and carrying on as though they had never known the like of

morose (mə rōs′): gloomy.

such grief, and there was an awful weeping and wailing the whole time.

He knew the one on the right-hand cross quite well. If by any chance the fellow saw him standing down here, he probably thought it was because of him, in order to see him suffer well and truly. He wasn't, he was not here because of that at all. But he had nothing against seeing him crucified. If anyone deserved to die, it was that scoundrel. Though not because of what he had been sentenced for, but because of something quite different.

But why was he looking at him and not at the one in the middle, who was hanging there in his stead? It was because of him he had come. This man had forced him up here, he had a strange power over him. Power? If anyone looked powerless, he did. Surely no one could look more wretched hanging on a cross. The other two didn't look a bit like that and didn't seem to be suffering as much as he was. They obviously had more strength left. He hadn't even the strength to hold his head up; it had flopped right down.

Now he did raise it a bit, all the same; the lean, hairless chest heaved with panting, and his tongue licked his parched lips. He groaned something about being thirsty. The soldiers who were sprawled over a game of dice a little further down the slope, bored because the men hanging there took so long to die, did not hear. But one of the relatives went down and told them. A soldier got up reluctantly and dipped a sponge in a pitcher, passing it up to him on a stick, but when he tasted the fusty, tainted liquid offered him he did not want it. The wretch just stood there grinning, and when he rejoined his companions they all lay grinning at what had happened. . . .

fusty: stale-smelling.

The relatives or whoever they were looked despairingly up at the crucified man, who was panting and panting; it was clear that he would soon give up the ghost. And just as well if the end came soon, Barabbas thought, so that the poor man would not have to suffer any more. If only the end would come! As soon as the end came he would hurry away and never think of this again. . . .

But all at once the whole hill grew dark, as though the light had gone out of the sun; it was almost pitch-dark, and in the darkness above, the crucified man cried out in a loud voice:

—My God, my God, why hast thou forsaken me?

It sounded horrible. Whatever did he mean? And why had it grown dark? It was the middle of the day. It was quite unaccountable. The three crosses were just faintly visible up there. It looked weird. Something terrible was surely going to happen. The soldiers had leapt to their feet and grabbed their weapons; whatever happened they always rushed for their weapons. They stood there around the crosses with their lances, and he heard them whispering together in alarm. Now they were frightened! Now they were not grinning any longer! They were superstitious, of course.

He was afraid himself. And glad when it began to get light and everything became a little more normal. It got light slowly, as it does at dawn. The daylight spread across the hill and the olive trees around about, and the birds that had been silent started twittering again. It was just like dawn.

The relatives up there were standing so still. There was no longer any sound of weeping and lamentation from them. They just stood looking up at the man on the cross; even the soldiers did so. Everything had grown so still.

Now he could go whenever he liked. For it was all over now, and the sun shone again and everything was just as usual. It had only been dark for a while because the man had died.

Yes, he would go now. Of course he would. He had nothing to stay for, not now that he, that other one, was dead. There was no longer any reason. They took him down from the cross, he saw before he went. The two men wrapped him in a clean linen cloth, he noticed. The body was quite white and they handled it so carefully, as if they were afraid they might hurt it, however slightly, or cause it pain of any kind. They behaved so strangely. After all, he was crucified and everything. They were queer people, to be sure. But the mother stood with dry eyes looking at what had been her son, and the rough, dark-complexioned face seemed unable to express her sorrow, only the fact that she could not grasp what had happened and would never be able to forgive it. He understood her better.

As the sorry procession moved past some little distance from him, the men carrying the shrouded body and the women walking behind, one of the women whispered to the mother—pointing to Barabbas. She stopped short and gave him such a helpless and reproachful look that he knew he could never forget it. They went on down towards the Golgotha road and then turned off to the left.

He followed far enough behind for them not to notice him. In a garden a short distance away they laid the dead man in a tomb that was hewn out of the rock. And when they had prayed by the tomb they rolled a large stone in front of the entrance and went away.

He walked up to the tomb and stood there for a while. But he did not pray, for he was an evil-doer and his prayer would not have been accepted, especially as his crime was not expiated. Besides, he did not know the dead man. He stood there for a moment, all the same.

not expiated: i.e., he had not paid the penalty.

Then he too went in towards Jerusalem.

For close reading

1 What feelings about Jesus does Barabbas express in this passage?

2 Besides Jesus, what other person does Barabbas seem strongly interested in?

For thought and discussion

3 Would you describe the style of this passage as simple or complex? Emotional or unemotional? Why do you suppose the author uses such a style?

4 In the Bible there is no further mention of Barabbas after he is released. Does Lagerkvist's portrayal of Barabbas seem reasonable to you? Why or why not?

5 Both Barabbas and Ben Tobit (in the preceding story) witness the sufferings of Jesus. What similarities and what differences do you find between the reactions of the two men? Why do you suppose the authors chose to present the crucifixion from the viewpoints of these characters?

Mouth of Hell, anonymous woodcut.

Jigo Soshi (Hell Scroll), paper, early Kamakura Period, c. 1200. Tokyo National Museum.
RIGHT: *Shepherd and Flock with Prancing Deer,* detail from a needlework chair back, American, c. 1725. The Metropolitan Museum of Art, New York, Gift of Mrs. J. Insley Blair, 1950.

THE
TOMB
IS
EMPTY

Luke

**first day of the
week:** Sunday.
they: the women from
Galilee who had
followed Jesus.

But on the first day of the week, at early dawn, they went to the tomb, taking the spices which they had prepared. And they found the stone rolled away from the tomb, but when they went in they did not find the body. While they were perplexed about this, behold, two men stood by them in dazzling apparel; and as they were frightened and bowed their faces to the ground, the men said to them, "Why do you seek the living among the dead? Remember how he told you, while he was still in Galilee, that the Son of man must be delivered into the hands of sinful men, and be crucified, and on the third day rise." And they remembered his words, and returning from the tomb they told all this to the eleven and to all the rest. Now it was Mary Magdalene and Joanna and Mary the mother of James and the other women with them who told this to the apostles; but these words seemed to them an idle tale, and they did not believe them.

That very day two of them were going to a village named Emmaus, about seven miles from Jerusalem, and talking with each other about all these things that had happened. While they were talking and discussing together, Jesus himself drew near and went with them. But their eyes were kept from recognizing him. And he said to them, "What is this conversation which you are holding with each other

Luke 24:1–11, 13–37, 44–53 (RSV).

as you walk?" And they stood still, looking sad. Then one of them, named Cleopas, answered him, "Are you the only visitor to Jerusalem who does not know the things that have happened there in these days?" And he said to them, "What things?" And they said to him, "Concerning Jesus of Nazareth, who was a prophet mighty in deed and word before God and all the people, and how our chief priests and rulers delivered him up to be condemned to death, and crucified him. But we had hoped that he was the one to redeem Israel. Yes, and besides all this, it is now the third day since this happened. Moreover, some women of our company amazed us. They were at the tomb early in the morning and did not find his body; and they came back saying that they had even seen a vision of angels, who said that he was alive. Some of those who were with us went to the tomb, and found it just as the women had said; but him they did not see." And he said to them, "O foolish men, and slow of heart to believe all that the prophets have spoken! Was it not necessary that the Christ should suffer these things and enter into his glory?" And beginning with Moses and all the prophets, he interpreted to them in all the scriptures the things concerning himself.

redeem: save and protect; literally, to safeguard the rights of a kinsman. God was regarded as a Redeemer, and Israel his first-born son.

So they drew near to the village to which they were going. He appeared to be going further, but they constrained him, saying, "Stay with us, for it is toward evening and the day is now far spent." So he went in to stay with them. When he was at table with them, he took the bread and blessed, and broke it, and gave it to them. And their eyes were opened and they recognized him; and he vanished out of their sight. They said to each other, "Did not our hearts burn within us while he talked to us on the road, while he opened to us the scriptures?" And they rose that same hour and returned to Jerusalem; and they found the eleven gathered together and those who were with them, who said, "The Lord has risen indeed, and has appeared to Simon!" Then they told what had happened on the road, and how he was known to them in the breaking of the bread.

constrained him: held him back.

the eleven: the original disciples minus Judas, who had committed suicide.

As they were saying this, Jesus himself stood among them. But they were startled and frightened, and supposed that they saw a spirit. . . .

Then he said to them, "These are my words which I spoke to you, while I was still with you, that

spirit: ghost.

everything written about me in the law of Moses and the prophets and the psalms must be fulfilled." Then he opened their minds to understand the scriptures, and said to them, "Thus it is written, that the Christ should suffer and on the third day rise from the dead, and that repentance and forgiveness of sins should be preached in his name to all nations, beginning from Jerusalem. You are witnesses of these things. And behold, I send the promise of my Father upon you; but stay in the city, until you are clothed with power from on high."

Then he led them out as far as Bethany, and lifting up his hands he blessed them. While he blessed them, he parted from them. And they returned to Jerusalem with great joy, and were continually in the temple blessing God.

For close reading

1 How do the disciples respond to the news the women bring?
2 At what point do Cleopas and his companion recognize Jesus?
3 When Jesus "stood among them" the disciples are frightened and think he is a ghost. When has this happened to the disciples before?
4 What final instructions does Jesus give to his followers?

For thought and discussion

5 Examine the series of events by which Jesus' resurrection is revealed. How do you think the story would have been affected if Jesus had suddenly appeared in a public display of glory?

6 Jesus explains the meaning of his life "beginning with Moses." What similarities and connections can you find between the lives of Jesus and Moses? Why is it significant that Jesus links himself with Moses?

7 Why do you think Jesus' followers are "slow of heart to believe"? When they finally realize that Jesus is with them again, which of the following feelings do you think is strongest: surprise, guilt, joy, fear, or confusion? Give reasons for your choice.

Activities

1 The celebration of Jesus' resurrection—Easter—involves many traditional symbols and practices, not all of which are based on the Bible story. List as many of these symbols and practices as you can, then choose one and try to trace its history.

2 In a painting, collage, or needlepoint, depict the ascension of Jesus into heaven.

3 Read the Gospel of Luke, giving special attention to the roles played by women. Report your findings to the class.

12

in
the end
of
days

Jeremiah, Isaiah

[*Certain biblical writings focus on "the end of days"
or apocalypse. These prophetic passages are vivid,
spectacular visions of world upheaval, judgment,
and God's final triumph over evil.*

*This chapter contains four groups of these visions,
including passages from the books of Jeremiah,
Isaiah, Daniel, and Revelation. Questions and activities appear after "A New Heaven, A New Earth."*]

I looked on the earth, and lo, it was waste and
    void;
and to the heavens, and they had no light.
I looked on the mountains, and lo, they were
    quaking,
and all the hills moved to and fro.
I looked, and lo, there was no man,
and all the birds of the air had fled.
I looked, and lo, the fruitful land was a desert,
and all its cities were laid in ruins
before the Lord, before his fierce anger. . . .

Jer. 4:23.

The earth mourns and withers,
    the world languishes and withers;
    the heavens languish together with the earth.
The earth lies polluted
    under its inhabitants;

Isa. 24:4.
languishes: becomes
weak.

Jeremiah 4:23–26. Isaiah 24:4–6, 12–13, 17–23 (RSV).
LEFT: *The Last Judgment,* detail from the west tympanum of the cathedral
of Saint-Lazare, Autun, France. Carved by Gislebertus before 1135. Bulloz.

transgressed: disobeyed.

covenant: agreement.

for they have transgressed the laws,
   violated the statutes,
   broken the everlasting covenant.
Therefore a curse devours the earth,
   and its inhabitants suffer for their guilt;
therefore the inhabitants of the earth are scorched,
   and few men are left. . . .

Desolation is left in the city,
   the gates are battered into ruins.
For thus it shall be in the midst of the earth
   among the nations,
as when an olive tree is beaten,

vintage: i.e., gathering
of grapes.

   as at the gleaning when the vintage is done. . . .

Terror, and the pit, and the snare
   are upon you, O inhabitant of the earth!
He who flees at the sound of the terror
   shall fall into the pit;
and he who climbs out of the pit
   shall be caught in the snare.
For the windows of heaven are opened,
   and the foundations of the earth tremble.
The earth is utterly broken,

rent asunder: torn
apart.

   the earth is rent asunder,
   the earth is violently shaken.
The earth staggers like a drunken man,
   it sways like a hut;
its transgression lies heavy upon it,
   and it falls, and will not rise again.

On that day the Lord will punish

host of heaven:
heavenly beings.

   the host of heaven, in heaven,
   and the kings of the earth, on the earth.
They will be gathered together
   as prisoners in a pit;
they will be shut up in a prison,
   and after many days they will be punished.

confounded: confused;
perplexed.

Then the moon will be confounded,
   and the sun ashamed;
for the Lord of hosts will reign
   on Mount Zion and in Jerusalem
and before his elders he will manifest his glory.

MARVELOUS VISIONS

Revelation, Daniel

After this I looked, and lo, in heaven an open door! And the first voice, which I had heard speaking to me like a trumpet, said, "Come up hither, and I will show you what must take place after this." At once I was in the Spirit, and lo, a throne stood in heaven, with one seated on the throne! And he who sat there appeared like jasper and carnelian, and round the throne was a rainbow that looked like an emerald. Round the throne were twenty-four thrones, and seated on the thrones were twenty-four elders, clad in white garments, with golden crowns upon their heads. From the throne issue flashes of lightning, and voices and peals of thunder, and before the throne burn seven torches of fire, which are the seven spirits of God; and before the throne there is as it were a sea of glass, like crystal.

And round the throne, on each side of the throne, are four living creatures, full of eyes in front and behind: the first living creature like a lion, the second living creature like an ox, the third living creature with the face of a man, and the fourth living creature like a flying eagle. And the four living creatures, each of them with six wings, are full of eyes all round and within, and day and night they never cease to sing,

"Holy, holy, holy, is the Lord God Almighty, who was and is and is to come!"

Rev. 4:1.

hither: here.

jasper: a quartz stone, usually red, yellow, or brown.
carnelian: a red or reddish-brown stone.

Revelation 4:1–11. Daniel 7:2–7, 9–14 (RSV).

And whenever the living creatures give glory and honor and thanks to him who is seated on the throne, who lives for ever and ever, the twenty-four elders fall down before him who is seated on the throne and worship him who lives for ever and ever; they cast their crowns before the throne, singing,

"Worthy art thou, our Lord and God,
to receive glory and honor and power,
for thou didst create all things,
and by thy will they existed and were created."

Dan. 7:2

. . . "I saw in my vision by night, and behold, the four winds of heaven were stirring up the great sea. And four great beasts came up out of the sea, different from one another. The first was like a lion and had eagles' wings. Then as I looked its wings were plucked off, and it was lifted up from the ground and made to stand upon two feet like a man; and the mind of a man was given to it. And behold, another beast, a second one, like a bear. It was raised up on one side; it had three ribs in its mouth between its teeth; and it was told, 'Arise, devour much flesh.' After this I looked, and lo, another, like a leopard, with four wings of a bird on its back; and the beast had four heads; and dominion was given to it. After this I saw in the night visions, and behold, a fourth beast, terrible and dreadful and exceedingly strong; and it had great iron teeth; it devoured and broke in pieces, and stamped the residue with its feet. It was different from all the beasts that were before it; and it had ten horns. . . . As I looked,

dominion: power to rule.

thrones were placed
and one that was ancient of days took his
seat;
his raiment was white as snow,
and the hair of his head like pure wool;
his throne was fiery flames,
its wheels were burning fire.
A stream of fire issued
and came forth from before him;
a thousand thousands served him,
and ten thousand times ten thousand stood
before him;
the court sat in judgment,
and the books were opened.

one . . . days: God.

raiment: clothing.

I looked then because of the sound of the great words which the horn was speaking. And as I looked, the beast was slain, and its body destroyed and given over to be burned with fire. As for the rest of the beasts, their dominion was taken away, but their lives were prolonged for a season and a time. I saw in the night visions,

and behold, with the clouds of heaven
   there came one like a son of man,
and he came to the Ancient of Days
   and was presented before him.
And to him was given dominion
   and glory and kingdom,
that all peoples, nations, and languages
   should serve him;
his dominion is an everlasting dominion,
   which shall not pass away,
and his kingdom one
   that shall not be destroyed."

SCENES FROM THE FINAL JUDGMENT

Revelation

Michael: archangel who protected Israel.

Now war arose in heaven, Michael and his angels fighting against the dragon; and the dragon and his angels fought, but they were defeated and there was no longer any place for them in heaven. And the great dragon was thrown down, that ancient serpent, who is called the Devil and Satan, the deceiver of the whole world—he was thrown down to the earth, and his angels were thrown down with him. . . .

Then I heard a loud voice from the temple telling the seven angels, "Go and pour out on the earth the seven bowls of the wrath of God."

So the first angel went and poured his bowl on the earth, and foul and evil sores came upon the men who bore the mark of the beast and worshiped its image.

The second angel poured his bowl into the sea, and it became like the blood of a dead man, and every living thing died that was in the sea.

The third angel poured his bowl into the rivers and the fountains of water, and they became blood. . . .

The fourth angel poured his bowl on the sun, and it was allowed to scorch men with fire; men were scorched by the fierce heat, and they cursed the name of God who had power over these plagues, and they did not repent and give him glory.

The fifth angel poured his bowl on the throne of the beast, and its kingdom was in darkness; men

---

Revelation 12:7–9; 16:1–4, 8–14, 16–20; 20:1–3, 7–15 (RSV).

gnawed their tongues in anguish and cursed the God of heaven for their pain and sores, and did not repent of their deeds.

The sixth angel poured his bowl on the great river Euphrates, and its water was dried up, to prepare the way for the kings from the east. And I saw, issuing from the mouth of the dragon and from the mouth of the beast and from the mouth of the false prophet, three foul spirits like frogs; for they are demonic spirits, performing signs, who go abroad to the kings of the whole world, to assemble them for battle on the great day of God the Almighty. . . . And they assembled them at the place which is called in Hebrew Armageddon.

The seventh angel poured his bowl into the air, and a loud voice came out of the temple, from the throne, saying, "It is done!" And there were flashes of lightning, voices, peals of thunder, and a great earthquake such as had never been since men were on the earth, so great was that earthquake. The great city was split into three parts, and the cities of the nations fell, and God remembered great Babylon, to make her drain the cup of the fury of his wrath. And every island fled away, and no mountains were to be found . . . .

Then I saw an angel coming down from heaven, holding in his hand the key of the bottomless pit and a great chain. And he seized the dragon, that ancient serpent, who is the Devil and Satan, and bound him for a thousand years, and threw him into the pit, and shut it and sealed it over him, that he should deceive the nations no more, till the thousand years were ended. After that he must be loosed for a little while. . . .

And when the thousand years are ended, Satan will be loosed from his prison and will come out to deceive the nations which are at the four corners of the earth, that is, Gog and Magog, to gather them for battle; their number is like the sand of the sea. And they marched up over the broad earth and surrounded the camp of the saints and the beloved city; but fire came down from heaven and consumed them, and the devil who had deceived them was thrown into the lake of fire and sulphur where the beast and the false prophet were, and they will be tormented day and night for ever and ever.

Armageddon (är′mə ged′n): place of the final battle between the forces of good and evil.

book of life: book
containing the names
of all the righteous.

Hades (hā′dēz′): place
of the dead; under-
world.

Then I saw a great white throne and him who sat
upon it; from his presence earth and sky fled away,
and no place was found for them. And I saw the
dead, great and small, standing before the throne,
and books were opened. Also another book was
opened, which is the book of life. And the dead
were judged by what was written in the books, by
what they had done. And the sea gave up the dead in
it, Death and Hades gave up the dead in them, and
all were judged by what they had done. Then Death
and Hades were thrown into the lake of fire. This is
the second death, the lake of fire; and if any one's
name was not found written in the book of life, he
was thrown into the lake of fire.

A NEW HEAVEN, A NEW EARTH

Revelation, Isaiah

Then I saw a new heaven and a new earth; for the first heaven and the first earth had passed away, and the sea was no more. And I saw the holy city, new Jerusalem, coming down out of heaven from God, prepared as a bride adorned for her husband; and I heard a loud voice from the throne saying, "Behold, the dwelling of God is with men. He will dwell with them, and they shall be his people, and God himself will be with them; he will wipe away every tear from their eyes, and death shall be no more, neither shall there be mourning nor crying nor pain any more, for the former things have passed away."

And he who sat upon the throne said, "Behold, I make all things new." Also he said, "Write this, for these words are trustworthy and true." And he said to me, "It is done! I am the Alpha and the Omega, the beginning and the end. To the thirsty I will give from the fountain of the water of life without payment. He who conquers shall have this heritage, and I will be his God and he shall be my son. But as for the cowardly, the faithless, the polluted, as for murderers, fornicators, sorcerers, idolaters, and all liars, their lot shall be in the lake that burns with fire and sulphur, which is the second death." . . .

Then he showed me the river of the water of life, bright as crystal, flowing from the throne of God and of the Lamb through the middle of the street of the

Rev. 21:1.

Alpha . . . Omega: the first and last letters of the Greek alphabet.

lot: fate.

Isa. 2:2.

Lamb: Jesus.

Revelation 21:1–8; 22:1–5. Isaiah 2:2–4 (RSV).

city; also, on either side of the river, the tree of life with its twelve kinds of fruit, yielding its fruit each month; and the leaves of the tree were for the healing of the nations. There shall no more be anything accursed, but the throne of God and of the Lamb shall be in it, and his servants shall worship him; they shall see his face, and his name shall be on their foreheads. And night shall be no more; they need no light of lamp or sun, for the Lord God will be their light, and they shall reign for ever and ever.

accursed: condemned by God.

It shall come to pass in the latter days
    that the mountain of the house of the Lord
shall be established as the highest of the moun-
      tains,
    and shall be raised above the hills;
and all the nations shall flow to it,
    and many peoples shall come, and say:
"Come, let us go up to the mountain of the
      Lord,
    to the house of the God of Jacob;
that he may teach us his ways
    and that we may walk in his paths."
For out of Zion shall go forth the law,
    and the word of the Lord from Jerusalem.
He shall judge between the nations,
    and shall decide for many peoples;
and they shall beat their swords into plow-
      shares,
    and their spears into pruning hooks;
nation shall not lift up sword against nation,
    neither shall they learn war any more.

Zion: hill in Jerusalem on which the temple stood.

pruning hooks: curved blades on handles, used for trimming branches and vines.

For close reading

1 In the first section, what images are used to describe the condition of the earth? According to this passage, why are the earth's inhabitants being punished?

2 How many different kinds of punishment are mentioned in the four sections?

3 In "Marvelous Visions," eight creatures are described. What differences are there between the four "living creatures" and the four "beasts" from the sea?

4 In "Scenes from the Final Judgment," what is "the second death"?

For thought and discussion

5 What would you say is the dominant mood or feeling expressed in each of the four sections? Which passage made the strongest impression on you? Why?

6 Thrones are mentioned throughout these passages. What is the effect of that repetition? Fire is also mentioned many times. What does fire seem to represent in these passages?

7 "I looked on the earth, and lo, it was waste and void." This phrasing recalls the Genesis account of creation, which describes the earth at the beginning as "without form and void." What other details in these passages seem to link the "end" with the "beginning"? (If necessary, reread the creation passages on pages 3 and 7.)

8 Angels pour out on the earth the "seven bowls of the wrath of God." Do any of the resulting disasters recall incidents from other Bible stories you have read? Explain.

9 One pattern in these visions is the locking up or the destruction of a terrible creature. How many episodes like this can you find? What is the effect of this pattern?

10 Throughout these passages, events and conditions on earth are related to events and conditions in heaven and vice versa. Why do you think this is so?

11 What three details in these passages seem most

nightmarish to you? What three details seem most comforting and pleasant?

Activities

1 There are many scientific theories, religious beliefs, and popularly expressed ideas about how the world will end. Research one or more of these and report to the class.

2 Make a collage of photographs showing the earth lying "polluted under its inhabitants."

3 Make a woodcut, ceramic, or mosaic representation of one of the beasts described in "Marvelous Visions."

4 Select or compose music to accompany a reading of "The Earth Is Broken" passages.

5 Using scraps of cloth, make a banner expressing a quotation from these passages.

EPISTLE
TO BE LEFT
IN THE EARTH

Archibald MacLeish

epistle: letter.

... It is colder now
        there are many stars
              we are drifting
North by the Great Bear
5   the leaves are falling
The water is stone in the scooped rocks
          to southward
Red sun grey air
       the crows are
10 Slow on their crooked wings
          the jays have left us
Long since we passed the flares of Orion
Each man believes in his heart he will die
Many have written last thoughts and last letters
15 None know if our deaths are now or forever
None know if this wandering earth will be found

We lie down and the snow covers our garments
I pray you
      you (if any open this writing)
20 Make in your mouths the words that were our names
I will tell you all we have learned
          I will tell you everything
The earth is round
      there are springs under the orchards
25 The loam cuts with a blunt knife
        beware of

Great Bear: group of stars forming the rough shape of a bear.

Orion (ō rī′ən): a group of stars near the equator.

loam: rich, fertile earth.

Elms in thunder
                    the lights in the sky are stars
We think they do not see
30   we think also
The trees do not know nor the leaves of the grasses
                                            hear us
The birds too are ignorant
                    Do not listen
35   Do not stand at dark in the open windows
We before you have heard this
                              they are voices
They are not words at all but the wind rising
Also none among us has seen God
40   (. . . We have thought often
The flaws of sun in the late and driving weather
Pointed to one tree but it was not so.)
As for the nights I warn you the nights are dangerous
The wind changes at night and the dreams come

45   It is very cold
                    there are strange stars near Arcturus

Voices are crying an unknown name in the sky

For thought and discussion

1 There are various theories about how our world will end. Which theory seems evident here?

2 What can you tell about the narrator from the list of "all we have learned" (beginning with line 23)?

3 "We are drifting." In what ways does the poem itself create a sense of drift?

4 What dominant feeling does this poem convey to you? What in the poem contributes most to that feeling?

5 The poem ends abruptly. What do you think might be the "unknown name" mentioned in the last line?

6 Suppose you could put a letter in a time capsule to be found by future generations, or in an unmanned missile to be sent deep into space. What would you say?

THE MASQUE
OF THE
RED DEATH

Edgar Allan Poe

The Red Death had long devastated the country. No pestilence had ever been so fatal, or so hideous. Blood was its avatar and its seal—the redness and the horror of blood. There were sharp pains, and sudden dizziness, and then profuse bleeding at the pores, with dissolution. The scarlet stains upon the body and especially upon the face of the victim were the pest ban which shut him out from the aid and from the sympathy of his fellow men. And the whole seizure, progress, and termination of the disease were the incidents of half an hour.

But the Prince Prospero was happy and dauntless and sagacious. When his dominions were half depopulated, he summoned to his presence a thousand hale and light-hearted friends from among the knights and dames of his court, and with these retired to the deep seclusion of one of his castellated abbeys. This was an extensive and magnificent structure, the creation of the Prince's own eccentric yet august taste. A strong and lofty wall girdled it in. This wall had gates of iron. The courtiers, having entered, brought furnaces and massy hammers and welded the bolts. They resolved to leave means neither of ingress nor egress to the sudden impulses of despair or of frenzy from within. The abbey was amply provisioned. With such precautions the courtiers might bid defiance to contagion. The external world could take care of itself. In the meantime it was folly to grieve, or to think. The Prince had provided all the appliances of pleasure. There were buffoons, there were *improvvisatori*, there were ballet dancers, there were musicians, there was

avatar (av′ə tär′): i.e., sign.

dissolution: i.e., death.

sagacious: shrewd, intelligent.

castellated: built like a castle.

ingress or egress: entering or leaving.

improvvisatori (ēm′prôv vē′zä tôr′ē): those who compose, recite, or sing on the spur of the moment.

Beauty, there was wine. All these and security were within. Without was the Red Death.

It was toward the close of the fifth or sixth month of his seclusion, and while the pestilence raged most furiously abroad, that the Prince Prospero entertained his thousand friends at a masked ball of the most unusual magnificence.

It was a voluptuous scene, that masquerade. But first let me tell of the rooms in which it was held. There were seven—an imperial suite. In many palaces, however, such suites form a long and straight vista, while the folding doors slide back nearly to the walls on either hand, so that the view of the whole extent is scarcely impeded. Here the case was very different, as might have been expected from the Prince's love of the bizarre. The apartments were so irregularly disposed that the vision embraced but little more than one at a time. There was a sharp turn at every twenty or thirty yards, and at each turn a novel effect. To the right and left, in the middle of each wall, a tall and narrow Gothic window looked out upon a closed corridor which pursued the windings of the suite. These windows were of stained glass whose color varied in accordance with the prevailing hue of the decorations of the chamber into which it opened. That at the eastern extremity was hung, for example, in blue—and vividly blue were its windows. The second chamber was purple in its ornaments and tapestries, and here the panes were purple. The third was green throughout and so were the casements. The fourth was furnished and lighted with orange, the fifth with white, the sixth with violet. The seventh apartment was closely shrouded in black velvet tapestries that hung all over the ceiling and down the walls, falling in heavy folds upon a carpet of the same material and hue. But in this chamber only, the color of the windows failed to correspond with the decorations. The panes here were scarlet—a deep blood-color. Now in no one of the seven apartments was there any lamp or candelabrum, amid the profusion of golden ornaments that lay scattered to and fro or depended from the roof. There was no light of any kind emanating from lamp or candle within the suite of chambers. But in the corridors that followed the suite there stood, opposite to each window, a heavy tripod, bearing a brazier of fire, that projected its rays through the

voluptuous: pleasing to the senses.

casements: windows.

depended: hung down.

tinted glass and so glaringly illumined the room. And thus were produced a multitude of gaudy and fantastic appearances. But in the western or black chamber the effect of the firelight that streamed upon the dark hangings through the blood-tinted panes was ghastly in the extreme, and produced so wild a look upon the countenances of those who entered that there were few of the company bold enough to set foot within its precincts at all.

precincts: areas.

It was in this apartment, also, that there stood against the western wall a gigantic clock of ebony. Its pendulum swung to and fro with a dull, heavy, monotonous clang; and when the minute hand made the circuit of the face, and the hour was to be stricken, there came from the brazen lungs of the clock a sound which was clear and loud and deep and exceedingly musical, but of so peculiar a note and emphasis that, at each lapse of an hour, the musicians of the orchestra were constrained to pause, momentarily, in their performance, to hearken to the sound; and thus the waltzers perforce ceased their evolutions; and there was a brief disconcert of the whole gay company; and, while the chimes of the clock yet rang, it was observed that the giddiest grew pale, and the more aged and sedate passed their hands over their brows as if in confused revery or meditation. But when the echoes had fully ceased, a light laughter at once pervaded the assembly; the musicians looked at each other and smiled as if at their own nervousness and folly, and made whispering vows, each to the other, that the next chiming of the clock should produce in them no similar emotion; and then, after the lapse of sixty minutes (which embrace three thousand and six hundred seconds of the Time that flies) there came yet another chiming of the clock, and then were the same disconcert and tremulousness and meditation as before.

disconcert: confusion.

pervaded: spread throughout.

tremulousness: trembling.

But in spite of these things, it was a gay and magnificent revel. The tastes of the Prince were peculiar. He had a fine eye for colors and effects. He disregarded the *decora* of mere fashion. His plans were bold and fiery, and his conceptions glowed with barbaric luster. There are some who would have thought him mad. His followers felt that he was not. It was necessary to hear and see and touch him to be *sure* that he was not.

piquancy: that which is stimulating.
Hernani: a drama by Victor Hugo.

appalls: horrifies.

He had directed, in great part, the movable embellishments of the seven chambers, upon occasion of this great fete; and it was his own guiding taste which had given character to the masqueraders. Be sure they were grotesque. There were much glare and glitter and piquancy and phantasm—much of what has been since seen in *Hernani*. There were arabesque figures with unsuited limbs and appointments. There were delirious fancies such as the madman fashions. There was much of the beautiful, much of the wanton, much of the bizarre, something of the terrible, and not a little of that which might have excited disgust. To and fro in the seven chambers there stalked, in fact, a multitude of dreams. And these—the dreams—writhed in and about, taking hue from the rooms, and causing the wild music of the orchestra to seem as the echo of their steps. And, anon, there strikes the ebony clock which stands in the hall of the velvet. And then, for a moment, all is still, and all is silent save the voice of the clock. The dreams are stiff frozen as they stand. But the echoes of the chime die away—they have endured but an instant—and a light, half-subdued laughter floats after them as they depart. And now again the music swells, and the dreams live, and writhe to and fro more merrily than ever, taking hue from the many tinted windows through which stream the rays from the tripods. But to the chamber which lies most westwardly of the seven, there are now none of the maskers who venture; for the night is waning away, and there flows a ruddier light through the blood-colored panes; and the blackness of the sable drapery appalls; and to him whose foot falls upon the sable carpet, there comes from the near clock of ebony a muffled peal more solemnly emphatic than any which reaches *their* ears who indulge in the more remote gaieties of the other apartments.

But these other apartments were densely crowded, and in them beat feverishly the heart of life. And the revel went whirlingly on, until at length there commenced the sounding of midnight upon the clock. And then the music ceased, as I have told; and the evolutions of the waltzers were quieted; and there was an uneasy cessation of all things as before. But now there were twelve strokes to be sounded by the bell of the clock; and thus it happened, perhaps, that more of thought crept, with more of time, into the meditations of the thoughtful among those who reveled. And thus, too, it happened, perhaps, that before the last echoes of the last chime had utterly sunk into silence, there were many individuals in the crowd who had found leisure to become aware of the presence of a masked figure which had arrested the attention of no single individual before. And the rumor of this new presence having spread itself whisperingly around, there arose at length from the whole company a buzz, or murmur, expressive of disapprobation and surprise—then, finally, of terror, of horror, and of disgust.

disapprobation: disapproval.

In an assembly of phantasms such as I have painted, it may well be supposed that no ordinary appearance could have excited such sensation. In truth the masquerade license of the night was nearly unlimited; but the figure in question had out-Heroded Herod, and gone beyond the bounds of even the Prince's indefinite decorum. There are chords in the hearts of the most reckless which cannot be touched without emotion. Even with the utterly lost, to whom life and death are equally jests, there are matters of which no jest can be made. The whole company, indeed, seemed now deeply to feel that in the costume and bearing of the stranger neither wit nor propriety existed. The figure was tall and gaunt, and shrouded from head to foot in the habiliments of the grave. The mask which concealed the visage was made so nearly to resemble the countenance of a stiffened corpse that the closest scrutiny must have had difficulty in detecting the cheat. And yet all this might have been endured, if not approved, by the mad revelers around. But the mummer had gone so far as to assume the type of the Red Death. His vesture was dabbled in *blood*—and his broad brow, with all the features of the face, was besprinkled with the scarlet horror.

out-Heroded Herod: i.e., gone beyond the extremes of the masquerade. This is a quotation from Shakespeare's *Hamlet.*

habiliments: clothing.

mummer: costumed person.
vesture: clothing.

When the eyes of Prince Prospero fell upon this spectral image (which, with a slow and solemn movement, as if more fully to sustain its role, stalked to and fro among the waltzers) he was seen to be convulsed, in the first moment with a strong shudder either of terror or distaste; but, in the next, his brow reddened with rage.

spectral: ghostly.

"Who dares?" he demanded hoarsely of the courtiers who stood near him—"who dares insult us with this blasphemous mockery? Seize him and unmask him—that we may know whom we have to hang at sunrise, from the battlements!"

It was in the eastern or blue chamber in which stood the Prince Prospero as he uttered these words. They rang throughout the seven rooms loudly and clearly—for the Prince was a bold and robust man, and the music had become hushed at the waving of his hand.

It was in the blue room where stood the Prince, with a group of pale courtiers by his side. At first, as he spoke, there was a slight rushing movement of this group in the direction of the intruder, who at the moment was also near at hand, and now, with deliberate and stately step, made closer approach to the speaker. But from a certain nameless awe with which the mad assumptions of the mummer had inspired the whole party, there were found none who put forth hand to seize him; so that, unimpeded, he passed within a yard of the Prince's person; and while the vast assembly, as if with one impulse, shrank from the centers of the rooms to the walls, he made his way uninterruptedly, but with the same solemn and measured step which had distinguished him from the first, through the blue chamber to the purple—through the purple to the green—through the green to the orange—through this again to the white—and even thence to the violet, ere a decided movement had been made to arrest him. It was then, however, that the Prince Prospero, maddening with rage and the shame of his own momentary cowardice, rushed hurriedly through the six chambers, while none followed him on account of a deadly terror that had seized upon all. He bore aloft a drawn dagger, and had approached, in rapid impetuosity, to within three or four feet of the retreating figure, when the latter, having attained the extremity of the velvet apartment, turned suddenly and confronted his pursuer. There was a sharp cry—and the dagger dropped gleaming upon the sable carpet, upon which, instantly afterward, fell prostrate in death the Prince Prospero. Then, summoning the wild courage of despair, a throng of the revelers at once threw themselves into the black apartment, and, seizing the mummer, whose tall figure stood erect and motionless within the shadow

impetuosity: rushing force.

of the ebony clock, gasped in unutterable horror at finding the grave cerements and corpselike mask, which they handled with so violent a rudeness, untenanted by any tangible form.

And now was acknowledged the presence of the Red Death. He had come like a thief in the night. And one by one dropped the revelers in the blood-bedewed halls of their revel, and died each in the despairing posture of his fall. And the life of the ebony clock went out with that of the last of the gay. And the flames of the tripods expired. And Darkness and Decay and the Red Death held illimitable dominion over all.

For close reading

1 Briefly describe the rooms in which the masquerade takes place.
2 How do the party-goers react to the chiming of the clock?
3 What do the party-goers discover when they seize and unmask the strange figure?

For thought and discussion

4 In your opinion, which seems most prominent in this story: plot, setting, or characterization?
5 All the party-goers are masked. What does this fact add to the story? Why do you think they are described as "a multitude of dreams"?
6 How would the story be changed if there had been no clock?
7 Compare "The Masque of the Red Death" with the Bible passages in this chapter. What similarities do you find? Which of the four biblical sections seems most similar to "Red Death" in imagery and mood? Give reasons for your choice.

RISE
AND
SHINE

Richmond Lattimore

At the big trumpet, we must all put on
our dentures, tie old strings to knees, adjust
shank upon socket, wig to cranium, bust
on ribbed architrave, fastidiously don
5 our properties, and blink to face the sun.
Farewell, dream image, cankered in our dust,
and sweets shrunk in the brain, farewell, we trust.
Uprise, O fragment brethren! We have won—
For, hallelujah, these dry graves are torn!
10 Thin bugles crash the valley of our bones
to rock the vultures wide away and scare
the griffin from his precipice as, worn
and damp, we crawl like grubs from under stones
to scarf our loves in paradisial air.

architrave: i.e., framework.
fastidiously don: i.e., carefully put on.
cankered: decayed.

griffin: mythical creature that is half eagle, half lion.

For thought and discussion

1 Who is the poet referring to when he says "we" in line 1?

2 Death and decay are sometimes regarded as gruesome or frightening. What seem to be the poet's feelings about these things?

3 The poet says "We have won" in line 8. What victory do you think the poem proclaims?

"Rise and Shine" (Copyright © 1957 Richmond Lattimore) which first appeared in *The New Yorker*, is reprinted by permission of Charles Scribner's Sons from *Poems from Three Decades* by Richmond Lattimore.

Pronunciation Key

The letters and signs used are pronounced as in the words below. The mark ⟋ is placed after a syllable with primary or heavy accent. The mark ⟋ after a syllable shows a secondary or lighter accent, as in **ab bre vi a tion** (ə brē⟋vē ā⟋shən).

Some words, taken from foreign languages, are spoken with sounds that do not otherwise occur in English. Symbols for these sounds are given in the key as "foreign sounds."

a	hat, cap	o	hot, rock	ə	represents:
ā	age, face	ō	open, go		a in about
ä	father, far	ô	order, all		e in taken
		oi	oil, voice		i in pencil
b	bad, rob	ou	house, out		o in lemon
ch	child, much				u in circus
d	did, red	p	paper, cup		
		r	run, try		**foreign sounds**
e	let, best	s	say, yes	Y	as in French *du*. Pro-
ē	equal, be	sh	she, rush		nounce (ē) with the
ėr	term, learn	t	tell, it		lips rounded as for (ü).
		th	thin, both		
f	fat, if	ᴛ͟ʜ	then, smooth	à	as in French *ami*. Pro-
g	go, bag				nounce (ä) with lips
h	**he, how**	u	cup, butter		spread and held tense.
		u̇	full, put		
i	it, pin	ü	rule, move	œ	as in French *peu*. Pro-
ī	ice, five				nounce (ā) with the lips
		v	very, save		rounded as for (ō).
j	jam, enjoy	w	will, woman		
k	kind, seek	y	young, yet	N	as in French *bon*. The
l	land, coal	z	zero, breeze		N is not pronounced,
m	me, am	zh	measure, seizure		but shows that the
n	no, in				vowel before it is nasal.
ng	long, bring				
				H	as in German *ach*. Pro-
					nounce (k) without
					closing the breath pas-
					sage.

The pronunciation key is from the *Thorndike-Barnhart Advanced Dictionary*, copyright © 1974 by Scott, Foresman and Company.

Index